27·50

KU-661-579

Cambridge Studies in French

SARTRE AND
'LES TEMPS MODERNES'

SARTRE AND
'LES TEMPS MODERNES'

HOWARD DAVIES

Principal Lecturer, Polytechnic of North London

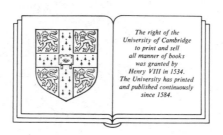

The right of the
University of Cambridge
to print and sell
all manner of books
was granted by
Henry VIII in 1534.
The University has printed
and published continuously
since 1584.

CAMBRIDGE UNIVERSITY PRESS

CAMBRIDGE

LONDON   NEW YORK   NEW ROCHELLE

MELBOURNE   SYDNEY

Published by the Press Syndicate of the University of Cambridge
The Pitt Building, Trumpington Street, Cambridge CB2 1RP
32 East 57th Street, New York, NY 10022, USA
10 Stamford Road, Oakleigh, Melbourne 3166, Australia

© Cambridge University Press 1987

First published 1987

Printed in Great Britain at
the University Press, Cambridge

British Library cataloguing in publication data
Davies, Howard
Sartre and 'Les temps modernes' –
(Cambridge studies in French)
1. Temps modernes
I. Title
805   PN5190.T4/

Library of Congress cataloguing in publication data
Davies, Howard.
Sartre and 'Les Temps modernes'.
(Cambridge studies in French)
Bibliography.
1. Sartre, Jean Paul, 1905–80 – Criticism and
interpretation. 2. Temps modernes. 3. French
periodicals – History – 20th century. 4. French –
Intellectual life – 20th century. I. Title. II. Series.
PQ2637.A82Z647   1987   848'.91409   86-19330

ISBN 0 521 32553 6

CE

For Toinha

La revue, nous y rêvions depuis 1943. Si la vérité est une, pensais-je, il faut, comme Gide l'a dit de Dieu, ne la chercher nulle part ailleurs que partout [...] Nous serions des chasseurs de sens ...

Jean-Paul Sartre, 'Merleau-Ponty', *Situations IV*

CONTENTS

GENERAL EDITOR'S PREFACE

This series aims at providing a new forum for the discussion of major critical or scholarly topics within the field of French studies. It differs from most similar-seeming ventures in the degree of freedom which contributing authors are allowed and in the range of subjects covered. For the series is not concerned to promote any single area of academic specialisation or any single theoretical approach. Authors are invited to address themselves to *problems*, and to argue their solutions in whatever terms seem best able to produce an incisive and cogent account of the matter in hand. The search for such terms will sometimes involve the crossing of boundaries between familiar academic disciplines, or the calling of those boundaries into dispute. Most of the studies will be written especially for the series, although from time to time it will also provide new editions of outstanding works which were previously out of print, or originally published in languages other than English or French.

PREFACE

Jean-Paul Sartre's monthly review *Les Temps Modernes* is an immediately attractive object of study. From 1945 to the present day it has promoted far-reaching debate in the fields of philosophy and political theory, in the arts and in those disciplines that the French know as the *sciences humaines*. Formerly, it was the vehicle chosen by some of the most prestigious intellectual authorities of post-war France; latterly, it has become much more the mouth-piece of those whom Régis Debray calls the *basse intelligentsia* – those, in other words, who offer radical critiques of contemporary French society from the 'coal-faces' of its various institutions rather than from the vantage points of the university mandarin or of the self-employed *littérateur*.

Fundamentally, however, this change in ethos, which dates from the aftermath of the upheavals of May 1968, came about in order to allow *TM*[1] to stay the same: it remains a journal clearly committed to a left-wing political programme. To regard any publication as a mere historical record of the years in which it appears is to misapprehend systematically the relationship of 'comment' to 'event'. *TM* has never allowed its readers to fall into this error; throughout forty turbulent years of French history it has striven, often turbulently, to render comment as eventful as it could possibly be and thus to usher in a socialist revolution.

One of the most fascinating aspects of *TM*'s history is the fluctuating height of profile of its founder and first *directeur*. Sartre may have been the high priest of existentialism for the rest of the French press in the years following the Liberation, but his own periodical never sought to purvey this image. It is simply not appropriate to view *TM* as the vehicle of a corpus of ideas elaborated, either within it or elsewhere, by one man. It has always been much more of a forum, in which Sartre moved between background and foreground, as indeed did many others. *TM* did not respond only to his initiatives; neither did it lose its dynamism whenever he gave it less than his full attention. Indeed, I hope to be able to demonstrate the extent of his dependence on it.

Of course, it is true that Sartre imposed on his publication certain moral and political parameters, but in practice his attitude seems to have been far removed from the authoritarian and the sectarian. If it is felt to be absolutely necessary to regard the review as an 'expression' of its prime mover, then it is best to perceive it as a celebration of the two moral values that underpin all of Sartre's philosophical project – reciprocity and generosity. Founder and review can be seen in the long term to influence each other immensely, but they do so in a specifically collective context in which the sense of all that is written is allowed to be modified by those who share the same aims. In this sense it is fair to say that *TM* is Sartre's greatest creation, by virtue of the extent to which it consistently redefines and escapes him. It is certainly all that he would have wanted of his progeny.

Despite its attractiveness, *TM* presents certain difficulties to the would-be analyst. The first is the problem of bulk: it is now approaching its 500th number, has grown to an overall size of 100,000 pages and has published articles by nearly 2,000 contributors (about one third of whom, incidentally, have been foreigners).[2] Secondly, there is the fact that while it ranges across a number of academic disciplines, it does so in order to contest their boundaries, their rationales and their methodologies.

There is thus a twofold danger: that students of *TM* may so disperse their attention across the range of material that all possibility of incisiveness disappears; or that they may be so far drawn into intractable epistemological problems that their investigations lose confidence and direction. Francis Mulhern, in his skilful analysis of the British periodical *Scrutiny*, modestly alludes to his 'over-strained authorial competence':[3] in the present study, a much greater strain is immodest enough to aspire to equal invisibility.

My methodological considerations proceed from the fact that Sartre's 'synthetic anthropology' – the *raison d'être* of *TM* – while phenomenological in inspiration and revolutionary in intent, is, in conventional academic terms, supra-disciplinary. The existing surveys of *TM*,[4] on the other hand, are resolutely sectoral (one is political and the other literary) and necessarily offer an incomplete view of the relationship of these parts to the whole. In doing so, they abandon the dialectical approach which Sartre spent so much time and energy promoting.

It is for this reason that I propose to focus closely on what I shall loosely call academic anthropology, and on its relations, established within *TM*, with Sartre's homonymous, 'synthetic' venture. My hope is not only that part and whole may illuminate each other, but also that the shifts of their interface may clearly be seen to impel invasions and mobilisations of other discourses such as historiography, political theory, psychoanalysis, linguistics, sociology, and so on. Any one of these disciplines, in fact, could theoretically be used to gain access to the whole. The choice of anthropology is thus arbitrary but not at all unjustified. Claude Lévi-Strauss and other prominent exponents contribute much to *TM*, but more important are the two long-standing editorial influences of Michel Leiris and Jean Pouillon. Academic anthropology, moreover, is the area in which Sartre's opposition to structuralism is most energetically expressed; in the particularly interesting period of the 1950s and 1960s, he succeeds in fusing his anti-structuralism with his anti-colonialism, to the point at which this dual enterprise becomes almost the principal motivation of the review.

I propose here, then, neither a history of Sartre's thought nor a sociology of a section of the French intelligentsia,[5] but rather something that approximates to a Sartrean view of *TM*. The juxtaposition of academic and synthetic anthropologies permits a segmentation of the forty years into five periods, which I shall examine in turn. The fifth period, ending with the fortieth anniversary of the review, will be covered in the Conclusion; given the decision of the Editorial Board to continue publication beyond 1980, Sartre's death is not treated as a landmark. Equally, his vast study of Flaubert is mentioned only in passing. This is not to say that *L'Idiot de la famille* represents wholly extraneous material – Flaubert, after all, in the first issue of *TM*, is assigned the crucial role of repudiated patron. It is simply that this particular symbiosis merits a study of its own. For similar reasons, I make little reference to other major texts by Sartre which are 'unknown', as it were, to *TM*, as a result of their posthumous and very recent publication.[6]

I should say that I hope very much to offer satisfaction to different categories of reader. Certainly, anyone eager to acquire a general knowledge of French intellectual activity since the war cannot afford to ignore the concerns and achievements of *TM*. Those with greater specialist knowledge than I, either of Sartre the philosopher or of French anthropology or of the French publishing industry, will, I trust, welcome the chance to relocate their expertise in the fascinating context that I shall endeavour to describe.

ACKNOWLEDGEMENTS

First, *meis et amicis*: to my parents, to family and friends in England and in Brazil, I express my deepest gratitude; without their love and support this project would not have come to fruition. For indispensable material help I am indebted to the Polytechnic of North London and to the Central Research Fund of the University of London. Many people have assisted me directly or indirectly, long ago or recently, with my work on *Les Temps Modernes*; I take this opportunity to express my thanks to Jean Benedetti, Jacques-Laurent Bost, Jeannette Colombel, Michel Contat, Claire Etcherelli, Jeanne Favret-Saada, John Gerassi, Geneviève Idt (and all the members of the Groupe d'études sartriennes), Octave Mannoni, Bernard Pingaud, Jean-Bertrand Pontalis, Patrice and Claudia Roucayrol, Fernande Schulmann-Métraux and Olivier Todd. I am particularly happy to acknowledge my debt to the following: Jean Pouillon, for his ready supply of information and assistance; Professor Malcolm Bowie, for his guidance and warm encouragement; and Professor Annette Lavers, who supervised the research from which this book derives, for her erudite counsel, her commitment and her unceasing and friendly support.

INTRODUCTION

The origins of *TM* can be traced to the short-lived Resistance group Socialisme et Liberté, founded by Sartre after his release from prisoner-of-war camp in 1941. Simone de Beauvoir, Jacques-Laurent Bost, Maurice Merleau-Ponty and Jean Pouillon were members and all were to become prominent in the *TM* team. By 1943, Albert Camus had become associated with the group and the idea of a post-war periodical had taken shape. Specifically, its vocation was to 'fournir à l'après-guerre une idéologie'.[1] In the event, Camus had become too involved with *Combat* by 1945, and the first Editorial Board consisted of Raymond Aron, Beauvoir, Michel Leiris, Merleau-Ponty, Albert Ollivier, Jean Paulhan and Sartre.

It is likely that purchasers of *TM* in October 1945 had little idea of what the review would contain. The name derived, none too obviously, from Chaplin's *Modern Times*, and the presence of Paulhan suggested that here was a publication to take the place of the disgraced *Nouvelle Revue Française*. The published work of Sartre promised a specialist interest in phenomenology and literature, but whether or how this would be translated into a particular political position was hard to predict.

A statement of intent, if not a manifesto, was clearly in order. It was bound to make explicit, as Beauvoir does in her autobiography, the lessons which had been learned in the war. To Sartre she ascribes the discovery of his implication in history,[2] the experience of solidarity in the Stalag and the realisation that his phenomenological ontology and its associated ethic would somehow have to become compatible with Marxism. These factors come together in the 'Présentation', the leading article of the first number, which urgently requires readers and writers to understand contemporary history and to embark on a programme of anti-capitalist reconstruction.

The editorial intention here is not difficult to appreciate: while

1

TM is manifestly to be a literary and political journal, its unique-
ness is to reside in the fact that the two designations are to be taken
as interdependent if not coterminous. Sartre's aspiration is categorical: he will become an anti-Flaubert, that is to say a writer
fully participant in, and avowedly responsible for, the political
history of his time.

There is no doubt that the quest for ideological legitimation
struck a chord both nationally and internationally:[3] 'Nous ne
voulons pas avoir honte d'écrire et nous n'avons pas envie de parler
pour ne rien dire.'[4] The formulation was admirably explicit.
Perhaps inevitably, however, the passage of forty years has clouded
the transparency of this urge to eschew the social status of 'rentier
de talent'[5] and a certain ambivalence has become visible. Gide and
Flaubert, for example, who are among those to whom the reproach
is addressed, prove to be objects both of antipathy and identification.[6] I mention this matter here because in three ways it touches on
one of the criteria by which *TM* requires itself eventually to be
judged – reflexivity. In the first place, the review will categorically
ask of ethnographers that they conduct their anthropological
fieldwork in full recognition of the extent to which the practice of
observation modifies both observer and observed; this stipulation
obliges Sartre himself to cultivate an equally critical awareness of
his own motivations. Secondly, because the assessment of the
proximity of antipathy to identification is the business of psychoanalysis, it is reasonable to expect *TM* to scrutinise Freudian theory
with considerable care and to measure how far it assists or inhibits
both reflexivity and political activity. Thirdly, and most importantly, it is arguably the principal task of Sartre and *TM* (given that
they intend to study and promote conflict) to develop a theory and
practice of conflict within which its ontological, psychological,
ethical, political and economic specifications are viewed in appropriately dynamic interaction.

A recent controversy shows how interesting the material opened
up by these lines of inquiry is. The eminent Jewish philosopher
Vladimir Jankélévitch asserted in a posthumously published interview[7] that Sartre became a 'grand homme de gauche' thanks to the
guilt that he felt for not having committed himself wholly to the
Resistance and for having pursued his intellectual career during the
Occupation. Michel Contat (in *Le Monde* of 28 June 1985)
endorsed this view at least in respect of 1943. He drew an angry
response from Beauvoir, Bost and Pouillon, who stressed the
degree of danger inherent in the Resistance activities of 1941.[8] The

truth is relevant to a history of *TM* and ought, in view of the premium set on reflexivity, to emerge from it. The question of whether Sartre, in particular, changed his priorities between 1941 and 1943 and whether he did so in a manner likely to induce subsequent remorse is now, however, a matter for a biographer, for *TM* has never tackled it head-on. It certainly had the opportunity in June 1948, when Jankélévitch used it to make the same accusation, thinly veiled.[9] It is difficult to believe that at the time the editors did not see through the veil; their decision to publish should perhaps be viewed as a tacit acknowledgement at least of the admissibility of Jankélévitch's views, an acknowledgement that offers no comment on their accuracy.

All this adds up to a moral and political problem of the sort that *TM* would recognise as the object of its continued reflection: should an honest appraisal of a particular situation be made if the appraisal itself reduces the moral credibility of the well-intentioned appraisers? In terms of the Sartrean avatar of the puritan ethic, it is a question of whether a possibly dubious motivation is purified by the achievement that it maximises: as far as the history of *TM* is concerned, all parties to the recent exchanges, Jankélévitch included, answer in the affirmative.

My intention at this stage is to reserve judgement. It is worth stressing, however, that the concern for *authenticité* is something that outlasts the vogue of existentialism; indeed, *TM* is established and flourishes very much as a regime that looks positively on the practice of *autocritique*. This is implied in the 'Présentation' when Sartre announces that 'nous concevons sans difficulté qu'un homme, encore que sa situation le conditionne totalement, puisse être un centre d'indétermination irréductible'.[10] We are born context-bound and everywhere we are free. It is from the platform of this paradox that *TM* takes off in 1945: 'Notre revue voudrait contribuer, pour sa modeste part, à la constitution d'une anthropologie synthétique. Mais il ne s'agit pas seulement [...] de préparer un progrès dans le domaine de la connaissance pure: le but lointain que nous nous fixons est une libération.'[11]

It is apparent from the allusiveness of the preceding remarks that Sartre's definitions are prospective. This is certainly true of the 'synthetic anthropology'. It is nonetheless worth pausing at both terms, for each has a certain Sartrean specification prior to 1945. 'Anthropology', to take the easier term first, is characterised by him very early as 'une discipline qui viserait à définir l'essence d'homme et la condition humaine';[12] rather than a branch of social science, in other words, it designates his own philosophical project.[13] The phenomenological ethic which he envisages will address itself to aspects of human experience – institutionalised reciprocity, for example – already studied by French academic anthropologists. Accordingly, the ontological and epistemological theories will be required to investigate the validity of academic anthropology as a body of knowledge. Sartre will never be shaken in his conviction that it is science that must seek its justification in philosophy and not the other way round. What is projected, in short, is a supra-disciplinary venture which, when invested with its full ethical force, will accomplish not only the fusion of literary and political activity but also the twin tasks set by Marx – the interpretation and the transformation of the world.

The notion of 'synthesis', however, is much harder to circumscribe. It recurs with great frequency, in conjunction sometimes with analysis, sometimes with thesis and antithesis, and derives from the work of antecedent philosophers, notably Descartes, Kant, Hegel, Comte, Bergson and Husserl.

Although the *cogito* does not go unquestioned, Descartes remains a great influence. The investigative method which *TM* is to promote at the end of the 1950s retains a Cartesian shape: diphasic, consisting of moments of regressive deduction and of progressive reconstruction, it will be presented as a procedure designed to complement analysis with synthesis. For Sartre, however, the second movement will be much more than one of verification, and its applicability will be not to mathematics but to the object of study of the social sciences.

From Kant Sartre inherits a great deal. Of broader significance than the categorical imperative, which is subsequently abandoned, is the ethical motivation itself. As was the case for Kant, the Sartrean ethic is to be based on logical conditions of possibility which are not those of the sciences. In other words, its power will lie in the fact that its prescriptions will remain out of reach of assertions validated by scientific method. In this connection, Sartre seems to deploy Kant's notion of synthesis – a dynamic one, inasmuch as it is applied to the unification of sense data by rational judgement – to counter what he regards as the apodicticity, or non-dialectical character, of Descartes's *cogito*. In Sartre's view, Descartes rendered, or surrendered, to God the crucial prerogative of humanity – the creativity of consciousness which is vested in its powers of negation.[14]

This dynamic sense of synthesis is obviously reinforced by the influence of Hegel, who divorced it from analysis, placing it at the apex of a ternary structure in which it is generated dialectically by tension between thesis and antithesis, then in its turn becoming thesis in a relentless forward movement.[15] It was Marx, of course, who stood this Hegelian model on its head, or on its feet, inverting the relative importance given within it to the material and the ideal. One significance of synthesis for Sartre is that he is in the historical and political position, subsequently at least, of being able to represent himself as the synthesis of Hegel and Marx. It is legitimate to see the development of *TM* in this light.

Prior to 1945, however, *L'Etre et le néant* offers the spectacle of Sartre as the synthesis of Hegel and Kierkegaard.[16] Following the latter, it assigns primacy to the ontologically insecure individual, in defiance of Hegel's assimilation of the intelligibility of history to the perfectibility of the transcendental mind. What Sartre takes up with enthusiasm, on the other hand, is the notion of the *pour-autrui*, which he introduces as the quantum of individual identity that is forever in the hands of the Other. This particular synthesis yields the interpersonal context in which the ethic becomes necessary. Kant is still needed, for Hegel is deemed quite wrong to conclude that the degree of reciprocity implied in interpersonal perception is sufficient to obviate the need for the ethic. The objection is one that will be extended to Husserl.

Despite the reservations, Hegel's conception of synthesis has much to recommend it to Sartre. It signifies a forward movement towards unity, resolving tension as it goes – and it is the relationship of partial elements to the ongoing totality which is important. The identification of the parts cannot be analytic if analysis means isolating allegedly discrete phenomena linked only by external chains of cause and effect; on this point, in the field of psychology, Sartre agrees with Bergson. Synthesis becomes possible precisely because each element implies and partakes of all the others: reality is far greater than the sum of its parts. And *TM* likewise, one might add.

Sartre is only being consistent when he insists that the philosopher should acknowledge the same degree of inherence in the object of study. His denunciation of Hegel's 'optimisme ontologique'[17] – the illusion that the accomplishment of history can be observed in practice from a position outside it – produces a further sense of 'synthesis'. Specifically, it is the emphatic refusal of the overview and of the *conscience de survol* which aspires to unconditional and context-free truth. When Sartre poses his fundamental question, 'Quel est le rapport synthétique que nous nommons l'être-dans-le-monde?',[18] he may thus be said to be using Hegel against Hegel.

The historical and academic pre-eminence of Descartes and Kant, together with the late discovery of Hegel, tend to push into the background the Comtean notion of synthesis. This is as it should be, for in Sartre's early writings on psychology the terms 'positivist' and 'synthetic' are taken to be mutually exclusive. The former carries strong negative connotations and is associated with 'mechanistic', 'atomistic' and 'analytic' when these are used to characterise what Sartre identifies as bourgeois ideology. Comtean synthesis is useful to Sartre only in the sense that it implies the integration of disparate bodies of knowledge at a higher level.

Perhaps it is the Husserlian notion of synthesis that is the closest ancestor of the synthetic anthropology.[19] Husserl initiated the return to the Cartesian *cogito* and its radicalisation. As a result, Sartre found himself with a philosophical method which set reflexivity at a premium and which did so in a manner incompatible with the ontological optimism of Hegel. Phenomenology, which is committed to the effective study of consciousness by provisionally placing in parenthesis (by *epoché*) the objective world, generates absolute knowledge only in respect of consciousness itself.

The operation of the *epoché*, the phenomenological reduction, reveals consciousness to be a continuously attentive (or intending) activity constituting the self. The *ego* conducts its *cogito* while addressing itself to *cogitata*. Not only is each movement one of recurrence, requiring integration if it is not to disassemble into a sequence of discrete consciential instants, but each has to be harmonised with the other in order to constitute the *ego* as agent of cogitation. To this perpetual bonding Husserl ascribes major importance: 'Only elucidation of the peculiarity we call synthesis makes fruitful the exhibition of the *cogito* (the intentional subjective process) as consciousness-of [...] and actually lays open the method for a descriptive transcendental–philosophical theory of consciousness (and naturally also for a corresponding psychological theory).'[20]

Synthesis, then, has now become the *sine qua non* of consciousness. Perhaps this is merely to say that Sartre's synthetic anthropology is a phenomenological anthropology. Indeed, it would be possible to stop here if it were not that his endorsement of Husserl is not at all unconditional. Husserl may be said to be Cartesian in that his philosophy claims not only to be the foundation of all future sciences, but also that it is in itself scientific. Sartre's ambitions for philosophy are not so self-effacing; he does not consider that the task of rendering the sciences philosophically acceptable is the same as conferring scientificity on philosophy. The reasons why the latter course is impossible are Kantian and Kierkegaardian.

Although Sartre warmly applauds Husserl for having placed philosophy in contact with the real world, his enthusiasm succeeds in shifting the emphasis of Husserl's work. The phenomenological reduction is crucial because, by refusing a naive acceptance of reality, it allows the opportunity of describing such acceptance in terms of consciential activity. It would seem, however, that Sartre is much more eager to suspend the *epoché* than is Husserl, much more anxious to delete the parenthesis in order then to be able to distinguish first of all between image and percept.[21] For Sartre, the crossing of the boundary between philosophy and psychology is a step that celebrates the subordination of the latter to the former. Husserl, less Kantian in this respect, sees the two as more consubstantial. The problem is that his philosophical argument from *cogito* to real world assumes that the Other is apprehended in an empathetic and non-agonistic manner; this, as is made abundantly clear in *L'Etre et le néant*, is an intuition incompatible with that of Sartre, who builds on a basis of Kierkegaardian anguish.

A glance at Husserl's venture into ethnographic territory reveals the significance of this for *TM*'s synthetic anthropology. 'To me and to those who share in my culture,' says Husserl, 'an alien culture is accessible only by a kind of "experience of someone else", a kind of "empathy", by which we project ourselves into the alien cultural community and its culture.'[22] The phenomenological terms of reference lead Sartre, on the other hand, to require that ethnographic science conform to overriding moral imperatives, without which it risks lapsing into the racialism consistently combated by *TM*. This is to say that because there is no inter-subjectivity that is pre-ethically non-agonistic, and because one cannot argue from science to ethics, one has instead to argue from ethics to science.

The importance that Sartre assigns to ethics thus impels him to seek contact with the real world and to found the sciences instead of foundering on them. He wishes to emerge from parenthesis into contingency, in order there to be able to tell the difference between percept and image, between what is and what yet might be, between *être* and *devoir-être*. The frontier between *epoché* and the real world is located, therefore, not between philosophy and science, but within philosophy – in the ethic that must inform all scientific activity.

It is this set of presuppositions that underpins the 'Présentation', giving it its evangelical fervour. It derives very much from *L'Etre et le néant*, rather than from the pre-war texts. In 1936 *La Transcendance de l'Ego* featured positions that would nowadays be described as close to those of Lacan. It argued against Husserl in favour of an *ego* which is not coextensive with consciousness but which is created by it on the basis of identifications that Sartre called 'poetic' because of their imaginary character. Here would seem to be a category of interpersonal transactions that pre-exist the embattled selfhood whose scenarios are described in *L'Etre et le néant*.

I do not suggest that Husserlian empathy is the same thing as identification, merely that in the pre-war period Sartre was presenting an apparently less conflictual ontological theory. I suggest this, not to pre-empt the debates that follow, but in order to show that there is something further that *TM* must be expected to synthesise, particularly as Sartre seemed – in his last years – to return to his earlier position, wishing, for example, to investigate the role of the maternal smile in the constitution of the individual.[23] *TM* is thus in a position to resolve the tension between the two models of human relations, the positivity of which is viewed alternately as pre-ethical and as dependent on the ethic. It is certainly a question that the historian has to bear in mind, even if, in the short term, the latter view dominates.

Having attempted to outline the scope and ethos of the synthetic anthropology projected by Sartre, I propose to assess briefly his proximity to academic anthropology in the years prior to 1945. The stage will then be set for a detailed study of all that unites and separates the two ventures.

I have mentioned already the dual status of Gide: the *rentier* and the man of goodwill. In the 'Présentation' he is invoked in a manner that establishes him as a committed intellectual to be ranked with Voltaire and Zola. 'L'administration du Congo était-ce l'affaire de Gide?',[24] asks Sartre, and this rhetorical question signals the sealing of what is virtually a contract, for the most consistent of *TM*'s positions are those that it adopts against colonialism, imperialism and racialism.

The historical conjuncture plays an important part in this. The colonial troops who had fought alongside the metropolitan Allied forces in the Second World War had been fighting for freedom; the establishment of the Union Française in 1946 was thus merely the prelude to acts of decolonisation undertaken, either by consent or under duress, by successive French governments. Indeed, the Resistance itself had been represented as an anti-colonialist struggle: Beauvoir offers a contemporary view in her fiction[25] and Sartre, speaking to the Russell Tribunal in 1967,[26] a retrospective one.

This is significant, not only as far as future contributors to *TM* are concerned – Tran Duc Thao, Albert Memmi, Frantz Fanon, Régis Debray – but also because the anti-colonialist struggle seeks to achieve lasting economic, political and social change in precisely those territories traditionally favoured by academic anthropology for its fieldwork. One of the main tensions between the two anthropologies, the synthetic and the academic, bears upon the shadowy identity of the latter, variously perceived as the liberator, the preserver, the administrator or the destroyer of colonised cultures.

In contrast with what is to come, the exclusiveness of Sartre's philosophical preoccupations in the pre-war years caused him to have little more than passing acquaintance with those anthropologists who were his contemporaries. While future authorities such as Roger Caillois, Leiris, Lévi-Strauss and Alfred Métraux moved in the outer circles of the surrealist movement as the result of a shared interest in non-Western cultures, Sartre's resistance to Freud kept him clear of this particular sphere of influence.[27]

The closest contact was Leiris, ethnographer, survivor of another short-lived Resistance group based in the Musée de l'Homme, and future editor of *TM*. Leiris had also participated in Georges Bataille's Collège de Sociologie, which had been active in the late 1930s. Denis Hollier's edition of the papers of the Collège[28] shows that, unlike Métraux,[29] he did not wholly share Bataille's position. The Collège nevertheless merits mention here. Bataille's wish was to radicalise the sociologists and the anthropologists of the French tradition, the students of Durkheim and Mauss. He urged them to become 'sorcerer's apprentices', to break with their own society and to live out the more meaningful experience of the sacred and the dangerous that they had identified in supposedly less alienated cultures. Sartre was not particularly tolerant of this. As far as he could see, the reflexivity of Bataille went no further than analytical observation of the Other followed by analogical reference to the self.[30] Of all the members of the Collège, only Leiris really escaped this judgement; his ethnography of *L'Afrique fantôme*,[31] in which the observer is neither denied, nor reduced to the status of mechanical objectifier, retains an exemplary value throughout the life of *TM*.

The Bataille connection takes the historian of *TM* back to the controversial work of Lucien Lévy-Bruhl.[32] Strange to say, both Gide's respected *Voyage au Congo* of 1927 and the young Sartre set some store by Lévy-Bruhl's theory of the 'pre-logical mentality', but whereas Gide sought evidence of it in French Equatorial Africa, Sartre strove to do likewise 'dans notre monde civilisé'.[33]

In the early part of the century, cultures lying outside the Western rationalist tradition were objects of great curiosity. To some extent, they became battlegrounds in which psychoanalysts, philosophers of various persuasions and sociologists like Lévy-Bruhl and Mauss all vied with each other in claims to greater descriptive and explanatory power. Themes of magic, sacrifice and possession, together with terms like 'mana', 'taboo' and 'totem' became common currency. The rise of nationalist irrationalisms no doubt stimulated this research. Lévy-Bruhl's particular contribution was to postulate two heterogeneous and geographically distinct types of dominant thought process. The prevailing mode in the '*sociétés inférieures*' was, curiously enough, described as 'synthetic' – that is to say it functioned with a high tolerance of contradiction and obeyed the 'law of participation', which prevented efficient differentiation of the constituent elements of reality. All thought was synthetic, according to Lévy-Bruhl, but pre-logical thought was characterised in particular by the fact that its syntheses were undertaken on the basis of no prior analytic intellection; there was no labour of definition, categorisation, abstraction or delimitation.

Sartre's use of 'synthesis' was not carried over directly from Lévy-Bruhl. On the contrary, as I have indicated, there were many more powerful influences. What is striking is the domestication, as it were, of the pre-logical mentality. In the long term, *TM* will pick up this intuition and give it a specific political context, but in the short term Sartre responded to the pre-logical mentality much as he did to the Freudian unconscious: both were to be incorporated into the phenomenological perspective as aspects of *mauvaise foi*. The process is best visible in the *Esquisse d'une théorie des émotions* of 1938. In this text the concept of magic was deployed to describe emotion as wishful thinking and as a believed denial of reality. A regime of magic was said to be instituted whenever consciousness was rendered passive by confrontation with an unwished-for state of affairs. Anticipating the bleak view of human community to be expounded in the ontological theory of *L'Etre et le néant*, Sartre declared that 'l'homme est toujours un sorcier pour l'homme et le monde social est d'abord magique'.[34]

Sartre, then, was fascinated at home by the exotic behaviour that his contemporaries believed was best observed abroad. It is thus only by radical incorporation that Lévy-Bruhl enters the synthetic anthropology. As far as the other founding father of French anthropology, Marcel Mauss, is concerned, Sartre seems to have been largely ignorant of his work. He might otherwise have noted Mauss's critiques of the atomistic character of such sociologies as that of Gabriel Tarde. The major texts of Mauss, the *Esquisse d'une théorie générale de la magie* of 1904 and the *Essai sur le don* of 1925, appear to have been investigated by Sartre only after being re-edited by Lévi-Strauss in 1950. Thereafter, the analyses of generosity and reciprocity in particular will be slowly absorbed into his thinking. (I have attempted elsewhere to show the important place they occupy in the autobiographical *Les Mots*.)[35]

Sartre's pre-war commerce with the academic anthropologists was not sufficient to deflect him from his philosophical trajectory; it does, however – and the history of *TM* will confirm this view – show him to be an alert *bricoleur*, not at all confined within a technical phenomenological discourse, but with an eye always open for notions worthy of salvage. Refusing Bataille's nostalgia for the Dionysian *potlatch*, Sartre opted instead for a resolutely Apollonian world-view, synthesising from a basis of clear-cut judgements and organised perceptions of a differentiated reality. The approach is rehearsed by Roquentin, hero of *La Nausée* and desperate ethnographer of Bouville, who seeks to extricate himself from the magical and the pre-logical and to construct reliable intellectual categories.

With the coming of the Second World War, the Sartrean project acquires a more overtly ethical and political character. Like Roquentin, Oreste (in *Les Mouches*) is no armchair anthropologist. Spurning the opportunity to produce a classical monograph of the city of Argos, he nevertheless achieves a sound understanding of its political institutions, its religious ritual and its ideology, not to mention certain aspects of the economy. Oreste is an intelligent tourist who resolves to intervene in a very voluntaristic manner on behalf of the down-trodden Argives. Leiris wondered in the

clandestine press[36] whether this made him a 'bouc émissaire' or a
'chaman guérisseur'. In 1985, as the Jankélévitch controversy has
shown, it is possible to ask the same question in respect of Sartre
himself.[37] Provisionally, as I have said, I reserve my judgement,
not because I fail to recognise the perennial urgency of the
question, but because I regard the interface of synthetic and
academic anthropologies as an excellent terrain in which to go in
search of edification.

In 1945, *TM*'s synthetic anthropology gets under way with the
following terms of reference: the legitimation of writing; supra-
disciplinarity and the rejection of conventional academic objectivity; a comprehensive view of the contemporary world, informed
by the phenomenological ontology and producing an appropriately
'synthetic' psychology and sociology; the promotion of reflexivity
as a moral imperative generating political action; the construction
of a socialist society.[38] In her 1944 essay 'Pyrrhus et Cinéas',
Beauvoir asserts that 'on ne peut assigner aucune dimension au
jardin où Candide veut m'enfermer'.[39] The remark is apt, for the
TM tribe will aspire not to be a people of sedentary farmers but a
band of hunters and gatherers (*chasseurs de sens*): production, in so
far as it is organised, will be geared to immediate consumption.
Sartre's famous comment on the bananas which 'ont meilleur goût
quand on vient de les cueillir'[40] implies a predilection for the wild
fruit and a hostility to banana republics.[41] *TM* offers him and his
foraging companions a territory in which to flourish, a regime of
exacting short-term deadlines and correlatively long-term flexi-
bility. Constrained, as long as it continues publication, to exist in
the present, it also offers the interested observer a view of his or her
intellectual and political horizons. This is as it should be, for *TM*
never ceases to believe that ethnography begins at home.

1

THE FIRST SIX YEARS: THE PARTICIPATION OF LEIRIS AND LEVI-STRAUSS

It is only in 1951 that structuralism first begins to be perceived as a rival methodology with terms of reference that are incompatible with the phenomenological approach. The first six years, although packed with incident, are years of harmony and co-operation as far as the synthetic and academic anthropologies are concerned. Little material of the latter category is to be found in the review – no more than 2% of *TM*'s output, in fact – and the reasons for this lie primarily in the state of the discipline. There are a number of significant factors that together prompt practitioners to engage in an urgent quest for disciplinary identity: the disruption occasioned by the war; the possibility that a change in the nature of the relationship of metropolis and colonies might affect the object of study, perhaps to the point of causing it to vanish altogether; the problematic character of the boundaries separating anthropology from other closely related areas; and, last but not least, anthropology's very tenuous foothold in French higher education. In 1945, the theoretical and methodological basis provided by Mauss stands in need of innovative consolidation. With *TM* seeking to establish itself at the same time, it is not surprising that mutual support should be offered and that certain influential figures should be prominent in both ventures.

Leiris is the first of these. Having travelled with Marcel Griaule on the 1931 Dakar–Djibouti expedition, a fieldwork programme regarded by historians of anthropology as a key event in the development of the discipline,[1] Leiris belongs to the senior generation of post-war anthropologists. Others, notably Georges Devereux, Roger Caillois and Alfred Métraux, also find their way into the pages of *TM*. The second major figure, however, is of course Claude Lévi-Strauss, whose enforced stay in New York during the Second World War stimulated anthropology as much as did that of Malinowski in Australian territory during the First. Lévi-Strauss, a close friend of Merleau-Ponty, had known Sartre and Beauvoir since the late 1920s.

13

Both Leiris and Lévi-Strauss find *TM* intellectually congenial because of their own readiness to transcend narrow disciplinary boundaries. Leiris's previous connections with Breton and with Bataille betoken a strong interest in literature, psychoanalysis and philosophy; Lévi-Strauss, for his part, perhaps because of anthropology's relatively weak specificity, is in a particularly ecumenical frame of mind in 1945.[2] In *TM*, both tend to range fairly widely and in a manner which more scholarly journals would no doubt find distasteful. This is why any quantitative measure of the review's anthropological content during the first six years is misleading. In fact, the influences of Leiris and Lévi-Strauss are powerful and suffusive. I intend, therefore, to highlight the presence of each by moving laterally across such territories as colonialism, literature, psychoanalysis and feminism, demonstrating as I go the extent to which each informs the developing synthetic anthropology.

The presence of Leiris

It may seem strange to commence this survey of *TM*'s performance with comments on poetry, but there are good reasons for doing so. The first is that poetry is Leiris's area of formal editorial responsibility. While no poet ever becomes a very regular contributor to *TM*, the list of those whose work appears sporadically in this period is not unimpressive: it includes Samuel Beckett, André du Bouchet, René Char, André Frénaud (who returns under Bernard Pingaud's editorship in 1964), Jean Lescure (the Resistance journalist who had published extracts from Sartre's *L'Age de raison* clandestinely), Henri Pichette, Francis Ponge and Raymond Queneau.

These poets are not to be regarded as militant existentialists. Leiris's editorial activities, in fact, have the effect of limiting the literary homogeneity of the review. Even though Sartre had written at length on Ponge in December 1944,[3] he and Beauvoir together display a very distant tolerance towards Leiris's field of responsibility.[4] She remarks of one of Ponge's contributions that it 'ne vaut pas grand-chose'[5] and Sartre's response to the suggestion that his lack of support might be construed as hostility is cryptic to the point of apparent *mauvaise foi*: 'On me reproche de la [poésie] détester: la preuve en est, dit-on, que *Les Temps Modernes* publient fort peu de poèmes. C'est la preuve que nous l'aimons, au contraire.'[6]

The truth is that at this time, and this is the second reason for considering it here, poetry comes to be for Sartre the linguistic and artistic activity into which he projects all the affective and ethical ambivalence that cannot be allowed to threaten the utilitarian effectiveness of prose. Poets in general (and the only real exceptions will be the poets of *négritude*), and Baudelaire, Mallarmé and Genet in particular, by opting for the aesthetic rather than for the instrumental, mark themselves out as candidates for existential psycho-analysis. Moreover, because this anti-Freudian practice is itself an adjunct to the most urgent and ambitious Sartrean aspiration – the elaboration of the phenomenological ethic – it has to be based on the ontological premiss which both permits and necessitates the ethic, namely the absence of pre-ethical non-agonistic relations between consciousnesses. It thus tends to exclude the possibility that the existential psychoanalyst might discover a participation in the object of study of the sort that Sartre has already, in *La Transcendance de l'Ego*, described as poetic. Poetry is repressed in two respects in *TM* in this period: not only is its publication not encouraged by the Director of the review, but neither is the review allowed to express the extent to which he might identify with the poets that he submits to existential psychoanalysis. The result is doubly negative: Sartre falls a long way from the standard of reflexivity that he so energetically sets and, in doing so, he plays into the hands of the Freudian analysts whom he so energetically opposes.

Here I am anticipating, but I do so for the sake of casting light on the role of Leiris. In a sense, and in the short term, he saves *TM*. A poet himself, he is respected by Sartre precisely because he brings to the poetic enterprise a high degree of reflexivity – higher than Sartre himself is prepared to afford at this time. In his 'Glossaire j'y serre mes gloses',[7] he explores what Sartre calls the 'ambiguïté du signe',[8] that is to say the range of possibilities, from transparency to opacity, that the signifier offers in its relationship with the signified. In what will later become *Biffures*, moreover, he exploits connotation in a programme of self-analysis. This labour of autobiography (assembled under the umbrella title of *La Règle du jeu*) dominates Leiris's contributions to *TM*. Of fourteen texts, appearing over some twenty years, seven are extracts from it. It is a work that has paradigmatic significance for Sartre: *Les Mots*, which might be described as his own belated attempt to come to terms with the poetic, owes much to the example of Leiris.

It is only in the hindsight made possible by *Les Mots* that the paradox of the situation becomes fully visible. In the immediate post-war years, as Sartre's existentialism becomes increasingly strident and soteriological, and as his quest for the ethic seems more and more to exclude the reflexivity on which it ought to be based, *TM* is guaranteed a certain literary openness by Leiris, the reflexive ethnographer–poet. This, at least, is a view offered by the published texts. Both the *Cahiers pour une morale* and 'L'engagement de Mallarmé'[9] show, however, that Sartre knows privately the difficulties to be encountered in the management of ambivalence. It is to his credit that he is prepared to learn from Leiris in the long term and to permit him to do what he himself is not ready to do in the short term. In any case, everybody benefits: Sartre is quickly transcended by the review that he directs, but in a manner that subsequently allows him to transcend himself; *TM*, meanwhile, fails to become a one-man band and thus takes a huge step toward commercial and intellectual success.

In addition to the poetic, Leiris is probably responsible for some of the anthropological material that is featured by *TM*. In December 1949, for example, the review carries a collection of Berber songs which illustrate the break-up of tribal structures by colonial rule. In July 1950, Emile Dermenghem presents a series of anecdotal accounts of prophets and seers in Morocco and Algeria. On other occasions, the ethnographic content is best placed under the heading of non-professional reportage, as when David Hare, the American sculptor, recounts his experiences in the Navaho and Hopi territories of New Mexico. In 1947 and 1948, the serialisation of Beauvoir's travel journal, *L'Amérique au jour le jour*, echoes the melancholy of Hare at the sight of the North American Indians' difficult absorption into a foreign culture.[10]

This material produces little evidence of any unified theoretical approach, on the part of *TM*, to matters anthropological. It is another American, however, who provides a more substantial insight into what committed ethnography might be. James Agee's documentation of poverty in the southern states is the work of a writer–photographer partnership, operating 'not as journalists, sociologists, politicians, entertainers, humanitarians, priests or artists, but seriously'.[11] *Let Us Now Praise Famous Men* is welcomed as a text that informs, galvanises, and testifies to the power of the written word.

Agee and Leiris have in common an unwillingness to edit out of the object of observation the influence of the observer. Even so, Leiris displays sufficient conformity to professional norms for his work to fall into two categories. On the one hand, there is the analytic work – articles presented to specialist journals or published under the auspices of the Institut d'Ethnologie.[12] This fieldwork is explicitly Maussian. On the other hand, there is the 'synthetic' account of the Griaule expedition, *L'Afrique fantôme*, which is ultimately concerned with the ethnography of the ethnographer, the necessity and the impossibility of maximum integration into the object of study.

The academic formalism of the first category contrasts vividly with the critical and self-critical verve of the second. *L'Afrique fantôme* predates *TM*, but, as I have hinted, may be said to haunt it. It explores the extent to which phenomena of different orders interconnect: life on another continent, sexual obsessions, the opportunism of the informants, Leiris's dreams of Breton, his sense of being a lackey of the colonial administration, the difficulty of reconciling the moral terms of reference of the observer with the magical terms of reference of the observed. Living with the adepts of the *zar* religion in Ethiopia, Leiris ends up not knowing whether to regard it as a mystical experience passing Western understanding or to rationalise it as a mixture of venality, neurosis and show business. His hesitation and his lack of detachment lead him to found an ethnographic uncertainty principle which undermines the validity of his formal fieldwork.[13] By the time that he codifies his position in 'L'ethnographe devant le colonialisme', however, the uncertainty occasioned by the immeasurability of subjectivity and of ethnocentricity is transformed into a programme wholly consistent with the spirit of *TM* – one that repudiates scientific 'objectivity' in favour of morally and politically committed interventions.

In this *profession de foi*, which *TM* publishes in August 1950, Leiris defines ethnography as an aspect of the cultural and social anthropology which has developed in an age of imperialism. Inasmuch as colonisation facilitates ethnography, and whether or not the converse is also true, the fieldworker is necessarily perceived by the colonised as an agent of the administration. This is a reality which conditions all professional activities and Leiris is right to seek to adopt a coherent attitude towards it. He therefore develops a number of points which together make up his assessment of the responsibility of the anthropologist. First, fieldworkers must bear in mind that the society under scrutiny has no cultural integrity: as the object of observation, administration and appropriation from without, it is necessarily dislocated and degraded. Secondly, they must become, in the metropolis, the advocates of the culture which is threatened; they must strive to eliminate racialism and to encourage the adoption of measures which favour the eventual political and economic autonomy of the colony. Thirdly, they must communicate all research findings to the society under investigation in order to increase its self-understanding and to liquidate whatever inferiority complex it might have. Fourthly, they must study the colony as an entity – economic, political and cultural – and not merely as a corpus of folklore to be seen in isolation from the social structures. Fifthly, they must contribute to the training, not so much of local informants, but of local ethnographers, and must attempt to establish links with local intellectuals. (As far as the training of ethnographers is concerned, *TM* gives a lead when, in November 1950, it publishes an analysis by Dominique Traore, from Upper Volta, of 'Mariage entre femmes chez les indigènes de tribu Niéniégué de la subdivision de Houndé'.) Finally, since colonialism cannot be brought to an end by radicalisation of the ethnographic profession alone, Leiris asks his French colleagues to fight for their own liberation within the metropolis.

This view of scientific and professional practice as an adjunct to a policy of decolonisation is consistently endorsed by *TM*. 1950, however, a year of repression in Madagascar and warfare in Indochina, offers little hope of rapid political change. The extent to which Leiris is able to fulfil his own terms of reference is limited by the global situation, by his comparative isolation within the profession and by the fact that ethnography is only one among his many interests. In *TM*, he publishes a small amount of material collected in visits to Martinique and to Guadeloupe, together with a sample of voodoo songs introduced by Métraux. Elsewhere, he produces a UNESCO paper entitled 'Race and culture', in which he gives to racialism the cultural, economic and political significance that he denies to the notion of race. In this paper, both Aimé Césaire and Richard Wright, future contributors to *TM*, are cited as exemplars of the moral and intellectual stature that is independent of race – a good indication of how far the attitudes of Leiris and Sartre towards poetry are reconciled in their support for *négritude* and in their hostility to colonialism.

There is no doubt that 'dès le début, *Les TM* ont pris une position nette sur les guerres coloniales, ont défendu les colonies contre les colonisateurs, sans ambiguïté d'aucune sorte'.[14] Events in Algeria are to prove very important, of course, but they merely confirm attitudes matured in the first six years in respect of Indochina. As early as December 1946, an editorial written by Pouillon announces its categorical disapproval of the French military action in South-East Asia. In the following years, the coverage is, if not massive, at least consistent and shows the review to be playing a dual role: concerned to inform, in the absence of adequate reporting by the press and in the face of metropolitan prejudice, it seeks at the same time to mobilise support for the Viet Minh. In January 1949, for example, it carries a petition signed by 53 prominent intellectuals calling for the cessation of hostilities and for negotiations with Ho Chi Minh.

The dominant figure in this connection is Tran Duc Thao. In February 1946, on his release from a French prison, he supplies the historical background to the conflict and goes on to conduct a polemic with Claude Lefort – *TM*'s first theoretical discussion of the strategies of liberation from imperialism.[15] The interest of the debate lies also in the fact that both men are Marxists with a real interest in phenomenology; both may therefore be regarded as assisting the implementation of the programme of the 'Présentation', at least insofar as it wishes to bring to Marxism a better understanding of the insertion of the individual into the collective.

Sartre recalls later that as well as being a member of the PCF, Tran Duc Thao was, like Lefort, an ex-student of Merleau-Ponty. 'Les penseurs officiels du Parti communiste', he observes. 'condamnèrent ses idées [i.e. Merleau-Ponty's] mais les meilleurs ont toujours su qu'il fallait les reprendre et que l'anthropologie marxiste avait le devoir de les assimiler. Sans Merleau, croit-on que Tran Duc Tao [*sic*] eût écrit sa thèse et tenté d'annexer Husserl à Marx?'[16] In fact, Tran Duc Thao's phenomenology, like Leiris's anthropology, becomes an important component of *TM*'s attitude to colonialism. It shifts the debate from the supposedly objective merits and demerits of colonial administration and poses the problem instead as one of perception and of the conflict of perceptions. The French are now urged to understand that 'la *situation* du colonisé est telle qu'il l'éprouve irréductiblement dans le sentiment d'appartenir à une autre communauté que celle du vainqueur'.[17] This affirmation allows the concept of a French international community to be denounced as an act of violence. The fact that the French deny the validity of the way in which the Vietnamese perceive their own situation legitimises, in Tran Duc Thao's view, the distinction between a 'racisme d'oppresseurs' and a 'racisme d'opprimés'.[18] Sartre's thoughts on *négritude* will draw heavily on this distinction.

The phenomenology of the colonial confrontation is an area into which *TM* is clearly eager to move. Francis Jeanson gives a warm welcome to Octave Mannoni's *Psychologie de la colonisation* and to its analysis of the 'dependence complex' in Martinique. It is Albert Memmi and Frantz Fanon, however, who will prove the most significant emulators of Tran Duc Thao in later years. Professional anthropologists, on the other hand, make little contribution to this project. The petition of January 1949 is signed by, among others, Louis Massignon, the sociologist of Arab cultures, but the task of communicating to readers the reality of the situation in Indochina is left to journalists. The only exception is Jeanne Cuisinier, a sociologist of religion who had worked with the Müöng tribe in northern Indochina, but her reports do not differ substantially from those of, for example, Claudine Chonez and Jean-Henri Roy.

Jeanson also celebrates the appearance of the Franco-Arab, anti-colonialist periodical *Consciences algériennes* in January 1951, and Leiris makes passing reference to the social structures of Martinique, Guadeloupe and Haiti in his presentation of the work of black poets. The best piece of in-depth reporting of the colonial question is, however, Roger Stéphane's coverage of the trials in Madagascar in 1947. It presumably does not escape Leiris's notice that Jacques Rabémananjara, one of the poets that he introduces to *TM*, is subsequently imprisoned in Tananarive.

With 'Orphée noir', published in *TM* in October 1948, Sartre turns his attention to poetry and to colonialism in the dual context established by Leiris. His ethnographer–poet colleague had visited the Ivory Coast in 1945 and Martinique in 1948 and, in the preface to the second edition of *L'Afrique fantôme* in 1950, celebrates the change that such journeys have brought about. It is as if the French West Indies represent the second moment of Leiris's development as an anthropologist: academicism is transcended and an understanding of colonialism is gained with the help of the intellectual elite of the colonised. In Martinique, he had met the man whom he describes as 'l'homme qui incarne aujourd'hui l'espoir de la masse martiniquaise: le grand poète Aimé Césaire'.[19] In *TM* in 1950, he introduces other black poets: Charles Calixte, Georges Desportes, Jean-Georges Guannel and René Ménil from Martinique, Henri Corbin from Guadeloupe, Roland Dorcély, Félix Morrisseau-Leroy and Magloire Saint-Aude from Haiti. Their poems counterpoint declarations of present humiliation with assertions of future dignity and are ethnographic in Leiris's committed sense of the term. They study a strange ancestral culture in order to rejoin it and, in doing so, they work for its liberation.

In the late 1940s, both Leiris and Sartre sit on the *comité de patronage* of the review *Présence africaine*, a duty which they share with the black American novelist Richard Wright.[20] It is from Wright that Sartre takes the eminently phenomenological formula, subsequently favoured by Malcolm X and by successive generations of Black Power leaders: 'il n'y a pas de problème noir aux Etats-Unis, il n'y a qu'un problème blanc'.[21] Beauvoir, meanwhile, having had first-hand experience of the black community in America, is well placed to perceive its significance for the Sartrean ethic. 'Il n'y a pas une minute dans la vie d'un noir qui ne soit pénétrée de conscience sociale', she notes; 'quoiqu'il fasse, un noir est "engagé". Il n'y a pas un écrivain noir à qui le problème de l'engagement ne se pose. Il est d'avance résolu.'[22] Wright himself, whose autobiography *Black Boy* is serialised in *TM* between February and June 1947, is able to write on behalf of the oppressed and to address the oppressors, thus making a literary and political commitment to his own culture which is nonetheless the result of a social and geographical detachment from it.

Given this glimpse of the possibility of a revolutionary literature, it is not surprising that Sartre should agree to preface Senghor's *Anthologie de la nouvelle poésie nègre et malgache* in 1948 and that his text, with a selection of poems by Césaire, Damas, Rabéarivelo, Rabémananjara, Roumain and Senghor, should be reproduced by *TM*. 'Orphée noir' provides him with the opportunity to clarify some of the issues which have been crystallising in the first years of the life of *TM*. What, for example, is the exact nature of the relationship of the synthetic anthropology and its academic counterpart? What is his own view of the psychology and politics of colonialism? What ethical lessons may be learned from the phenomenology of poetry and racialism? In a number of respects, the line of *TM* now becomes clearer.

In particular, the approach of Tran Duc Thao is endorsed. Underpinning the phenomenology of both writers is the presupposition that human beings are intelligible to each other. Jeanson, writing for African readers, aptly quotes a passage from *L'Existentialisme est un humanisme*, in which Sartre declares that 'tout projet, quelque individuel qu'il soit, a une valeur universelle [. . .] Tout projet, même celui du Chinois, de l'Indien ou du nègre, peut être compris par un Européen.'[23] This principle, it is implied, is of unlimited applicability, transcending ethnocentricity in the anthropocentrism of certain moral imperatives. In 'Orphée noir', Sartre is thus able to write specifically for the whites, aiming to change their point of view in order that their oppression of the blacks might

cease. The emphasis is ethical before being political, something
which is confirmed by the fact that Sartre's thoughts on 'Le noir et
le blanc aux Etats-Unis' are published in *Combat* in 1949 as extracts
from the non-forthcoming *Morale*. 'Pour voir clair dans une situation injustifiable', he observes, 'il n'est pas suffisant que l'oppress-
eur la regarde honnêtement, il faut aussi qu'il change la structure
de ses yeux.'[24] Thus, when black poets write to celebrate their own
power of expression, suddenly – in a traumatic manner redolent of
the analysis of shame in *L'Etre et le néant* – the perceiver is
perceived.

It is noticeable that Sartre is concerned not so much to describe
cultural relativisation in terms of the experience of the groups
involved, but rather to explain how and why the process has
occurred through poetry. His own comprehension of others is
achieved through existential psychoanalysis and it is indeed in this
category that 'Orphée noir' is best placed. *Négritude* is a project, a
'complexe rebelle à l'analyse',[25] and its study requires an appropriately synthetic methodology, namely the existential psychoanalysis which addresses itself almost exclusively to writers. That which
draws the West Indian and African poets into the ambit of the
synthetic anthropology – their literacy – thus tends to carry them
out of reach of an academic anthropology which prefers to investigate societies that have no forms of writing. Not that this indicates
the existence of an agreed division of labour – far from it; Sartre's
most insistent ethical and political question of the period,
'Qu'est-ce que la littérature?', has already revealed that he considers the desirable reading public as coextensive with the species.

Négritude is hailed so vigorously because 'pour une fois au
moins, le plus authentique projet révolutionnaire et la poésie la
plus pure sortent de la même source'.[26] The power of expression
becomes the expression of power, yielding an 'écriture automati-
que engagée',[27] so designated because the black poets affirm
themselves by subverting the metropolitan language that oppresses
them. They 'surréalise' it, temporarily denying it any instrumental
value, in order then to proceed to a synthesis in which poetry,
normally the opposite of action, becomes the action of opposition.
Active poets, they represent a contradiction of Sartrean terms and
are greeted by him with the thrill that he always derives from
Hegelian chiasmus.

The fact that Sartre should warm to literature which he regards as
surrealist is interesting in itself. It is clear that its exportation to a
colonial context, in which it acquires political efficacy, accounts for

its new acceptability. In undergoing this displacement, moreover, the poetry can be seen to derive its energy from the experience of a socio-economic reality, rather than from the volcanic, but very private unconscious celebrated by Breton. There is no doubt that Sartre welcomes the opportunity to show by implication not only that Freudian determinism (as he sees it) can be discarded in favour of other more powerful conditioning factors, but also that, like all apparent determinisms, it is a dubious initiative calculated to pervert the moral autonomy of others.

There is a Lévy-Bruhl connection to be made here. It might be supposed that an ethnocentric impulse leads Sartre to project out of France the surreal and the non-rational, depositing them in cultures deemed to be more suffused by them. But it is the opposite that is the case. His familiarity with the theses of Lévy-Bruhl, which inspire him to track down all that is 'magical' in his own culture, effectively reverses the tendency to ethnocentricity. His attitude to *négritude* resembles his attitude to madness: it consists in showing to be rational what his compatriots might prefer to regard as manifestations of *mentalité pré-logique*. The function of the black poets is thus to reveal that the essence of poetry is colonisation. By virtue of their evident socio-economic and linguistic dispossession, they highlight the quantum of ontological possession which is inherent in the poetic attitude and which, in the case of Western aesthetes, is normally limited to possession by parental figures and by literary antecedents. Such is the urgency of his ethical project, however, that Sartre fails to address the white poet within him. As I have said, reflexivity takes place only in private (in the essay on Mallarmé) or by proxy (thanks to Leiris). Even so, because poetry is an expression of a practico-inert, the otherness of self imposed from without, 'Orphée noir' succeeds in specifying its object of study in terms which anticipate the *Critique*: 'comme toutes les notions anthropologiques, la Négritude est un chatoiement d'être et de devoir-être; elle vous fait et vous la faites: serment et passion, à la fois'.[28]

In the short term, however, ethical considerations are given the highest priority. Nowhere is this more true than in the area of the theory of literature, where once again Leiris plays a key role. The preface to the post-war edition of *L'Age d'homme*, entitled 'De la littérature considérée comme une tauromachie', appears in *TM* in May 1946, and its aesthetic of asceticism makes a useful bridge between the 'Présentation' and *Qu'est-ce que la littérature?*[29] Even so, although *TM* comes to be known as the purveyor of *littérature engagée*, it is less than clear to some of those on the inside what this actually means. Etiemble, who is resident literary critic for the first six years, strenuously resists all theoretico-ethical formulations. Merleau-Ponty displays puzzlement and rather unhelpfully suggests that 'au sens étroit et sectaire, la littérature engagée serait celle qui oublierait d'être littérature, la littérature dégagée celle qui ne dit rien de rien'.[30] The problem is essentially whether literature is a sector within the synthetic anthropology or whether it is its be-all and end-all. If the latter, then it has little taxonomic usefulness. Beauvoir's early article 'Littérature et métaphysique' (April 1946) does not shed a great deal of light on this question.

For all its ebullience, the 'Présentation' was vague in its assertion of the identity of literature, supra-disciplinarity and political activity. *Qu'est-ce que la littérature?*, on the other hand, turns out to be a welcome clarification of *TM*'s rationale.[31] Providing normative definitions of prose and poetry and thereby repressing the ambivalence that was permitted to inform *La Nausée* (at least at the level of the narrated),[32] it is a moralisation of literature rather than a theorisation. Acceptable writing is revealed to be synthetic, inasmuch as its naming of aspects of the world discloses them as potentially modifiable by the exercise of human freedom. *Qu'est-ce que la littérature?* is thus a contribution to, or even a substantial substitute for, the formal existentialist ethic. By its very force it manages to give the impression that at this time the synthetic anthropology is held together by repeated acts of faith in literature. 'Nous voulons', says Sartre, 'que l'homme et l'artiste fassent leur salut ensemble, que l'œuvre soit en même temps un acte; qu'elle soit expressément conçue comme une arme dans la lutte que les hommes mènent contre le mal.'[33]

Salvation, asserts Sartre, will follow from the reciprocity established between writer and readers and from the extent to which their several freedoms are interdependent. Reciprocity, of course, is a phenomenon studied in Mauss's *Essai sur le don* and given pride of place in Lévi-Strauss's *Les Structures élémentaires de la parenté*. In *Qu'est-ce que la littérature?* the anthropological references are non-existent. They do, however, appear in *Saint Genet* and in *Les Mots*, to name but two of the later texts which take quite a different view of the ethical project. For all Sartre's discussion of readership and the fascinating passages on the social history of literature, the high valuation of literature renders impossible a thoroughgoing anthropology or sociology of literature. (When Merleau-Ponty, in his 'Commentaire' on Lukács's *autocritique*, notes that 'Engels disait que la courbe des idéologies est beaucoup plus compliquée que celle de l'évolution politique et sociale',[34] he is going where the review is not ready to follow.) More importantly, the high valuation of literature actually inhibits the elaboration of the ethic which is supposed to validate literary production. Sartre's anxiety to justify his own activity leads him to hasty justifications and he is fortunate that both Leiris and Lévi-Strauss help him to broaden his view, particularly after 1950. Only then, in the atmosphere of the Cold War, will it become fully apparent how much anthropology assists in reining back his more voluntaristic impulses and how much it restores to social structures the weight that he himself had ascribed to them when waiting at the Front in 1940.[35]

Although Director of *TM*, Sartre is, in other words, only one among a group of editors and influential contributors. However pressing his prescriptions are, the literary life of the review proceeds, thanks to Leiris, Beauvoir and others, on a much more catholic basis than his programme would suggest. A concept of commitment has to be fairly broad if it is to embrace such writers as Nelson Algren, Samuel Beckett, Bertolt Brecht, William Faulkner, Michel de Ghelderode, Franz Kafka, Pierre Klossowski, Ignazio Silone, Boris Vian and Elio Vittorini. On the other hand, the Sartrean concept of commitment has to be seen to be wider than that of socialist realism. Its own realism derives in large measure from the experiences of war. As a result, much of the material marries well with the prevailing pre-eminence of existential anguish. This is true (to name only the best known) of the work of Antonin Artaud, Colette Audry, Béatrix Beck, Jacques-Laurent Bost, Jean Cayrol, Marguerite Duras, Jean Genet, Violette Leduc, Robert Merle, Jean-Bertrand Pontalis, Raymond Queneau and Maurice Sachs. In certain cases, and Carlo Levi's *Christ Stopped at Eboli* is perhaps the best example, committed ethnography of the standard of Leiris and Agee is conducted under duress.

No writer, however, may be said to be implementing in a precise way the precepts of *Qu'est-ce que la littérature?* unless it be Sartre himself with the third and unfinished fourth parts of *Les Chemins de la liberté*. It is striking that so many of the writers listed above operate on the interfaces of autobiography, reportage, political history, sociology and psychology. So weak have literary boundaries become, and so flourishing are the *témoignages* and the *récits de vie*, that Sartre's own contributions stand out as anomalous and conservative. It is fair to say that his narrowly literary output does not match his enthusiasm. *Les Mains sales*, which is serialised in the review, is interesting because it embodies the tension between the ethic as existentialist commitment and the ethic as ideological superstructure, and thus points forward to the abandonment of the *Morale* and to the 1950s.

Once again, the work of Leiris is of outstanding relevance. Extracts from the autobiographical *Biffures* appear in February and March 1946, displaying both a high valuation of literary activity and a high degree of reflexivity. The two are fused, moreover, in an anthropological intertext to which Sartre does not yet have ready access. Unlike Sartre, Leiris is able to offer a model of literary reciprocity that does indeed draw on the *Essai sur le don*, as in the following passage which solicits retransmission less abrasively than the moral injunctions of *Qu'est-ce que la littérature*? Leiris writes:

> Car pour celui qui écrit toute la question est là: faire passer dans la tête ou dans le cœur d'autrui les concrétions – jusque-là valables seulement pour lui – déposées, par le présent ou le passé de sa vie, au fond de sa propre tête ou de son propre cœur; communiquer, pour valoriser; faire circuler, pour que la chose ainsi lancée aux autres vous revienne un peu plus prestigieuse, tels ces boucliers des Indiens du Nord-Ouest américain qui se trouvent doués d'une valeur d'autant plus grande qu'ils ont fait l'objet de plus nombreux échanges cérémoniels.[36]

The giving of words, the receiving and the giving in return – Leiris transcribes Mauss's threefold obligation, in which reader and writer achieve greater authenticity. In doing so, he anticipates the study of the transaction of the linguistic sign which will loom large in Lévi-Strauss's structuralism.[37]

Biffures effectively synthesises literature with the practice of the synthetic anthropology, yet thanks to its complexity it does so ambivalently; as it moves slowly towards the mapping of a personal *pensée sauvage*, it never knows whether it is constructing constraints or a liberation. If Sartre probes the double-edged character of freedom, Leiris may be said to do the same for intelligibility. Neither of them, in this period, comes to terms with the element of counter-productivity in his respective activity, but Leiris gets closer to it than Sartre. Where ethnography is concerned, he is in no doubt at all and I quote his comments as a marker for future reference:

> l'ethnographie n'a abouti qu'à faire de moi un bureaucrate [...] son caractère de science exigeant objectivité et patience va finalement à l'encontre de mes espérances (bris de mon armature logique par le contact avec des hommes vivant dans l'obédience d'autres normes) [...] le voyage

enfin, tel que je le concevais (une prise de distance solitaire), loin d'être une façon de se faire autre que ce qu'on est en changeant de décor n'est que pur déplacement d'un personnage toujours identique à lui-même, nomade rien que spatial qui traîne derrière soi – renforcés plutôt que diminués par son isolement relatif – ses inquiétudes, son narcissisme et ses manies.[38]

Leiris's autobiography, for all its commitment, is not at all anti-Freudian. It presumably draws, after all, on the analysis undertaken with Adrien Borel between 1929 and 1935. Existential psychoanalysis, on the other hand, is resolutely hostile to all mechanistic psychologies, and for Sartre this includes Freudian theory. Initially, the Sartrean rival venture is developed as a way of confirming the validity of the phenomenological ontology. *L'Etre et le néant* (part 4, chapter 1) presents it as resting on synthetic postulates – refusing the analytic representation of the person as the sum of characterological elements. Instead, stress is placed on the *projet originel*, which is coterminous with existence and is a movement of perpetual transcendence. Although the method is not set out in detail, it appears to consist of processes of comparison and reduction, each minor project being rewritten in terms of the project into which it can be integrated, until such time as the rewriting can go no further. The *projet originel* is then identified and comprehended in a manner that eliminates causal models (in the manner of Jaspers's notion of *Verstehen*) together with all that pre-exists the lived experience of the person concerned.

In *L'Etre et le néant* Sartre chooses not to engage with Freudian psychoanalysis at a theoretical level. Parallels are noted in passing and go relatively unexplored – that, for instance, between *choix originel* and complex – or else the Freudian concepts are subjected to a perfunctory incorporation, as when libido is relegated by the primacy of the ontology to the status of a second-order project. Sartre favours psychoanalysts who lend themselves to translation into existential terms (Stekel, for example) and leans heavily on philosophers such as Scheler who prefer to handle 'Freudian' realities at the level of moral consciousness. *Mauvaise foi*, an ontological category that is never able to disguise the importance of its place in the future *Morale*, functions in precisely this fashion. If there is such a thing as pathogenesis for Sartre, it is more closely related to evil than to sickness. If there is any therapy it is volunta-ristic and closer to Nietzsche than to Freud (the Nietzsche, indeed, that Freud chose not to read). Reciprocity, when it finally finds a theorised place in Sartre's thought, will appear as the possibility of transcending what Nietzsche had identified as resentment.

Leiris is quite correct when he classifies Sartre's *Baudelaire* (featured in *TM* in May 1946) as a philosophical work.[39] The same is true of *Réflexions sur la question juive* (December 1945) and *Saint Genet* (July to December 1950), as well as of Jeanson's studies of Constant (June 1948) and of Gide (October 1948).[40] The ethical preoccupation which dominates *Baudelaire* but which is much more diffuse in *L'Idiot de la famille* leaves no room, as Beauvoir says, for the 'étude psychanalytique qui eût expliqué Baudelaire à partir de son corps et des faits de son histoire'.[41]

Beauvoir's remark suggests a subsequent *rapprochement* with Freud. It is not opportune at this stage to assert that this does or does not take place. That it may prove even to be possible is due in large measure to Leiris. He and Sartre are in complete accord concerning colonialism; on the subject of poetry they agree to differ except in the case of *négritude*. The two issues, however, are not distinct and together they implicate psychoanalysis and render Leiris's presence in *TM* one of crucial importance. For if the 'poetic' identifications that constitute the ego are perceived by Sartre as colonisations, then this is likely to be all the more true of the movement of transference that makes of the Freudian analyst a temporary constituent of the analysand. Doubtless there are analysts who colonise their patients, and this is one of the strands in Sartre's periodic attacks on the profession. Leiris, however, is both the object of permanent respect and a testimony to the liberating potential of Freudian theory. In this as much as in anything else, he exerts a durable influence over *TM* and over the trajectory of its Director.

The presence of Lévi-Strauss

Sartre's unwritten ethic founders on its dependence on the Kantian categorical imperative and on its problematic relationship with the political and with the literary. It is not true, however, to say that it is partially abandoned before 1951. The famous footnote in *Saint Genet*, which declares that 'toute *Morale* qui ne se donne pas explicitement comme *impossible aujourd'hui* contribue à la mystification et à l'aliénation des hommes',[42] probably dates from 1952, that is to say after Sartre's quarrel with Camus and after the critique of Lévi-Strauss by Claude Lefort which marks the end of this first period. This is not the case, however, with the lengthy quotation, in *Saint Genet*, from Lévi-Strauss's introduction to the works of Mauss, the very text with which Lefort takes issue. It is reasonable to suppose that Sartre cites it before being fully appraised of the moral and political implications of structuralism. At this time, he is becoming interested, because of the glimpse of the moral impasse that they afford, in individuals caught between incompatible value systems (Heinrich in *Le Diable et le Bon Dieu* and Kean in the play of the same name prove the best examples); these are individuals forced by the community at large to 'figurer certaines formes de compromis irréalisables sur le plan collectif, de feindre des transitions imaginaires, d'incarner des synthèses incompatibles'.[43]

Even though both the *Réflexions sur la question juive* and *Saint Genet* operate in the universalist context presupposed by the ethic, they have an anthropological interest: both undertake the existential psychoanalysis of victimisers and scapegoats. The *Réflexions*, however, although very precise in the phenomenology of antisemitism, lack both an understanding of institutionalised racialism and a recognition of Jewish cultural specificity. In *Saint Genet* the conjunction of poetry, racialism and colonialism is visible once more; firmly fixed in the nexus of elements which link Sartre to Leiris, it nonetheless displays evidence of the Lévi-Straussian interest in the shaman. Genet, oppressed by the Other's objectification of him, seeks subjective expression in, among other things, antisemitism. The propensity of existential psychoanalysis to select morally reprehensible literary figures – 'antisémite, Flaubert et Baudelaire, antisémite Villiers; antisémite, hélas! Mallarmé'[44] – in order to repudiate them in the name of a literary ethic aspiring to reciprocity, thus remains strong. Sartre is all the more elated when Genet, coloniser and colonised, discovers in the magic of poetry the means by which to reverse society's perceptions of him. Like 'Orphée noir', *Saint Genet* celebrates 'la revanche du bouc émissaire'.[45]

Existential psychoanalysis is perhaps not the obvious point in this lateral survey at which to embark on a discussion of Lévi-Strauss. The reason for doing so is that his anthropology is available to be mobilised as an ally in the struggle against Freudianism. This, at least, is how Sartre perceives the situation initially, largely because Lévi-Strauss's attitude to Freud is in fact one of great ambivalence, and because the negative pole is more clearly visible in the late 1940s. Lévi-Strauss at this time is anxious to find a clear disciplinary identity and one of the strategies that he adopts is the assertion of the primacy of the anthropological over the psychological. In order to foreground the anti-Freudianism which he shares with Sartre, I shall first comment on *TM*'s attitude to psychoanalysis.

'Nous ferons, dans nos chroniques, la plus large part aux études psychiatriques lorsqu'elles seront écrites dans les perspectives qui nous intéressent.'[46] Thus ran the 'Présentation' of 1945 and on the whole it must be said that the promise is fulfilled. Beauvoir's views on the abuse of psychoanalysis in the USA hint that it may also be used in the service of authenticity. I have already mentioned Sartre's belief in the rationality of madness; *TM* sets out to verify it with an attitude of active, non-sectarian inquiry. The diary of a schizophrenic, for example, appears significantly early, in May 1946.

Much of the initial stimulus does, in fact, come from America. Moreno's ideas on psychodrama appear in September 1950 and are followed in the next month by an analysis of the antisemitic personality by Frenckel-Brunswik and Sanford. It falls to Georges Devereux to give an overview of psychoanalysis in the USA. He considers the European philosophical tradition to be an encumbrance which the American analysts have been fortunate enough to shed – not a view that would endear him to Sartre or Lacan. His admiration for Ruth Benedict tempts him to try to fuse anthropology and psychoanalysis, and in later years he goes on to develop his own specialist area of 'ethnopsychiatry'.

TM also publishes the psychoanalyst Racamier on psychosomatic disorders (September 1950) and features Charles Mauron's 'Introduction à la psychanalyse de Mallarmé' (with which Sartre will later take issue in his own study) in September 1948. If the review has anyone who can claim to be its resident psychoanalyst, however, it is Francis Pasche, a member of the Anna Freud wing of the Société Psychanalytique de Paris. In his articles on 'les psychoses affectives et la guerre' (October 1945) and on sublimation (February 1948), his general purpose is to represent Freudianism as existentialist, that is to say as a mode of intervention designed to restore patients to their original state of autonomy. Ego-psychology seems at this stage to be acceptable to *TM* as long as it is not concerned merely with the adaptation of the individual to bourgeois norms.

The most significant indication of *TM*'s openness is its publication in May 1948 of extracts from the third part of Freud's *Moses and Monotheism*. This is an explicit act of homage, although the prefatory note makes the predictable assertion of the subordination of the psychological to the ontological: 'au lieu d'*expliquer* le conflit humain par le conflit sexuel, on pourrait réintégrer la haine du père à l'agressivité humaine'.[47] It is worth noting that *Moses and Monotheism* is a significant addition to *TM*'s dossier on antisemitism. At the same time, it has political implications, coming in the same year as the PCF's denunciation of Freudianism as a reactionary ideology.

More important in the present context is the fact that Moses the Egyptian (in Freud's hypothesis) is a man whose marginal status is used by the Jews to construct their own collective identity. He is of the category to which Genet and the shaman analysed by Lévi-Strauss in his essay on 'Le sorcier et sa magie' (March 1949) also belong. In this article, for once 'plus psychologique que sociologique',[48] Lévi-Strauss discusses the levels of belief that sustain the power of the shaman – his own, that of his patient or victim, and that of the collectivity. He finds that the actions of the shaman are validated by the consensus, but only in such a way that neither the sorcerer nor his society are able clearly to demarcate real magic from simulation.

Both Sartre and Lévi-Strauss owe a debt to Leiris's formal and informal reports of his fieldwork in Ethiopia. Here is Sartre, for example, describing Genet as a man possessed by the collective representation of him: 'Tels sont au fond les zars qui "possèdent" certains indigènes d'Ethiopie: rien d'autre que les possédés eux-mêmes mais objectivités [*sic*] et sacralisés. Et Genet fait ce que font ces Ethiopiens: il rend un culte à son zar.'[49] Leiris influences Lévi-Strauss's thinking on these matters even after the publication of 'Le sorcier et sa magie', for a footnote to its 1958 republication tells us that 'j'ai été amené par d'opportunes critiques de Michel Leiris à préciser ma pensée dans "L'Introduction à l'œuvre de Marcel Mauss"'.[50]

Leiris and Lévi-Strauss are much more interested than Sartre is in the relationship of shamanism and psychoanalysis. Despite the fact that Sartre had borrowed the Saussurean notions of signifier and signified in an earlier discussion of Freud,[51] he is now manifestly more concerned by the relation of the sign to the referent in the context of literary production. Lévi-Strauss, on the other hand, in attempting an account of the shamanistic cure in psychosocial terms, steps onto the linguistic terrain so fleetingly occupied by Sartre. It is here that is to be found the methodological watershed, the effects of which so deeply mark *TM*.

Lévi-Strauss's use of the Saussurean model yields the following account of magic: the culture in which the shaman operates is non-scientific and is characterised by a deficit of signifieds; the pathological behaviour of the shaman and of his patient, meanwhile, constitute a reality that may be conceptualised only by tapping the excess of signifiers supplied by the sorcerer. Shamanism thus entails the quantitative adjustment of signifieds to signifiers; in doing so, it renders the consensual and the pathological inter-dependent. Is not psychoanalysis, suggests Lévi-Strauss, potentially just as magical? The argument is carried further in 'L'efficacité symbolique'.[52] In Lévi-Strauss's view both shaman and psychoanalyst furnish signifiers which render suffering mythically intelligible to the community – the former by elaborating a social myth, and the latter by becoming a partner in the production of an individual myth. The conclusion to this article brings a clearer view of what linguistic references might give to psychoanalysis, for the effectiveness of the interaction in both shamanism and psychoana-lysis suggests to Lévi-Strauss the existence of a common psychic apparatus, in which the subconscious might play the role of personal lexicon and the unconscious that of a shared grammar characterised by universal laws. These laws would be those identi-fied by Jakobsonian phonology.

Historically, of course, these two essays mark a turning-point in French psychoanalysis – the emergence of Lacan as a radical force. The irony is that Lacan's structuralism derives from Lévi-Strauss's attempt to anthropologise Freud. Pasche is thus quite correct to sense a hostile intent on the part of Lévi-Strauss towards psycho-analysis in general. Pasche's response,[53] however, which affirms the scientific vocation of psychoanalysis as well as its potential contribution to radical social change, is of less use to *TM* than is Lévi-Strauss's preference of reason to magic. As a result, Pasche vanishes from *TM*; even when Pontalis begins his slow movement from Sartrean to Lacanian positions, Pasche does not return, for by then he has been left on the side of the intellectually unadventurous orthodoxy after the 1953 schism in the French psychoanalytical movement. Lévi-Strauss, on the other hand, remains for much longer, primarily because Pouillon moves into anthropology much as Pontalis does into psychoanalysis. Even so, the success of Lacan is one of the things that reveals to Sartre the pro-Freudian or para-Freudian features of structural anthropology. This is why, in the consideration of the growing tensions between Sartre and Lévi-Strauss, psychoanalysis is a factor that must not be forgotten.

Lévi-Strauss's assertion in 1945 that linguistics was 'la route qui mène à la connaissance positive des faits sociaux'[54] is not a conviction shared by *TM*. Sartre chooses not to pursue his own deployment of Saussurean categories and although Merleau-Ponty lectures on Saussure at the Ecole Normale Supérieure in 1948–9, nothing of his thinking in this area reaches the review. The attempt by R.-L. Wagner[55] to move towards a phenomenological socio-linguistics similarly comes to naught, at least in *TM*. Sartre's view has changed little since 1944, when he said of language that 'les questions qu'il pose sont techniques, politiques, esthétiques, morales [...] mais il n'y a pas de problème métaphysique du langage'.[56] Language is held to be a second-order phenomenon which mediates, in a purely instrumental way, specific courses of action which have already been chosen and which are already significant; its only mysteries are those projected onto it by the morbidity of poets.

In the late 1940s, then, Lévi-Strauss is perceived as an ally to be mobilised in anti-Freudian polemics. His commitment to linguistics is not really held against him, simply because the review does not take linguistics seriously. More significantly, he and Sartre share the wish to be incorporated into a post-Stalinist Marxism. In Lévi-Strauss's case this is articulated rarely and obliquely; in Sartre's frequently and directly. Even so, the political complicity is taken to be there, and this is sufficient to maintain a bond between them. In respect of Lévi-Strauss's politics, however, there is little to say. Sartre's campaign against the dogmatism of the PCF does nevertheless have implications for *TM*'s view of anthropology, and without wishing to reproduce in detail the political history of the review provided by Burnier, I shall briefly mention certain factors which will assume relevance in due course.

Merleau-Ponty's formulation is perfectly clear: 'Un marxisme vivant devrait "sauver" la recherche existentialiste et l'intégrer, au lieu de l'étouffer.'[57] Increasingly, however, the PCF prefers confrontation to recuperation. *TM* has no qualms about offending its sensibilities: it publishes the testimonies of Silone and Wright in respect of 'the god that failed' and seeks out Marxists from beyond the French orthodoxy, notably Walter Benjamin and Antonio Gramsci. The major texts, however, are the following: Sartre's 'Matérialisme et révolution' (June–July 1946), those by Merleau-Ponty that later became known as *Humanisme et terreur* (October 1946 to January 1947, and June 1947) and Sartre's preface (not published in *TM*, but crucial nonetheless) to Louis Dalmas's essay on *Le Communisme yougoslave depuis la rupture avec Moscou* (1950).

Sartre's 1946 article is an attack on the doctrine of the PCF.[58] He sees it rather as he sees Freudianism – as a mechanical determinism evolved in this case for dubious political purposes and wholly incapable of accounting for itself in its own terms. Sartre looks initially to Merleau-Ponty for the elaboration of the living Marxism that the Party is so unlikely to produce. *TM*'s political editor, however, becomes increasingly doubtful whether the task can be accomplished in the existing circumstances. By 1950 his political contributions cease (the immediate cause being disagreement over Korea)[59] and it is Sartre himself who renews the call for this living Marxism in his preface to the study by Dalmas. His celebration of the early years of Titoism reasserts in Hegelian terms the tension between materialist and existentialist positions, calling for the resolution of 'cette antinomie nouvelle; thèse: le subjectif est une structure secondaire de l'objectivité – antithèse: l'objectivité dépend d'une subjectivité qui apprécie et prévoit les phénomènes et qui les modifie en fonction de ses appréciations'.[60]

The synthesis required of the Sartrean anthropology is formulated quite clearly, therefore, in terms of the possible transcendence of social situations by subjects conditioned in those situations. *TM* may thus be expected in future to be attentive to whatever academic anthropology may offer in the way of theories of social change. Moreover, its own moralistic universalism will in due course be tempered by an increasing awareness of cultural specificity, due in large measure to the need to discover roads to freedom other than those signposted by Moscow. Gramsci and Tito herald a much wider interest in alternative models of revolution, all of which will be notable for their evident incompatibility with the static properties of the societies studied by structuralist anthropology. The political reticence of Lévi-Strauss in the 1940s will not be without consequence in *TM*.

Lévi-Strauss, however, does contribute to one strand of political struggle in which the PCF, and the French left in general, is inactive: feminism. Between May 1948 and July 1949, *TM* publishes eight extracts from Beauvoir's *Le Deuxième Sexe*.[61] Such articles as had already appeared in this area (the 'Journal d'une prostituée', for example, and material by Colette Audry, Violette Leduc and Geneviève Serreau) are made use of in it. It is a work that clearly belongs to the synthetic anthropology and, although it relies heavily on the psychoanalytical data of Helene Deutsch and of Stekel, its terms of reference are unmistakable, rehearsing the familiar quest for liberation from the position of being alienated in the *pour-autrui*. It is better researched than Sartre's work on the antisemite and the black poets, even though the sociological aspect is not strong. Most effective are the existential psychoanalyses of projects like those of the narcissist and the *amoureuse*. Without extending the theoretical power of the synthetic anthropology, Beauvoir widens its scope so that it comes to include the largest group of marginalised members of all known communities. This is not an insignificant development.

Her encounter with Lévi-Strauss predates his debate with Pasche. Early in the second part of *Le Deuxième Sexe*, she has recourse to *Les Structures élémentaires de la parenté*, to which, thanks to Leiris,[62] she has access prior to its publication. It must be said that she respectfully misuses Lévi-Strauss, calling upon him to endorse a diachronic account of the origins of male domination. She agrees that the institutions of exogamy are a function of group self-preservation, that men establish reciprocity primarily by the exchange of women (who represent both labour power and the potential reproduction of labour power) and that the incest prohibition is an expression of this economic practice. Prior to these mechanisms of group interaction, however, she postulates the transcendence, in reciprocity, of the fundamental consciential conflict that establishes the Other as Other. It is at the level of *pour-soi* and *pour-autrui* that she locates sexual differentiation, that is to say in the various perceptions of the biological constraints (*facticité*) which limit the scope of female transcendence. Her argument leads to the following account of male supremacy: the nomadic tribes settled, alienating individual consciousness in group identity; they assimilated the fertility of the women to that of the land and consequently overvalued the former; then, achieving their neolithic revolution and evolving tools with which to master nature, they devalued the women and established universal patriarchy. In the beginning, therefore, was husbandry.

Lévi-Strauss would no doubt say that Beauvoir, like Freud in *Totem and Taboo*,[63] supplies just another origin myth. She, however, regards him as much more readily assimilable to the synthetic anthropology than Freud is. In her review (in November 1949) of his thesis on kinship, she pronounces herself 'singulièrement frappée par la concordance de certaines descriptions avec les thèses soutenues par l'existentialisme'.[64] By this she means that the reciprocity which binds man to man (but not man to woman, or even woman to woman), and which Lévi-Strauss inherits from Mauss, is consistent with what little has been formulated of the existentialist ethic. At this stage, she too avoids the question of the pertinence of the linguistic model, even though it is Lévi-Strauss's analogy of woman and sign that permits its use. It is probable in her case, too, that his critique of Freud is mistakenly read as a repudiation of the unconscious.

The underlying tensions between Lévi-Strauss and *TM* are finally brought into the open by Claude Lefort, when the main lines of the emergent structuralism are clarified in 1950. Curiously enough, structuralist anthropology attains an influential position within the social sciences thanks to the republication of the major works of Mauss, most of which had appeared between 1900 and 1930. Georges Gurvitch, the senior academic in the field, having invited Lévi-Strauss to supply an introduction to the volume, is presented with a text which he describes rather reservedly as 'une interprétation très personnelle'.[65] Its eccentricity lies in the fact that it speaks of Mauss as the precursor of structuralism rather than as the founding father to whom total respect is due. Its relaxed attitude to academic protocol and to sociological orthodoxy combines with its promotion of linguistics to make of it a radical statement of aims for a new anthropology. I shall mention some of its salient features.

At first sight, there is much that seems acceptable to the synthetic anthropology. Mauss, says Lévi-Strauss, helps us see that phenomena of possession and shamanism should not be regarded as pathological in their local contexts. Societies must be viewed as sets of interlocking symbolic systems which are often slightly out of phase with each other. These temporary incongruencies engender misfits whose social role is the potentially prestigious one of embodying the resultant social tensions. This is the argument that Sartre borrows in *Saint Genet*. It leads Lévi-Strauss to believe, like Sartre, that the problem of the relation of the individual to the group is not usefully discussed in simple causal terms. In his view, the psychological and the social are epistemologically inseparable: the former expresses the latter such that the latter can be verified only in its expression by the former. This, however, poses a problem of method which brings Lévi-Strauss apparently close to one of the bases of the Sartrean anthropology, namely the acknowledgement that '*l'observateur est lui-même une partie de son observation*'.[66]

The convergence is not real, however, for Lévi-Strauss is not thinking of the particular social interactions of observer and observed which, in optimal circumstances, would impel political change. He is concerned instead with the more abstract consideration that the ethnographic encounter involves parties of the same very broad category – human beings. To use the Jaspersian terms which Sartre will later employ in his own thoughts on 'questions de méthode', one might say that the fieldworker is empowered to explain (*erklären*) and to understand (*verstehen*) a human subject who is living out certain specific social possibilities theoretically open to all. Lévi-Strauss seems to envisage a partially empathetic stance, such as that adopted by Sartre in *L'Idiot de la famille*, but is bothered by the prospect of erroneous interpretations. He goes on as follows: 'Cette difficulté serait insoluble, les subjectivités étant, par hypothèse, incomparables et incommunicables, si l'opposition entre moi et autrui ne pouvait être surmontée sur un terrain, qui est aussi celui où l'objectif et le subjectif se rencontrent, nous voulons dire l'inconscient.'[67]

This is indeed the crux of the matter. Lévi-Strauss's article is seminal in a significant respect. Rather like Sartre's *Morale* and his own thoughts on anthropology and Marxism, his view of the methodology and epistemology of ethnographic fieldwork is never fully developed. What happens instead is that the unconscious is promoted from its role as mode of control of hypotheses to the status of prime object of study. This movement is clearly visible in 1950 when Lévi-Strauss reconsiders the *Essai sur le don*.

He regrets that Mauss had to import the Maori notion of *mana* to explain the motive power of the separate obligations to give, to receive and to give in return. He should have realised, says Lévi-Strauss, that the discrete actions are less important than the system of exchange itself, and that the latter is a 'nécessité inconsciente'.[68] To the extent that exchange is a complex system of mechanical reciprocity, it is amenable to precise description in the same way as is the oppositionality of phonemes in the phonology of Jakobson. The manifest is thus describable in terms of its latent organisation, and the task of the anthropologist is to 'distinguer un donné purement phénoménologique, sur lequel l'analyse scientifique n'a pas de prise, d'une infrastructure plus simple que lui, et à laquelle il doit toute sa réalité'.[69] Had Mauss had access to linguistics, suggests Lévi-Strauss, he would have recognised in *mana* the equivalent of Jakobson's 'zero phoneme', that is to say an entity which enters into no binary relations with others in order to generate meaning, but which instead simply marks a contrast with an absence of meaning. Like such terms as *machin* in French, its function is to bridge the gap between signifiers and signifieds; it is evidence of the surplus of the former, a surplus which will disappear completely only when humanity accedes to total scientific knowledge.

The 'Introduction à l'œuvre de Marcel Mauss' is underdeveloped in the sense that it can merely affirm, without real demonstration, that linguistic models can be used to understand the unconscious processes which, it is also affirmed, inform non-linguistic aspects of social reality. What models may be selected, whether they are consistent with each other, how they may be deployed, how far their usefulness extends – these are questions that remain unanswered. Enough has been asserted, however, for *TM* to realise that Lévi-Strauss proposes scientistically to preserve the unconscious rather than to dissolve it.

Lefort's response is by no means such a substantial document. He concentrates on the *Essai sur le don* and asks of Mauss that he serve a specific purpose – that of contributing to a new Marxism purged of Leninism and of Stalinism. In this context, the Mauss constructed by Lévi-Strauss has to be denied in order that Lefort might reveal another, committed to the study of the lived intentions of the agents of exchange. Lefort draws two important conclusions. First, that exchange has economic, juridical, moral, religious and aesthetic significance: the economic is thus not a discrete sector or infrastructure, but something much more diffuse, the correct localisation of which implies a departure from vulgar economistic Marxism. Lefort here voices a thought which gains wide acceptance only fifteen years later with the work of the PCF philosopher Louis Althusser, and for which the Marxist anthropologist Maurice Godelier will give credit to the Lévi-Strauss of *Les Structures élémentaires de la parenté.*[70]

Secondly, Lefort refuses to allow Lévi-Strauss to 'se donner artificiellement une rationalité totale, à partir de laquelle les groupes et les hommes sont réduits à une fonction abstraite, au lieu de la fonder sur les relations concrètes que ceux-ci viennent à se nouer entre eux'.[71] Because his own terms of reference are close to those of the phenomenological ontology (he belongs to the group called Socialisme ou Barbarie),[72] he brings to the fore the agonistic aspects of the practice of exchange. Seeking his own explanation for the triple obligation to give, to receive and to give in return, he moves onto ground covered by Sartre in his analyses, in *Saint Genet*, of the destructive power of aristocratic generosity. In giving, the subject is said to assert its difference from others; in receiving, it learns its similarity. '*On ne donne pas pour recevoir; on donne pour que l'autre donne.*'[73] Out of conflict is born reciprocity, and out of reciprocity, community.

The situation is a curious one; Lefort and Lévi-Strauss agree that structural anthropology has become incompatible with phenomenology; each, in recognition of the conflict, seeks to appropriate reciprocity from the other. Even so, the flashpoint is not reached in 1951. The main thrust of the synthetic anthropology has been so exclusively ethical and literary that it can hardly be expected to rush headlong into analyses of the systems of exchange of non-literate peoples. On the other hand, in the future, when its commitment to an ethic of literary production begins to wane, it might be expected to concern itself with theories of ideology, theories to which academic anthropology should also be attracted. Conditions might then not be unfavourable for both Sartre and Lévi-Strauss to bring their own work closer to the Marxism to which both are committed. In 1951, however, the claims of each to Marxist consistency are not sufficient to permit comparison. All that can be said is that, thanks to Lefort, it is now clear that while for Sartre social structures are the expression of the interaction of individual purposes, the converse is true for Lévi-Strauss.

The outlook for convergence is thus bleak, and for a number of reasons. First, because mention of the unconscious tends to close doors in *TM* rather than open them. Secondly, because the participation of the potentially conciliatory Merleau-Ponty is declining. And thirdly, because *TM* is not well placed to examine the bases of structuralist anthropology. Indeed, it is sufficiently unattracted to linguistics for it to remain unable to assess Lévi-Strauss's analogical use of certain aspects of the work of Saussure and Jakobson.

The likely tendency is therefore for Sartre and Lévi-Strauss to move further apart. (As this happens, it represents a great intellectual and editorial challenge to Pouillon.) Both men speak of the place where subjectivity and objectivity meet, but for the former it is in history, for the latter in the unconscious. Lévi-Strauss claims that scientificity is guaranteed by a contemplative empathy of the ethnographer with the object of study; Sartre claims to remain beyond science and asks the fieldworker to assume a role in the labour of socio-political change. It does not seem, therefore, that Lévi-Strauss will be able to supply what Leiris believes anthropology should offer: theories of social transformation based on the phenomenology of the colonial confrontation; an active commitment to anti-colonialist and anti-racialist struggles; an acute moral consciousness, capable of raising ethnocentricity to a level of reflexivity at which it will found mutual comprehension and an existential reciprocity.

2
FROM 1951 TO 1956: THE RISE OF STRUCTURALISM

These are the years of the consolidation of Lévi-Strauss's innovations in anthropological theory. This does not prevent him from maintaining a presence in *TM* and, in July 1956, Pouillon undertakes a respectful evaluation of his work, one which usefully highlights all that separates it from the synthetic anthropology. Leiris, for his part, makes only literary contributions, but with Georges Balandier, Verrier Elwin and Margaret Mead, the review is able to feature other ethnographic research. Quantitatively, there is no increase in anthropological material and the main emphasis of this half-decade is political.

A brief comment on the editorial personnel is relevant here. Of the original Board, Aron and Ollivier had resigned in June 1946. Thereafter, and in fact until January 1954, no Board is named, effective control and political editorship passing initially to Merleau-Ponty. After 1949, however, the year in which he gives up the legal responsibility of the position of *gérant*, Merleau-Ponty chooses to slip steadily into the background. So much so that when this second period opens there is a general loss of direction which Sartre subsequently describes in the following way: 'Ainsi découvrions-nous l'un et l'autre que la revue avait au cours de ces six années acquis une sorte d'indépendance et qu'elle nous menait autant que nous la menions. Bref, pendant l'interrègne, entre 1950 et 1952, un navire sans capitaine recruta lui-même des officiers qui en évitèrent la perdition.'[1] Sartre had begun to adopt precisely the political positions and ambitions that his colleague was relinquishing. This led to such a degree of inhibition that, recalls Sartre, 'nous avions désaffiché la politique'.[2] In public, each deferred to the other:

Chacun de nous, sans rien en dire même à soi, s'était approprié la revue. Il y avait, d'un côté, comme dans le *Cercle de craie caucasien*, une paternité officielle et nominale, la mienne – en tout ce qui touchait la politique, elle n'était que cela (dans les autres domaines, je ne dirais pas que la situation

40

se renversait mais que nous travaillions ensemble) – et, de l'autre, une paternité d'adoption, cinq ans de soins jaloux.[3]

In due course, however, Sartre takes hold, convinced now that the fulfilment of the ethic is contingent upon a prior investment, both theoretical and practical, in the political. It nevertheless takes three or four years for a new editorial team to become established. Beauvoir notes that Claude Lanzmann and Marcel Péju 'aidèrent Sartre à repolitiser la revue et ce furent eux surtout qui l'orientèrent vers ce "compagnonnage critique" avec les communistes que Merleau-Ponty avait abandonné'.[4] The interregnum is nonetheless a long one. Although Lanzmann and Péju begin contributing in 1952, it is only in January 1953 that Merleau-Ponty finally leaves, and only in January 1954 that an Editorial Board is once again named on the front cover of the review. It consists of Jean Cau, Lanzmann, Péju (General Secretary) and Sartre (Director), with Jeanson as *gérant*.

The story of the loss and recapture of political momentum is told by Burnier. Unfortunately, his account lacks a sense of the extent to which the repoliticisation is achieved by running counter to the current of structuralism which gains strength at the same time. It is certainly true to say that Merleau-Ponty becomes disaffected with Sartrean voluntarism and departs, but this does not mean that the level of intellectual debate falls or that the rivals to existential Marxism retreat. On the contrary, Lacanian psychoanalysis acquires an increasingly insistent spokesman, Pontalis, while Pouillon, equally insistently, refuses to give up hope of reconciling the positions of Sartre and Lévi-Strauss. In this chapter, I propose to scrutinise the activities of Merleau-Ponty, Pontalis and Pouillon – not in order to relegate the political to a secondary role but in order to explore its context in other discourses. I shall do so, as before, by reviewing different categories of material in turn.

The contribution of Merleau-Ponty

Merleau-Ponty's profile fades within *TM* only to sharpen again after his departure when, uninhibited by former loyalties, he gives the reasons for his withdrawal. Both the reasons and the editorial traces which he leaves are best located in the areas of sociology, history, political theory, linguistics and philosophy. I shall begin with the first of these, the closest to anthropology.

Prior to 1951, *TM* contained no academic sociology; instead, it published a considerable amount of primary material that a sociologist might well have been able to use – first-hand accounts of the daily life of a prostitute, a magistrate, a miner, a legionnaire, and so on. The priority given to the direct documentation of the individual's lived experience is not difficult to understand; the absence of sociologists more so, perhaps. The reason lay in the state of the discipline, which was parlous. Durkheim had lost his first generation of students in the First World War; in 1945, following the death of Halbwachs in Buchenwald, a similar situation existed. Balandier spoke in 1949 of 'la crise actuelle de la sociologie française' and of 'le petit nombre de personnalités de premier plan'.[5] The only prominent name was that of Gurvitch, who owed less to the French sociological tradition than to philosophy and who, as I have indicated, was to look askance at the birth of structuralism.

Only in 1951, then, does *TM*'s first professional sociologist, Michel Crozier, make his appearance. He is quick to complain, perhaps because of the celebrity that is beginning to attend the work of Lévi-Strauss, that 'la sociologie sérieuse répugne encore à abandonner l'étude des sociétés primitives et les réflexions méthodologiques'.[6] Provocatively, he ascribes this to a fear of the real world. The fact that he should write at all in *TM* is therefore doubly significant. It indicates the rise of a new French sociology and shows that the review is interested in it. This is just as it should be, given that, with *Saint Genet*, attention has begun to shift from the contents of the ethic to its social conditions of existence.

Crozier's most important contribution, anticipating the influential editorship of André Gorz in later years, is his article on 'Human engineering' in July 1951. It is a consideration of the uses made of social psychology by American capitalism and could well be taken as the first allusion to the images of Charlie Chaplin working on the production line in *Modern Times* – and for *TM*, therefore, a long-awaited return to source. Crozier's conclusion makes a timely reassertion of the radicalism of the review: 'Nos psychanalystes et nos sociologues doivent s'attaquer aux problèmes du travail et du commandement, se placer sur le terrain même du Big Business américain et critiquer impitoyablement toutes les déductions tendancieuses qu'il oblige à tirer des progrès des disciplines sociales et humaines.'[7]

'Human engineering' merits close attention because its preface, signed '*TM*', is sufficiently substantial to be taken as one of the rare restatements of the rationale and the focus of the synthetic anthropology. I therefore quote it at length:

Le 'culturalisme' et certaines recherches de la psychologie sociale américaine, que les *TM* ont contribué et contribueront à mieux faire connaître
en France, sont une acquisition importante dans toute la mesure où ils
s'attachent à révéler les rapports tacites, officieux, mais vécus, entre les
hommes, par delà des idées ou les devises officielles qui les masquent au
moins autant qu'elles les expriment [. . .] Ils entreprennent d'appliquer ce
principe incontestable que la vérité d'un système social est dans le type de
rapports humains qu'il rend possibles. La corrélation dans une seule vie
humaine des conceptions morales, juridiques, religieuses avec les techniques, le travail et les forces de production, la sociologie marxiste l'avait
bien constatée, mais beaucoup d'auteurs paraissent la fonder sur une
causalité mystique de l'économie, au lieu que la notion de la *culture* comme
d'une totalité qui a ses lois d'équilibre, ses changements moléculaires, ses
crises, ses re-structurations – et celle d'une *structure de la personnalité de
base*, tantôt stéréotypée, tantôt travaillée par un principe de changement
dans chaque groupe humain, – vient éclairer la connexion des 'pensées' et
des 'faits économiques'.[8]

It has to be said that *TM* is here overstating its achievements: apart
from extracts from Mead's *Male and Female*, to which I shall turn
shortly, and a not particularly warm review of Benedict's *Patterns
of Culture*,[9] it has done little to promote American culturalism. As
a future programme, the text has a similarly dubious status, for it is,
in fact, the last editorial material to be placed in the review by
Merleau-Ponty.[10] The directions, new and not so new, which he
suggests, are thus being spelt out for him and not necessarily for
TM.

It is unfortunate that the programme should be so short-lived, for
although Sartre's positions have changed considerably, he still
cannot be regarded as having tried to find a prominent place in his
phenomenology for sociology and anthropology. Contact with
structuralism has not meant close co-operation, and when Merleau-
Ponty moves towards Lévi-Strauss,[11] he clearly feels obliged to
move away from *TM* at the same time. The significance of this
development is that it creates a space for Pouillon to take up the
task of conciliation.

In the short term, after the editorial crisis of 1951–3, the
sociological policy and content of *TM* cannot be said to display any
consistency. In the absence of 'Questions de méthode', which does
not arrive until 1957 and which shows that Sartre has in the
meantime gained some familiarity with the work of the American
cultural anthropologist Abram Kardiner – although not from any
articles in *TM* – the review seems at a loss as to how to proceed.
Only one sociologist, the Brazilian Gilberto Freyre, makes a mark,
and that is by virtue of his exemplary eclecticism. Pouillon's review

of Freyre's outstanding study of slavery and agriculture, *Casa Grande e Senzala*, allows him to formulate the line which he will ultimately follow:

Que le réel soit compréhensible ne signifie pas qu'il relève d'une seule explication, cela veut dire qu'il faut en pousser la description assez loin et selon les méthodes particulières que requièrent ses divers aspects sans craindre la pluralité des systèmes d'interprétation. Assez loin, c'est-à-dire jusqu'au point où cette pluralité fait apparaître une vérité effective et non préfabriquée, où la rivalité des méthodes fait place à leur convergence.[12]

Pouillon's faith in the ultimate complementarity of different approaches is what distinguishes him from Merleau-Ponty. Both agree, and Sartre with them, that what is needed is a means of thinking through the relationship of the individual to the group in a non-determinist manner, with a view to conceptualising what Pouillon calls 'l'indissoluble corrélation de la liberté et de l'alié-nation de l'homme dans le monde'.[13] Freyre's success, in Pouillon's view, lies in the fact that his methodological eclecticism is justified by the primacy that he accords to diachrony. For Merleau-Ponty, on the other hand, it is not possible to dissolve all differences in an appeal to history, precisely because there are different conceptions of history and because the Sartrean is unacceptable.

At least this means that it is idle to ascribe Merleau-Ponty's withdrawal either to disagreements over Korea or to disagreements over Saussure. Whole sets of intellectual terms of reference are involved and the gap between them prompts first the divergence and then the criticisms addressed to Sartre by his ex-colleague. Looking at *TM* in the light of the polemic, one is forced first of all to note a singular absence of context in respect of the main point of contention, history. For while both men have from time to time offered philosophical considerations, articles by professional historians have proved rarer than those written by linguisticians. This reflects badly on the editorial activities of both philosophers and leaves Sartre in a particularly weak position. The lack of historiography and the growing influence of Lévi-Strauss mean that the synthetic anthropology is forced to defend the diachronic principle against the synchronic without ever having sought to research it: it seemed, like language, to go without saying. The great respect shown to the social historian Freyre simply underlines the failure to keep the promises of the 'Présentation', where, in 1945, Marc Bloch of the *Annales* school had been cited as an author capable of avoiding the temptation to segment history into discrete political, economic and social histories and capable of recognising that 'l'époque s'exprime dans et par les personnes et que les personnes se choisissent dans et par leur époque'.[14]

The reasons for this failure are no longer mysterious: there is the recent traumatic acquaintance with historicity in the war and a degree of amnesia in respect of the pre-war period, the high valuation of literature, the primacy of the ontology and the moral urge to produce an ethic. But in this second period, not all of these factors are quite so powerful; given the more sociological attitude towards the ethic, the way seems clear for historical analyses and for explorations of collective temporality more extensive than the imaginative reconstruction of the recent past in, for example, *Les Chemins de la liberté*. Sure enough, November 1954 marks the beginning of a long sequence of articles by Henri Guillemin, two-thirds of which are extracts from his voluminous study of *Les Origines de la Commune*; this collaboration continues until 1967. *TM* obviously attaches great importance to Guillemin's research, with its detail, its range, its interest in literature and in the role of key individuals and its lack of dependence on theory. Sartre has recourse to it in his essay on Mallarmé and in 1956 draws up an interesting list of 'les livres qui ont fait avancer la connaissance, ceux de Bloch, de G. Lefebvre, de Guillemin, les ouvrages ethno-graphiques de Lévi-Strauss, les travaux de Francastel sur la pein-ture etc.'.[15]

It is Sartre himself, however, who supplies the most significant work of the period, operating in a field which is primarily that of political theory, but which in his case serves a dual purpose: that of legitimising the political position which he holds between 1952 and 1956, namely anti-anti-communism and critical support of the PCF, and that of working towards an existential Marxist historiography, that is to say an understanding of history in terms of the dialectic of individual and group. Historiography in this sense is just another word for the synthetic anthropology, but the change in stress should not pass unnoticed. The quest for the ethic had previously induced a focus on contemporaneity, but now that it is necessary to come to terms with Marxism, now that there is a danger that contempo-raneity might be confused with structuralist synchrony, and now that anthropology has afforded a glimpse of how sociality harbours forces greater than the Freudian parameters of ontogenesis – now, therefore, Sartre can allow himself to perceive that the here and now implies a there and then.

The days when history played only the smallest part in a synthetic anthropology so intent on emphasising historicity now themselves become a recent past. Hitherto, it made little difference, from the methodological point of view, whether the object of study was situated in a previous epoch (Baudelaire, Sade) or in the present (Genet, the poets of *négritude*). What Sartre does now, however, is to modify his approach in quite a radical way: his investigations henceforth take the form of existential psychoanalyses of groups in conflict. The move from personal histories to public history, in other words, passes by way of the sociological, but only to the extent that social classes undergo a process of personalisation. Lefort is quite right to point out that the French bourgeoisie is assessed in the third part of 'Les communistes et la paix' (April 1954) as if it were an individual.[16]

On the other hand, and fortunately for Sartre – because the temptation to psychologise recedes accordingly – it is less easy to speak in the same way of the proletariat. This is because, like the colonised, it has, in Sartre's term, been 'massified' – reduced to isolated and demoralised units by the economic practices and the atomistic ideology of the bourgeoisie. Sartre deems it important, therefore, to look at the way in which such separated individuals may come together as a newly potent group. Consistent with the transcendence already outlined in 'Orphée noir' and elsewhere, the proletariat is now said to define itself in the movement of synthesis by which objectified subjects discover their multiple objectifications and assert their subjectivity through a collective objectification of their antagonist. It is the Party which enacts this mediation between fragmentation and unity and between despair and resolve. This extended line of argument derives directly from the analyses of colonialism in the late 1940s; it will undergo further elaboration in the *Critique de la raison dialectique*.

It is a line which both Lefort and Merleau-Ponty greet with perplexity. They cannot decide whether 'Les communistes et la paix' makes general theoretical statements or whether it simply addresses the political events of the moment (the summer of 1952); their puzzlement turns quickly to annoyance. Lefort insists that Sartre appears still not to have taken proper cognisance of the determining power of social and economic conditions. Merleau-Ponty endorses further reservations which are formulated specifically to show how the premisses of Sartrean philosophy predispose it to overlook such factors. His opinion may be summarised as follows: Sartre is limited by the extent to which he is dependent on the dualism of subject and object, as well as by his reduction of all human relations to consciential conflict and of all historical activity to voluntarism; this voluntarism, in the last analysis, is amenable only to ethical evaluation and can never hope to understand the dialectic of human and material factors from which it derives.[17]

Since Lefort and Merleau-Ponty refuse to accept the existence of the void out of which they consider Sartrean consciousness to spring, they hold his representation of history to be grossly inadequate. What is missing, for them, is a realm of experience and determination interposed between the individual and the event, influencing the scope, the nature and the effect of particular actions, pre-existing them and shaping the consciousness that perceives itself to be the locus of moral and political choices. In retrospect, it is possible to see a lack of frankness in these exchanges, certainly on the part of Sartre. Such is the political tension of the period, in the view of all the parties concerned (and Audry, Beauvoir, Camus, Jeanson and Pierre Naville all enter the fray at one stage or another), that Sartre does not reveal the extent to which his continuing thoughts on ethics have grappled with the problems that Lefort and Merleau-Ponty place before him. In essence, their allegations of defective epistemology amount to an accusation of a lack of reflexivity, the moral judgement lying on occasion very near the surface of their critiques. They view the synthetic anthropology much as Sartre views vulgar Marxism – as incapable or unwilling to account for itself in its own terms. Perhaps unbeknown to them, however, Sartre is fully aware of his wish to emerge *ab nihilo* as *ens causa sui*; he is aware, too, of his tendency to regard all social antecedents as poetic colonisations to be denied either vehemently or, even more effectively, in silence. This is why *Les Mots*, which comes to terms to some extent with the poetic and the parental, is the real reworking of the then unpublished *Cahiers pour une morale*. Yet even *Les Mots*, which at this time is in the process of composition, remains unpublished until 1963. For as long as Cold War vehemence is appropriate, that is to say until his anger at the Soviet intervention in Hungary in 1956, Sartre does not fully acknowledge the extent to which the substantial critiques of Lefort and Merleau-Ponty assist in impelling him towards the next theoretical threshold of the synthetic anthropology, the *Critique de la raison dialectique*. Ironically, it will be Merleau-Ponty's death in 1961 that both facilitates amicable recognitions and allows Sartre to engage in the historiography of the early years of *TM*.

The present context offers a way of bringing these general remarks into focus. When, in his 'Réponse à Claude Lefort',[18]

Sartre evokes the workers prior to their organisation into a militant group, that is to say massified and abject in their suffering, he asserts that it is in this condition that bourgeois sociology describes them – in order to maintain them there. The analytic thus separates what the synthetic wishes to bring together. Dismissing in rather a vague way 'la sociologie "fourre-tout"',[19] he adds elsewhere that 'ce qui rend les choses encore plus suspectes c'est que la sociologie des primitifs ne tombe *jamais* sous ces reproches . . . on étudie là de véritables *ensembles signifiants*'.[20]

It is striking that although Sartre's views lead him away from Lévi-Strauss, his references are often disconcertingly complimentary. This poses the problem of how closely he had read the work that he mentions. It is not clear from the quotation above, moreover, whether he is distinguishing between sociology and anthropology, or between two different types of society, or whether he is eliding the two distinctions. Balandier takes up the first option, contrasting the sociologist, who observes from within, with the anthropologist, who observes from without and who is therefore better placed to assign and to grasp meanings: 'c'est ce qui a frappé J.-P. Sartre analysant la démarche ethnologique, et qui l'a conduit à accorder un privilège à l'ethnologue, au détriment du sociologue'.[21]

But this does not seem to be at all what Sartre has in mind. His objection to those observers who do not recognise the extent to which they impinge on the object of study applies as much to ethnographers as to sociologists. The evidence suggests that he is distinguishing between two types of society, opposites in the sense that they display certain characteristics in complementary distribution: conflict and consensus, dynamic and static histories, the absence and presence of unifying symbolic systems. It is not specified what the *ensembles signifiants* might be. What is clear is that when conflict supervenes, cultural unity is broken and massification ensues; this latter can be transcended only by the formation of a class consciousness capable of resolving the conflict. It is in this sense that Sartre deploys his one ethnographic reference in the 'Réponse à Claude Lefort'.[22] Here his position emerges as follows:

Dans un milieu social structuré qui possède ses traditions, ses institutions, ses propagandes et sa culture, on peut bien imaginer la réciprocité car l'individu sera forgé dès sa naissance par le milieu social, il en recevra les coutumes et les techniques, la culture etc. Mais la réalité sociale est en chacun et en tous comme un 'pattern' culturel qui n'a de vie que celle qu'on lui donne, qui se *maintient* comme tradition, et n'évolue jamais comme mouvement intentionnel. Si le prolétariat est sujet, s'il écrit son histoire, il a une autre réalité que cette unité idéale: ce n'est pas un 'pattern' c'est un pouvoir réel d'intégration. Donc vous n'échapperez pas: il faut revenir à la synthèse.[23]

Sartre borrows Benedict's concept of pattern to refer to the ethos of a stable, consensual society, held in place by a system of equitable exchange. Consciential conflict is here transcended in a reciprocity that extends to the whole of the community. Divided, conflictual societies, on the other hand, await synthesis by the proletariat; in the meantime, in these societies there can be no system of reciprocity or of symbolism coextensive with the society as a whole. It thus does not seem that this argument is simplistic enough to allow Lefort to claim that Sartre completely ignores social reality. At the same time, Sartre's apparent assimilation of symbolic systems to systems of material reciprocity – no doubt influenced by Lévi-Strauss's conflation of woman and linguistic sign – leads to confusion. What is required, and what nobody provides, is the phenomenological description of social realities like language and ideology, which exist also in divided societies and which, however inequitably distributed they might be, constitute the factors without which division cannot be observed and experienced.

I hope that I have shown that the political differences of Lefort, Merleau-Ponty and Sartre are located in an explicitly anthropological context. It is easy to sense an appeal to this in Merleau-Ponty's later critique, a passage from which I shall quote *in extenso*:

Tout ce qu'on peut savoir sur l'histoire et sur les hommes, cette encyclopédie des situations, cet inventaire universel que les *TM* entreprenaient, ne pouvaient diminuer d'un pouce la distance de la liberté radicale et sauvage à ses incarnations dans le monde, établir une équivalence entre telle et telle civilisation, telle nation, telle entreprise historique. Car on ne s'engage que pour se défaire du monde [...] On pouvait donc bien dénoncer des faits d'oppression, parler des Noirs, des Juifs, des camps soviétiques, des procès de Moscou, des femmes, des homosexuels, on pouvait habiter en pensée toutes ces situations, s'en faire personnellement responsable, montrer comment en chacune la liberté est bafouée, – mais non trouver à la liberté une ligne politique, parce qu'elle s'incarne autant ou aussi peu dans les diverses actions politiques qui se disputent le monde, dans la société soviétique que dans la société américaine.[24]

In the view, then, of the departing political editor of the review, *TM*'s policy of *dévoilement* is based on ethical intuitions which have little purchase on reality, precisely because of the social disincarnation of its Director. The curse of the bourgeois intellectual, which Sartre has struggled so energetically to lift, is once again visited upon him, this time by a philosopher of incarnation. Rightly so, in view of the record of *TM*'s early years, but less justifiably if one considers the provisional removal of the ethic in the early 1950s to a position of lower immediate priority. It is possible to imagine that Merleau-Ponty might have remained within *TM* had he not been political editor. Had he written purely on aesthetics, say, then he might well have been able to flourish in the increasingly structuralist ethos being built up by Pontalis. Unhappily, the atmosphere of antagonistic reciprocity that prevailed allowed the rift between him and Sartre to widen. Beauvoir is quick to defend Sartre,[25] but her response to Merleau-Ponty is merely the last in a series of articles in which all parties concerned push each other's arguments to beyond their logical limits. That she should defend Sartre rather than *TM* is tacit acknowledgement that the corporate identity of the editorial team is weakening.

I do not mean to imply that aesthetics is either politically neutral or independent of philosophy. I mention it because Merleau-Ponty's final contribution to *TM* is his long discussion of 'Le langage indirect et les voix du silence',[26] ostensibly an assessment of André Malraux's *Le Musée imaginaire*. Dedicated and addressed to Sartre, it is written with none of the acerbity of *Les Aventures de la dialectique* and is the best indication to *TM*'s readers of Merleau-Ponty's increasing distance. The relative softness of tone is a good reminder that the Merleau-Ponty–Sartre separation has little in common with that of Sartre and Camus. In no way is Merleau-Ponty perceived as having regressed to where Sartre has already been, something which is very much the case with Camus, who turns to moral solutions to political problems exactly when *TM* resolves to do the opposite.[27]

'Le langage indirect et les voix du silence' begins by invoking Saussure's distinction between *langue* and *parole* and the theory of the diacritical nature of the linguistic sign. What interests Merleau-Ponty is the nature of the change from one synchronic state to another, a change which Saussure held to be arbitrary and contingent upon invention in utterances. Modification of *langue*, he notes, can take place only through *parole*, even though the latter is a manifestation of the former. Moreover, because the crucial relationship is that entertained by sign with sign and not that by sign with referent, the view of language as primarily utilitarian is no longer tenable; gone, as far as he is concerned, is the Sartrean notion of the transparency of language, and gone with it is the role of language as the mediator of non-linguistic content. The pre-eminence of code over utterance means that all linguistic production is foreshadowed, as it were, by a set of limited possibilities. It is with this pre-eminence in mind that Merleau-Ponty comes to conflate individual speech-acts with the diachronic alteration of the language. What he calls the incubatory or gestatory quality of the system – its susceptibility to conditioned modification – then becomes its dominant characteristic.

Linguistic history thus becomes coterminous with history *tout court*:

Car l'intimité de toute expression à toute expression, leur appartenance à un seul ordre, obtiennent par le fait la jonction de l'individuel et de l'universel. Le fait central auquel la dialectique de Hegel revient de cent façons, c'est que nous n'avons pas à choisir entre le *pour-soi* et le *pour-autrui*, entre la pensée selon nous-mêmes et la pensée selon autrui, mais que dans le moment de l'expression, l'autre à qui je m'adresse et moi qui m'exprime sommes liés sans concession.[28]

Merleau-Ponty not only anticipates the major bone of contention between Sartre and structuralism – the nature of history – but does so contentiously, by making of Hegel a structuralist historian. The message to Sartre is clear: expression does not have to be ascetic in order to be constructive; all *parole*, prosaic or poetic, engages with the dialectic by virtue of its relation to *langue*: 'L'histoire est chez Hegel cette maturation d'un avenir inconnu, et la règle de l'action chez lui n'est pas d'être efficace à tout prix, mais d'abord d'être féconde.'[29]

Merleau-Ponty's last word in *TM* is therefore a last word only in the most local and immediate sense. It deliberately makes its potency explicit in such a way that the resonance is shown to be more important than the source. Merleau-Ponty remains in *TM* as a *voix du silence*.

The contribution of Pontalis

The pointed silence of Merleau-Ponty is reinforced by the substantial articles emanating from Pontalis. He publishes more in this period than he does as a member of the Editorial Board between 1961 and 1970. Curiously enough, though, the first complimentary mention of Lacan in *TM* comes not from him but from one of the long-standing associates of Beauvoir, Colette Audry. In July 1953, she reviews Karen Horney's discussion of *Self-Analysis*; without making clear whether her objections to Horney are Lacanian or Sartrean, she quotes Lacan's view that 'celui qui omet que toute parole est une parole *donnée* ne peut rien comprendre à la dialectique de l'analyse'.[30] The idea evidently derives from Lévi-Strauss's *Les Structures élémentaires de la parenté*, but, as it stands, is not incompatible with Lefort's reading of the Maussian theory of the gift. Historically, Audry's piece is best regarded as a prologue to the eventful fifteen years during which Pontalis writes on psychoanalysis in *TM*.

By the time he contributes his first specialist article in January 1954, his name is already well known to readers. An ex-student of Sartre, his participation extends from the birth of *TM* until 1970. As I have suggested earlier, it is instructive to pursue the comparison with Pouillon. Both move from existentialist positions into the structuralist sphere of influence: Pontalis turns from Sartre to Lacan and ultimately detaches himself from both; Pouillon develops and retains a dual allegiance to Sartre and to Lévi-Strauss. Many of Pontalis's articles discussed in this chapter are later collected in the volume entitled *Après Freud*,[31] and it is noticeable that significant emendations stress the Lacanian positions while eliminating all Sartrean resonances.

1954 is one of the years that he later describes as his '"années d'apprentissage" psychanalytique'.[32] It is also the beginning of a new epoch in the history of the profession in France, following as it does the decision of the Société Psychanalytique de Paris in 1953 to found an Institut de Psychanalyse, an institute intended to operate within the medical faculty of the university. A breakaway group, the Société Française de Psychanalyse, was subsequently formed by Lacan and Daniel Lagache (who, incidentally, had supplied Sartre with mescalin during the years in which *La Nausée* was being written). These developments have a significance for *TM*: with Pontalis, it moves to the Lacan side of the schism, with the result that former contributors who remain loyal to the original Society either make no further appearance (like Pasche) or else write only to challenge the positions adopted by Pontalis (as in the case of Racamier).

In his 1954 articles, Pontalis is very concerned with the status of psychoanalysis in two respects: first, he wishes to prevent its object of study from being dissolved in either the social or the biological, a fate that it would meet were it to be totally absorbed into the medical faculty; secondly, he is anxious to preserve its freedom to develop, not merely as a therapy, but as a wider enterprise of exploration. For him, this means a return to the spirit of Freud, who never lost interest in the progress of neighbouring disciplines. 'Cette intuition', he remarks, 'n'a fait que se vérifier depuis: des travaux comme ceux de Lévi-Strauss et de Dumézil ne transforment pas seulement l'horizon du psychanalyste mais son travail.'[33] He feels very strongly that the non-mechanistic, non-biologistic writings of Freud have been institutionalised and dogmatised, with the result that analysands have been alienated in a therapy based on simplistic definitions of health and sickness. His view of this intellectual decline recalls the phenomenological critique of the positivist social sciences and anticipates the theorisation of the *pratico-inerte* in the *Critique de la raison dialectique*: 'c'est une règle du savoir que de tendre à l'objectivation [...] il transforme par exemple les intentions en processus naturels, les relations signifiantes en rapports stricts de causalité, réduit à des éléments ou à des forces des structures mouvantes'.[34]

The implication is that a return to Freud through Lacan is compatible with the prescriptions of the synthetic anthropology, at least inasmuch as both reject mechanistic psychologies. Pontalis's gravitation towards Lacan initially endows *TM* wiith a certain continuity – in the hostility towards American psychoanalysis, with its concern to 'readjust', as well as in the anxiety (manifested by Lévi-Strauss in 1949) that psychoanalysis should not become a machine for the production of myth. This is why Lacan is welcomed into the tradition that *TM* is committed to uphold:

la tradition d'un humanisme inspiré de Socrate, de Hegel et de la phénoménologie; pour lui la parole n'est certainement pas une 'conduite verbale' mais ce don qui fait émerger le sens et la vérité dans l'histoire du sujet; il ne décrirait pas la relation analytique comme une réduction progressive de tensions mais bien plutôt comme une phénoménologie de l'esprit, une sorte de triomphe dialectique.[35]

In the February issue of 1954, in the conclusion to his own article on Horney – worth quoting *in extenso* because it is dropped from *Après Freud* – Pontalis brings Lacanian psychoanalysis into the framework of Sartrean existentialism:

Or, la relation analytique 'qui n'a de nom dans aucune langue' permet de vaincre cette forme d'aliénation systématique de la conscience qu'est la névrose et de sortir de ces cercles toujours recommencés de l'intersubjectivité: narcissisme et agressivité, dépendance et abandon, etc. ... ; c'est qu'elle constitue une forme de communication privilégiée qui rend possible une reconnaissance par un autre – qui ne soit ni juge, ni maître, ni ami, ni rival; elle établit une réciprocité non symétrique par la médiation du langage qui rouvre cette langue morte qu'est une névrose, où les éléments varient quand la structure demeure immuable, cette langue que personne n'entend plus. Dans l'analyse le névrosé redécouvre le pouvoir créateur de la parole qui le libère de ses mythes qu'il prenait pour des êtres réels, suspend ses adhérences au passé et le rend aux autres et au monde qu'il avait voilés de ses craintes. N'est-ce pas une 'condamnation' à la liberté que donne en définitive l'analyse, plutôt qu'un certificat d'adaptation et de normalité?[36]

This incorporation is undoubtedly more than a polite invocation of the Sartrean concept of freedom, yet there is nothing to reconcile the *pour-soi* and *pour-autrui* modes of existence with the identifications that Lacan regards as the key to the construction of the ego. In spite of the apparent intention to mediate, Pontalis fails to specify the exact relation between the Sartrean view of interpersonal perception and of the subject and the Lacanian view of the ego. In the summer of 1956, however, he is given further opportunity, when he celebrates both the centenary of the birth of Freud and the first issue of Lacan's new review, *La Psychanalyse*. His long article, published in three parts in May, June and July, merits close attention.

Pontalis begins his 'Freud aujourd'hui' in general terms, recapitulating earlier statements, but soon embarks on the discussion of the ego. He notes that, while most psychoanalysts prefer a topographical definition, there is a further 'genetic' view (to which in *Après Freud* he adds the qualification 'structural'), according to which the ego results from the alienation of the subject in imaginary representations of itself. This approach, which sets subject and ego in a dynamic interrelationship, is, he suggests, in no way 'étrangère à la méthode phénoménologique; comme elle, elle fait de l'avènement du sens un problème mais n'implique aucune répudiation du perçu'.[37] Once again, there is an assertion of compatibility, but without a detailed comparison of Sartrean and Lacanian theory – despite the evident proximity of *le stade du miroir* to *La Transcendance de l'Ego*. This time, however, the assertion is dramatically qualified as Pontalis publishes his arrival at the watershed; henceforward, the current that bore Merleau-Ponty away runs strongly through the pages of *TM*. Pontalis is now obliged to put a greater distance between himself and his philosophical antecedents:

Nous sommes plus imprégnés que nous ne le pensons de concepts hérités de ce mélange de logique et de psychologie qui fait de la conscience l'unique ressort de l'existence. Imagine-t-on un linguiste, un ethnologue opposant aux hypothèses freudiennes, comme le firent nos philosophes, d'Alain à Sartre, des objections de principe? Leurs méthodes de travail les préparent mieux à les recevoir. Un mythe, une langue sont des structures qui ont leur logique interne, des systèmes partiels porteurs de significations. Leur analyse conduit à ne pas tenir pour vraies les représentations que s'en font ou les explications qu'en donnent les hommes qui les utilisent.[38]

As I have suggested, Pontalis seems reluctant to effect a contrastive study of Sartre and Lacan. Instead, he opts for the now familiar ploy of invoking Lévi-Strauss as an ally, neatly turning the tables on what appeared to be Sartre's tactic in the late 1940s. His own mode of recuperation is to describe the psychoanalytic cure in a manner reminiscent of the valid ethnography postulated by Lévi-Strauss in 1950. Underlying the ethnographic encounter, it is supposed, is an unconscious which is collective in the sense that its structure (although not its contents) is everywhere the same. Here he turns explicitly to the 'Introduction à l'œuvre de Marcel Mauss':

Une société en effet n'est que l'ensemble de ses institutions par lesquelles elle organise les expériences, ouvre et régularise les histoires personnelles et collectives; elle est donc éminemment symbolique et, par son être même du côté du signifiant; alors que les comportements individuels se situent du côté du signifié. Simplement ils peuvent être happés par le signifiant.[39]

This last rather enigmatic sentence (which is deleted in *Après Freud*) is a transcription of Lévi-Strauss's assertion that abnormal behaviour appears symbolic, while normal behaviour does not, precisely because it deviates from the symbolic system that defines the norm. Pontalis adds in a footnote that 'en fait un tel clivage n'existe pas; chacun s'établit des institutions personnelles qui organisent, orientent, lient, les divers moments de son histoire affective et ne relèvent ni de ce que Saussure – cité par Lacan – nomme "la masse amorphe du signifié" ni du pur signifiant'.[40] This section of his article, which predates Lacan's 'L'instance de la lettre dans l'inconscient' by one year, attests to a certain confusion of the categories of *langue* and *parole* with those of signifier and signified. Pontalis probably does well to conclude that 'c'est dire encore que l'analogie, souvent proposée aujourd'hui, entre la langue et les autres systèmes sociologiques, ne rend que plus nécessaire une théorie du symbolisme'.[41]

It may be doubted whether Lacan's position is very clear to readers of *TM* at this stage. What is now quite apparent, on the other hand, is that Pontalis can no longer be reckoned a Sartrean. 'La conscience ne mesure pas l'homme,' he concludes, 'il faut le confronter, et justement pour saisir ce qu'il porte de plus irréductible, à une "réalité transindividuelle".'[42] Psychoanalysis has to attend to 'un rapport *singulier* comparable à celui d'une parole et d'une langue; ses opérations font apparaître à la fois l'efficacité structurante des champs symboliques et la responsabilité du sujet dans la position qu'il y occupe'.[43] The allusion to responsibility may or may not be a *lapsus*; whichever the case, it is replaced in *Après Freud* by the more vague and less Sartrean term *initiatives*.

Lacan, then, does not represent the means by which Freud may best be brought back within the synthetic anthropology. On the contrary, he serves only to increase the tensions with structuralism. Lacan himself seems never to have doubted this; his analysis of *le stade du miroir* in 1949 gave existentialism very short shrift. On the other hand, Sartre is not insensitive to the extent to which identification renders problematic the boundaries between self and other. The ethic of literary production is abandoned ultimately, not only because of the factors that I have indicated, but also as a result of reflection (perhaps stimulated by his work on John Huston's film on Freud in the early 1950s) on the degree of his identification with his grandfather and on the persistence of the grandpaternal *voix du silence*.

The growth of Pontalis's influence is a fascinating spectacle because it is gradual and tactically astute. He tends to avoid theoretical confrontations, preferring a programme of encroachment and appropriation. This period contains two examples of the subtle promotion of psychoanalysis which saps the strength of the Sartrean project. The first concerns Leiris and the second the author of supreme importance – Flaubert. I shall look at each in turn, digressing from time to time in order to maintain contact with the ongoing context of *TM*.

Between 1951 and 1956, the review publishes four extracts from Leiris's *Fourbis* (the second volume of *La Règle du jeu*). It also features, presumably thanks to him, Césaire's poem 'Aux îles de tous les vents'. It carries nothing concerning his visit to China in 1955 and it does not reproduce his contribution to Sartre's dossier on the *affaire Henri Martin*,[44] a text which is wholly consistent with 'L'ethnographe devant le colonialisme'. *Fourbis* is equally in line with the precepts of reflexive and committed ethnography and furthers Leiris's self-analysis by reconsidering his experiences of Cairo, Haiti, Ethiopia, Guadeloupe, Algeria, Senegal and the

Ivory Coast. The evils of colonialism are briefly rehearsed but their denunciation plays a relatively small part in the labour of self-comprehension.

It is this aspect that Pontalis assesses in his 'Michel Leiris ou la psychanalyse interminable'.[45] In *L'Age d'homme*, *Biffures* and *Fourbis* he recognises three moments in a largely successful dissolution of anxiety. The first moment consists of the circumscription of the ego as a psychic entity created by the subject but distinct from it; this involves Leiris, in *L'Age d'homme*, in the painstaking dismantling of the mythology of himself. *Biffures*, the second moment, is taken to embody the disappointment of the hope that through language the extra-linguistic truths of identity might be revealed. Leiris, says Pontalis, discovers the diacritical nature of the sign and the impossibility that one single lexical item might ever emerge as the key for which he is searching. The investigation, although slowly losing momentum, moves from the rehearsal of the objectification of the self by death towards an intuition of the limitlessness of the human subject. *Fourbis* accordingly effects a synthesis in which death, previously perceived as an arbitrary frontier, is now integrated and accepted. As the obsession is liquidated, so Leiris's language, in the opinion of Pontalis, loses its oracular character and regains communicational effectiveness.

It is not the case that future instalments of *La Règle du jeu* (which recollect Leiris's attempted suicide) necessarily prove that Pontalis overestimated the success of the self-analysis. He specifies quite clearly that the operation can proceed only in continued oscillation between fascination and detachment, between exhilaration and depression. He regards this cyclothymic rhythm as a structural feature of the *journal intime*. It is a feature, he says, which correlates closely with the polar possibilities open to the ethnographer – extreme ethnocentricity and total identification with the object of study. Pontalis shares Lévi-Strauss's view that there is no resolution of this tension and that caution and compensation merely minimise the dangers without removing them.

From the point of view of the synthetic anthropology, Pontalis says too little about Leiris. In particular, he does not admit the third possibility, adumbrated in 'L'ethnographe devant le colonialisme', which is that of the constructive and reciprocal relationship to be entered into with representatives of the foreign culture. This is a relationship, after all, that might effectively provide a way out of the cycles of projection and identification, aggression and narcissism. Pontalis omits to credit the anti-imperialist struggle with the same therapeutic force that he ascribes to psychoanalysis; in this respect, he fails to wrest Leiris from Sartre.

Moreover, while it is no doubt reasonable to attribute to self-analysis an oscillatory structure (indeed, both *La Nausée* and *Les Mots* exhibit it), there seems no reason to assume that ethnography must be similar. This is something that *TM* will pursue in due course: Jeanne Favret-Saada, from her post-1968 vantage point, will diagnose cyclothymia in the practice of certain anthropologists (Lévi-Strauss being the best example) of publishing both academic research and *journaux intimes* while failing to perceive that the methodological implications of this are unacceptable.

The Leiris purveyed by Pontalis is thus a long way from being an effective political agent. This is the price that is paid for singling him out as an explorer of a selfhood whose boundaries dissolve in an exemplary manner. Pontalis polarises where Merleau-Ponty might well have mediated; in doing so, he helps confer on structuralism, much more than does *TM*'s former political editor, its reputation of apoliticism.

Before considering his handling of Flaubert, I shall comment briefly on the literary content of *TM* in this period. A number of interesting texts, notably those by Beauvoir, Sartre and Albert Memmi, bear, in one way or another, on the new direction taken by the synthetic anthropology and on its relationship with its academic counterpart. In addition, despite a decrease in the quantity of literary material, the review publishes for the first time work by writers of the stature of Heinrich Böll, Jorge Luis Borges, Ray Bradbury, Scott Fitzgerald, T. E. Lawrence, Pablo Neruda and Cesare Pavese.

But what of the high valuation of literature that had characterised the early years? It had been dangerous for the synthetic anthropology in three respects: in the first place, it limited the study of the relation of individual and group to those instances of formal communication instituted by the production and consumption of literature; in the second place, it persistently subordinated the proposed ethic to the extrapolation of moral values from the consideration of exemplary individuals who were all authors; in the third place, although it promoted the concept of *situation* with great energy, it drew from it only the convenient advantages (the extent to which co-ordinates of time and place guaranteed the individual's contact with the real world) without recognising the disadvantages (the extent to which the real world might limit the expression of individual freedom).

The change comes in 1951 and 1952, immediately prior to the publication of *Saint Genet* in book form. As literature loses some of its prestige, anthropological reference is allowed to increase in significance: it is during the early 1950s that Mallarmé joins Genet in the ranks of the shamans[46] and that Sartre first suggests *Les Griots* (the wandering story-tellers of West and Central African tribes) as the title of what will later become *Les Mandarins*.[47] But what evidence is there in *TM* of a change in policy? At first sight, Beauvoir's 'Faut-il brûler Sade?' (December 1951 and January 1952) suggests that the answer is none at all, for it operates within the familiar paradigm of existential psychoanalysis and literary morality. On the other hand, the study definitely postdates *Saint Genet*. The history of Sade, like that of Genet, is traced to a sudden, traumatic point at which the spontaneous activity of the individual is abruptly inserted into a social context and deemed a crime. Similar choices are made: if society is against Sade and if an evil nature is against society, then Sade will embody that evil nature. Through the eyes of the marginalised aristocrat, Beauvoir perceives that 'aucune morale universelle n'est possible puisque les conditions concrètes dans lesquelles vivent les individus ne sont pas homogènes'.[48]

This is exactly the conclusion that informs *Le Diable et le Bon Dieu* (serialised from June to August 1951); it also legitimises the political alignment out of which comes the Cold War farce *Nekrassov* (July to September 1955). The first of the two plays is the more important in terms of Sartre's evolution. It enacts the dissolution of absolute concepts of good and evil in contexts of economic and political conflict. It represents the discovery in literature of the realities of counter-productivity and confirms the abandonment of the Kantian categorical imperative and the partial devaluation of the concept of intention. Goetz's trajectory takes him from the illusions of the ethic to the political *praxis* that is required to achieve the ethic's material precondition – the equitable distribution of wealth.

The same shift in emphasis is visible in the choice of authorities that inform Sartre's thinking. He had already availed himself, in *L'Etre et le néant*, of Scheler's phenomenology of resentment: in *Le Diable et le Bon Dieu* the resentment felt by Goetz towards God is explicitly made the stimulus for his programmes of good- and evil-doing. Here, however, it is incorporated into the framework of the *Essai sur le don*, for it is God's generosity that Goetz resents, and he likewise brings resentment on himself by giving his land to the poor and by killing them with kindness. The gifts of both God and Goetz are acts of violence: they differ so much in degree from what the recipient is able to offer in return that they cannot be reciprocated. A social interaction is thus set up in which the third of Mauss's obligations (to give in return) has no viability. Retroactively, receipt becomes a sufferance, and the act of giving is revealed to be only the semblance of generosity. God and Goetz give feudally, in order to diminish and to obligate; they remain forever *anciens riches* and in no way modify the real distribution of wealth. What is crucial, however, is that out of resentment (out of the reciprocal resentments of Goetz and Hilda, for example) may come a positive reciprocity capable of being called love, but this happens only when the participants are equally endowed with possibilities of giving, receiving and giving in return.[49]

'L'attitude morale apparaît quand les conditions techniques et sociales rendent impossibles les conduites positives. La morale, c'est un ensemble de trucs idéalistes pour vous aider à vivre ce que la pénurie des ressources et la carence des techniques vous imposent'.[50] So runs the unpublished note which calls a halt to the quest for the ethic. The change of direction is usually ascribed to lessons learned in the political arena (the RDR's relations with the PCF and the bourgeois press, and so on), but anthropological considerations clearly have a major role to play as well. Intuitions of reciprocity are helped towards formulation by the frameworks supplied by Mauss, Lévi-Strauss and Lefort; in the course of this, generosity ceases to be solely a moral value and becomes at the same time an ideological practice which must be combated. Sartre still needs to bring to his views on the *don* all that ethnography can tell him of spiritual or psychological possession. Here there will be a role for Frantz Fanon, Leiris, Métraux and Pouillon to play: they will help Sartre call both for the dispossession of the rich by the poor (the redistribution of material goods) and for an end to the possession of the poor by images of wealth.

Sartre's literary contributions in the period are limited to the two plays. Two major texts in progress – 'L'engagement de Mallarmé' and *Les Mots*, which have so much in common – leave no trace in *TM* and their existence is unsuspected. It had been generally known, on the other hand, that Sartre had wished to write more on Flaubert than had been contained in the 'Présentation' and in *Qu'est-ce que la littérature?* Beauvoir reports that in the early part of 1956, at the suggestion of Roger Garaudy, 'Sartre écrivit une longue étude fouillée, mais de forme trop négligée pour qu'il envisageât de la publier.'[51] In due course, the aborted contest with Garaudy leads to 'Questions de méthode', but it would be wrong to stop at this point in an investigation of the genesis of *L'Idiot de la famille*: Pontalis's discussion of 'La maladie de Flaubert' (March and April 1954) must have been equally stimulating.

Pontalis's article marks another shift away from Sartre and also from the ethico-literary positions of the first period. It goes much further than either Sartre or Beauvoir in the study of the high valuation of literature. By implying a parallel between Sartre and Flaubert, it decentres the synthetic anthropology and quite correctly absorbs the producer of literary ethics into the field of inquiry. It is hard to read the following remarks, for example, without thinking of existentialism: 'Flaubert partageait avec pas mal de ses contemporains l'idée d'un absolu littéraire qui réclame en principe un dévouement inconditionnel; il *gueule* ses phrases comme un moine ses chants de gloire: l'art sauvera le monde et l'artiste avec. Mais est-il dupe?'[52]

If the *cogito* of the synthetic anthropology is really a *scribo*, then Pontalis is here subverting it, going 'behind'[53] it in order to show that it is a construction based on an identification. He notes that *Madame Bovary* is sometimes seen as an attempt by Flaubert to suppress his spontaneous lyricism. Once again, it is difficult not to recall that *TM* was born in just such a regime of linguistic repression. The conflation of Flaubert and Sartre assumes prophetic proportions in Pontalis's conclusion: 'Si l'art doit, en définitive, nous délivrer de la nausée, il commence par l'accentuer. Et puis l'art n'est peut-être qu'une suggestion hystérique (Emma) ou un vice un peu morne.'[54] The hegemony of the symptomatic reading now threatens to engulf the synthetic anthropology; I shall take up the story of Sartre's reaction in later chapters. For react he was bound to do: nobody would have made a worse analysand, which is no doubt one reason why Pontalis, when requested, declined to analyse him. In any case, in one sense Pontalis has said enough and need say no more. Sartre's move from an antipathetic to an empathetic view of Flaubert in *L'Idiot de la famille* is a cautious acknowledgement of his implication in the object of study, and Pontalis can take some of the credit for this. In this way, too, Freudianism impels Sartre a little further along the road to reflexivity. As for Pontalis, he never again ventures so near an implied diagnosis; it may be that his stay in *TM* is sustained by a professional wariness of the counter-transferential.

The contribution of Pouillon

Despite all the developments recorded above, literature does not vanish from the review and there is no reason to suppose that Pontalis would have wished that it might. *TM* maintains its interest in material offering broad support to its anti-imperialist positions and accordingly promotes work by Jorge Amado, Basil Davidson, George Lamming and Richard Wright. Of particular significance is Albert Memmi's autobiography, *La Statue de sel*, serialised from October 1952 to March 1953. Memmi does not resemble Sade and Genet. He is not the negation of a homogeneous community, but a problematic individual raised at the point of intersection of a variety of cultural groups – Berber, Jewish, Tunisian and French. He sees himself as the sum of irreconcilable parts: 'indigène dans un pays de colonisation, juif dans un univers antisémite, Africain dans un monde où triomphe l'Europe [. . .] Comment faire une synthèse [. . .] de tant de disparités?'[55] He is satisfied that writing is no solution to the problem: as it increases his self-awareness it increases his solitude, obliging him to opt for one language and one community in preference to the rest.

Like Wright, he is the informal ethnographer of the ghetto from which he emerges, one of the local intellectuals designated by Leiris as the hope for the future. His advice to the metropolitan is interesting: 'Dépaysez-vous si le jeu vous plaît, visitez des contrées lointaines, goûtez à des nourritures étranges, instruisez-vous dans des aventures dangereuses, mais que votre âme vous appartienne. Ne devenez pas un inconnu à vous-même car ce jour-là vous serez perdu.'[56] This word of warning seems to argue in favour of the psychological security of a measure of ethnocentricity. The victim of colonisation, in other words, strives to attain precisely what professional ethnographers seek to eliminate from their academic work, but which infallibly emerges when they permit themselves the luxury of a *journal intime*. It is a mark of success for the synthetic anthropology that when the colonised speak they either move completely outside the field of activity of orthodox ethnographers (as did the poets of *négritude*) or confound the methodological bases of the discipline.

This is the reason for Sartre's support for Memmi, and it is easy to see how the preoccupations of each come together in the ethics and the politics of the gift. The suppressed ethnocentrism of the French academic, however well intentioned the suppression might be, is regarded by the colonised as counter-productive: born of an indulgent exoticism, it nevertheless comes across as an imposition of language, of intellectual and professional terms of reference, with all the moral and political values that these imply. Equitable cultural exchange is impossible to achieve as long as generosity, in the form of one-way cultural *prestations* and appropriations, is the basis of the relationship. In Memmi's perspective, the ethnocentricity avoided by metropolitan ethnographers is avoided for good reason and with guilty conscience, for it has been stolen from the colonised. Even Leiris's vision of reciprocity makes light of this intrinsic difficulty. Its solution lies ultimately in the intuition that informs Montesquieu's *Lettres persanes* – the creation of a situation in which French and non-French visit and study each other and from which the cultural domination of one by the other is absent. Memmi belongs to the synthetic anthropology by virtue of his assumption that the road to valid ethnography goes by way of anti-colonialism. He confronts the academic world with a political question and introduces an urgency into the activities of those like Pouillon who are committed to exploring the space between Sartre and Lévi-Strauss.

It is unfortunate that *TM* carries nothing on the Bandung conference of non-aligned countries in 1955 which did much to focus and to link a number of liberation struggles. Even so, between 1951 and 1956, it covers a much wider geographical range than in the first period, devoting articles to Indochina, Morocco, Algeria, Tunisia, the Ivory Coast, Togo and the French West Indies. Attention is confined to French possessions and tends to be aroused by a rise of the political temperature in the area concerned. Algeria, for instance, is mentioned only cursorily in the years prior to 1955, whereas after that date nearly every issue contains important material. Once again, there is no need to reproduce the details recorded by Burnier. *TM*'s commitment continues to be dual: to inform the metropolitan reader and to support the liberation movements. It is worth mentioning that relevant articles come from two professional anthropologists: Paul Mus, specialist in Cambodian and Cham religions, friend of Ho Chi Minh and adviser to General Leclerc in 1946, discusses the 'Insertion du communisme dans le mouvement nationaliste vietnamien' in April 1952; Marcel Ner, expert on the kinship structures of the Moi and of the Cham and erstwhile teacher of General Giap, writes on 'La république démocratique du Vietnam' and on 'Le Vietnam et la Chine de 1945 à 1953' in the August/September special issue in 1953. These texts resemble those of Cuisinier in the previous period; they are pieces of historical and political commentary which do not draw on ethnographic material.

In addition to the colonial case histories, *TM* features items of broader focus. One example is Claude Bourdet's 'L'équilibre social et le fait colonial', which argues that colonisation is an intervention which worsens the 'natural' balance of oppressors and oppressed. Jeanson's 'Logique du colonialisme' seeks to dispel the illusion that the French colonial territories are administered on a democratic basis. Henri Moscat and Marcel Péju, meanwhile, turn their attention to the half-million North African immigrants working in France. *TM*'s general policy is set out in five points preceding Jeanson's article in June 1952.[57] Colonial reality, it affirms, will not be reduced to economic factors, but neither will these factors be ignored. Capitalism and racialism will always constitute a dual framework for discussions of colonialism. There will be no mechanical reduction of nationalist movements to expressions of class struggle. Finally, colonialism will always be seen in the context of the Cold War.

An example of work undertaken along these lines is Daniel Guérin's two-part study 'Un futur pour les Antilles?' (January and February 1956). Guérin looks forward to the formation of a Caribbean Federation independent of the United States. This is a reminder that in the mid-1950s there is no concept, in *TM* at least, of *neo-colonialism* as it is understood today (that is to say, economic domination effected in the absence of direct political control). Indeed, Sartre, in an important article which I shall now consider, uses the term to refer to the beliefs of those who hold that colonial injustices can be removed by enlightened metropolitan administration.

On 27 January 1956, both Césaire and Sartre addressed a public meeting of the Comité d'Action des Intellectuels contre la Poursuite de la Guerre en Afrique du Nord. Their speeches appear in the March/April issue of *TM*, and while Césaire's is a moral denunciation of colonialism, Sartre's contains new synthetic anthropological formulations. It is based on two premises: that colonialism is systematic and that it has recently become counterproductive. The system, says Sartre, involves the implantation on foreign soil of settlers who dispossess the indigenous peoples of land and who sell their produce to the metropolis; their real function, however, is to constitute an expanding market for the industrial goods produced in the metropolis. The stability of the system is ensured by the extent to which its mechanisms constrain the human agents concerned: 'car le colon est fabriqué comme l'indigène: il est fait par sa fonction et par ses intérêts'.[58] Settlers and original inhabitants, both marginalised in terms of the metropolis, come to resemble Genet, the shaman, women and Jews, in the sense that they inhabit a macro-social logic which incapacitates them. It is the spirit of 'analysis', the atomistic liberalism of the metropolis, which has a particularly damaging effect on local populations. Sartre therefore determines to describe it synthetically, in terms which damage the metropolis:

En Algérie, la république française ne peut pas se permettre d'être républicaine. Elle maintient l'inculture et les croyances de la féodalité, mais en supprimant les structures et les coutumes qui permettent à une féodalité vivante d'être *malgré tout* une société humaine; elle impose un code individualiste et libéral pour ruiner les cadres et les assises de la collectivité algérienne, mais elle maintient des roitelets qui ne tiennent leur pouvoir que d'elle et qui gouvernent pour elle. En un mot, elle *fabrique* des 'indigènes' par un double mouvement qui les séparent de la collectivité archaïque en leur donnant ou en leur conservant, *dans la solitude de l'individualisme libéral*, une mentalité dont l'archaïsme ne peut se perpétuer qu'en relation avec l'archaïsme de la société. Elle crée des *masses* mais les empêche de devenir un prolétariat conscient en les mystifiant par la caricature de leur propre idéologie.[59]

Practices of analysis in the Sartrean sense (those which refuse to allow that an entity is greater than the sum of its parts), when expressed in political policies, make of a group a mass of discrete and alienated individuals. The sudden search for liberation from analytic constraints is celebrated as a moment of synthesis, and it is the synthesis of these separate moments that now becomes the political aim of Sartre. If 1956 is a key year in this respect, it is because of Algeria as much as of Budapest. The theoretical project of the *Critique de la raison dialectique* is prefigured here in the highlighting of systematic counter-productivity. 'L'unique bienfait du colonialisme', says Sartre, 'c'est qu'il doit se montrer intransigeant pour durer et qu'il prépare sa perte par son intransigeance.'[60] The protection required by the settlers ultimately becomes so expensive that the whole enterprise loses its economic viability.

Sartre's descriptions are specific. There is no attempt to make general statements about serialisation and the *pratico-inerte*. The article's anthropological significance is nevertheless immense, since it strikes at the heart of the widespread academic assumption that the colonised peoples constitute living and healthy cultures threat-

ened by absorption. On the contrary, says Sartre, bearing out what
Leiris had affirmed in 1950, the original culture is unobservable, for
a 'native' has been constructed by colonialism. There can be no
domination without degradation; neither can there be any ethnography which can 'bracket out' the colonial reality.

The political position of academic anthropology, never completely comfortable, now begins to look untenable, unless, of
course, it can reshape itself along the lines suggested by Leiris.
Onto Pouillon devolves the task of seeing whether this can be done.
It is thus time to look at the specifically ethnographic material
carried by *TM* in this period. I have already mentioned Margaret
Mead, who seems to be preferred to Benedict, and whose *Male and
Female* appears in extract in April and May of 1951. It is a text that
is addressed to the non-specialist and motivated by a didactic intent
– that of communicating evidence of cultural relativity in the hope
that it might lead to a liberalisation of the moral code prevalent in
the United States.

Mead concentrates on the acquisition of sexual roles in childhood. Her review of seven South Sea cultures recognises certain
psychological universals defined in Freudian terms (Oedipal tensions, stages of infantile sexual development, etc.). At the same
time, it records a high degree of cultural variation and confers on
each pattern such designations as 'womb-envying' and 'money-
minded'. The book leads on to a comprehensive critique of North
American sexual and familial mores and shows Mead's cultural
relativism to be less sceptical than Benedict's. It asserts that the
degree of alienation from the physiologically and psychologically
healthy is variable; it holds in particular that diminished sexual
stereotyping will alleviate a great deal of suffering among her
compatriots. It is easy to see why her anthropology should not be
grossly unacceptable to *TM*. Although it fails to fall completely
within Leiris's terms of reference and says nothing of colonialism, it
is sufficiently reflexive not to wish to disguise its value judgements.

After *Male and Female*, Mead appears no more in *TM*. The fact
that her work helps to fill the interregnum may indicate that there is
no one editor engaged in keenly promoting her. Leiris shows no
great interest, and while there may have been contact through the
Métraux family, the most visible connection between Mead and
TM is her translator into French, René Guyonnet, who also sends
coverage of the McCarthy hearings in the United States. Lévi-
Strauss's familiarity with British and American anthropology
meant that Mead's work had been known in France for some years

– Balandier had reviewed it in *Critique* in July 1946 – but not in accessible French translation; he would therefore have welcomed *TM*'s initiative. It is also possible that *Male and Female* appears on the recommendation of Beauvoir, for its theses would have been usefully invoked in *Le Deuxième Sexe* had they been available. There is, however, no mention of Mead in Beauvoir's autobiography.

There exists in *TM* during this period one other fascinating text, Verrier Elwin's *The Muria and their Ghotul*, extracts from which are published in the first two months of 1956, in advance of the incomplete French edition put out by Gallimard. The study of the Indian Muria tribe had first appeared in English in 1947; it consisted of two parts, the first a detailed account of the geo-political, economic and social parameters of Muria life, and the second a description of the village dormitory, the *ghotul*. Only the second part is translated into French and a Mead connection is made by *TM*'s subtitle: 'une méthode d'éducation sexuelle et sociale dans une tribu de l'Inde';[61] Elwin's authorities included Havelock Ellis, Freud, Melanie Klein and Stekel.

The village dormitory is located at the centre of a culture which Elwin portrays as gentle and tolerant. He ascribes its existence to the desire of parents that their children should not witness the primal scene in the family dwelling. The children therefore reside in the *ghotul* until after adolescence, when they are ready for marriage. In it they learn sexual roles, techniques and manners, as well as comradeship and the communal organisation of labour. Elwin is at pains to stress that the *ghotul* is not an erotomanic environment; it offers facilities for friendly initiation and is the cornerstone of a successful monogamous society. It seems likely that, after Beauvoir and Mead, readers of *TM* will not object to this alternative to Western sexual education. Certainly, the comments of Lévi-Strauss are startlingly heartfelt: 'Tous ceux qui liront cet admirable livre se demanderont jusqu'au jour de leur mort s'il n'eût pas été préférable que l'humanité payât d'une vie simple le luxe de pouvoir offrir à tous ses membres, au temps de leur plus grande perfection physique et morale, quelques années de Paradis.'[62] Sartre's own hostility to the bourgeois family has not yet reached its peak of explicitness. A fleeting mention of the *ghotul* in 'Questions de méthode' suggests that the fantasies awakened by Elwin's ethnography are as strong in him as in Lévi-Strauss.[63]

Elwin's work is subsequently reviewed in *TM* in August 1959 by Pouillon, who cautions readers against judgements of Muria culture as either promiscuous or liberated. The argument used is the one developed by Lévi-Strauss in *Les Structures élémentaires de la parenté*, where it is asserted that no society is closer than any other to nature, since the nature–culture relationship is not a continuum but an opposition based on the presence or absence of rules. Elwin also offers Pouillon the chance to comment on what is already becoming a contentious issue – the apparent absence of historicity in the societies studied by academic anthropology. Pouillon, in a manner quite foreign to him, ventures a culturalist and psychoanalytic explanation, ascribing Muria immobilism to an arrested narcissism. This seems an unprofitable way of mediating between Sartre and Lévi-Strauss and is probably why the culturalism of Elwin and Mead is allowed to recede from view.

One other anthropologist merits brief consideration, and that is Georges Balandier. Like Lévi-Strauss, he elects to complement his formal academic work with contributions to *TM* which seek a wider readership. His professional career had begun immediately after the Second World War and had involved him in fieldwork in French West Africa. By the 1950s, he had become the leading proponent of a new anthropology committed to the study of colonialism; as such his appearance in *TM* is hardly surprising. Like Crozier, he implies that Lévi-Strauss is reluctant to face the facts of post-war change and that French anthropology can no longer afford to seek refuge in primitivism. He acknowledges the 'analyse critique extrèmement serrée'[64] provided by Leiris in 1950 and points at the same time to its lack of academic follow-up, for although there is substantial British and American material on colonialism, in French there is virtually nothing. Balandier can cite only Bourdet's articles in *TM* and Sartre's 'Orphée noir', together with Mannoni's *Psychologie de la colonisation*. This is a good indication of the extent to which *TM* had been offering an intellectual lead.

Balandier follows Mannoni in choosing to delimit his object of study in terms of models of dependence, specified objectively as political, economic and social structures, and subjectively as attitudes characteristic of the parties involved. He follows Crozier in using sociological studies of capital–labour relationships, so as to understand better the integration of African economies to the Western European industrial metropolis. His first contribution in 1952 has no theoretical pretensions and simply tells the story of the messianic Gabonese leader Benoît Ogoula Iquaqua. *Afrique ambiguë*, which appears four years later, is a *journal intime* inasmuch as it traces Balandier's own movement from exoticism and primitivism and his discovery that primitive Africa does not exist. His intention is to assist in Africa's transformation by rendering it intelligible. Radical in a technocratic sense, he regards the colonial societies as victims of arrested development and considers that they have to detribalise and evolve national economic bases. He consequently eyes *négritude* with some caution, reluctant to tolerate the mobilisation of the past in the construction of the future. These views are curious, coming as they do from one of the founders of *Présence africaine*; they show that his support for the black intellectuals is much less qualified than is that of Leiris and Sartre. Just as his appearance in *TM* is unsurprising, his departure is equally so.

Mead, Elwin and Balandier: these are specialists who are easily absorbed or discarded by the synthetic anthropology. Lévi-Strauss is altogether harder to grapple with, for not only are the political situation and Sartre's understanding of it changing rapidly, Lévi-Strauss too has not stayed in the same place. The 1951–5 period is for him one of considerable development and productivity. His output includes virtually half of the essays that will go to make up *Anthropologie structurale*, as well as other formal articles and the much more personal *Tristes Tropiques*. None of this work brings him into open conflict with *TM*. Broadly speaking, his position *vis-à-vis* the review is one of continued collaboration and increasing divergence, and it proves difficult for Pouillon to rationalise in his study of 'L'œuvre de Claude Lévi-Strauss', which closes the period in July 1956.

Pressing on with his exploration of the pertinence to anthropology of models taken from linguistics, Lévi-Strauss deepens the concept of structure and introduces that of mytheme. In respect of methodology, he reaches the conclusion (which Balandier mistakenly ascribes to Sartre) that 'alors que la sociologie s'efforce de faire la science sociale de l'observateur, l'anthropologie cherche, elle, à élaborer la science sociale de l'observé'.[65] This comment rewrites the division of labour deriving from Durkheim and Mauss. Lévi-Strauss, however, is obliged to bring the tensions between sociology and anthropology into line with the disciplinary redefinitions occasioned by the advent of linguistics. Postulating that anthropology is the science that 'se veut *science seméiologique*' (*sic*),[66] he seizes this chance to endorse Sartre's invocation of the *ensembles signifiants*. On two occasions – in the article cited here ('Place de l'anthropologie dans les sciences sociales' (1954)) and in his reply to Roger Caillois in *TM* – Lévi-Strauss manages to give his

anthropology a Sartrean gloss. It is said not to be content to gather
statistical data in the manner of the sociologists, 'car elle sait que
ces éléments ne sont rien, sinon dans la mesure où ils se réintègrent
dans une expérience vécue'.[67]

The situation is confused not merely because Lévi-Strauss is
constantly seeking new ways of distinguishing his anthropology
from the *ethnologie* of his predecessors. The additional problem is
that when he and Sartre allude to each other positively, it is
typically in the context of the separate disputes of each with third
parties such as Caillois and Lefort. The nods and winks imply no
deep agreement; they merely disguise the extent to which the two
men would disagree were they to thrash out the issues.

In any case, Sartre does not distinguish between two professions
and their methodologies, but between two types of society, the
consensual and the conflictual. What is striking is that Lévi-Strauss,
in the 1954 article quoted above, proceeds to agree with Sartre on
this second question, proposing, as a criterion of classification, a
concept of authenticity to designate social organisations characterised by direct reciprocity. What can one conclude from this
convergence? More apparent than real, more wished for than
achieved, it arises from the conjunction of the notions of authenticity and reciprocity. The fact that Lévi-Strauss does not fully
elaborate the former and that Sartre does not fully elaborate the
latter is enough to cast doubt on the solidity of the conjunction.
Authenticity, in any case, is for Sartre a moral value that in this
period loses its unambiguous status; Lévi-Straussian reciprocity, on
the other hand, is a structural feature that has no place in the
ontology. Despite the evident goodwill, the common ground is no
more than terminological.

In *Tristes Tropiques*, in a brief sketch of his intellectual history,
Lévi-Strauss soon dispels any suggestion of close affinity between
the two men: 'La phénoménologie me heurtait, dans la mesure où
elle postule une continuité entre le vécu et le réel [...] Quant au
mouvement de pensée qui allait s'épanouir dans l'existentialisme, il
me semblait être le contraire d'une réflexion légitime en raison de
la complaisance qu'il manifeste envers les illusions de la subjectivité.'[68] What brings Lévi-Strauss to *TM*, as I suggested in my
previous chapter, is a combination of personal contact and political
sympathy, and of the two it is the latter that still requires elucidation.

Lévi-Strauss's attitude to history has hitherto been exclusively
concerned with its study. In 1949,[69] he chose to institute a division

of labour between history and anthropology, whereby the latter was to study the unconscious aspects of social life and the former the conscious aspects. Lefort, writing in 1952,[70] disagrees with this and moves the discussion back to the object rather than the method of study. Lefort's view is that while all societies have a history, they differ in the attitudes that they adopt towards it, change either being absorbed into the existing social structures or else being actively promoted. Simultaneously, Lévi-Strauss begins thinking along the same lines in his UNESCO pamphlet *Race and History* which, having been criticised by Caillois, is summarised in his *TM* reply, 'Diogène couché'. In it, two different types of history are specified: 'une histoire progressive, acquisitive, qui accumule les trouvailles et les inventions pour construire de grandes civilisations, et une autre histoire, peut-être également active et mettant en œuvre autant de talents, mais où manquerait le don synthétique qui est le privilège de la première'.[71] The gift of 'synthesis' (and this has to be recorded as a Sartrean rather than as a Lévy-Bruhlian usage) possessed by the first type is a gift of circumstance: it is stimulated by the contacts, exchanges and appropriations that take place when cultures exist in close proximity one with another. Contact is therefore the precondition of progress.

This view is partially consistent with Saussurean diachrony as interpreted by Merleau-Ponty: it sees the systematic as a moment of the random, even if it cannot envisage an internally stimulated transition from one organised state to another. 'Ma conception est pessimiste', says Lévi-Strauss, 'dans la mesure où le système, à quelque moment qu'on le considère, est dominé par une tendance à l'inertie.'[72] Pessimism is a curious term here, for in fact the inert social state is a happy one, in Lévi-Strauss's opinion. The possibility of immunity from exogenous cultural contact appears utopian when considered in the light of the alternative, the global monoculture so feared in *Tristes Tropiques*.

Sartre's view is different: for him, instability and change do not have to come from the outside; they derive also from internal pressures. Moreover, synthesis (a term which, like authenticity and reciprocity, obscures the divergences) is for Sartre a welcome and a triumphant phenomenon, transcending the conflictual and heralding the entry into consensus. For Lévi-Strauss, it is a disaster, a state of degradation into which healthy communities fall. Both men doubtless place high value on the *ensembles signifiants* of the so-called primitive societies – Sartre because they represent an image of future universal socialism, Lévi-Strauss because they represent a lingering denial of future totalitarian capitalism. While logic can reduce the two positions to one, it can do so only at the cost of ignoring a vast difference in temperament and outlook.

If Lévi-Strauss and Sartre were really in agreement, it would be possible to identify a common anticolonialism consistent with that of Leiris. But although Lévi-Strauss is able to describe cultural contact, he is unwilling to study it – as Balandier correctly observed – still less to use it as the basis for an analysis of imperialism. His is not an anthropology with any direct political application. A militant anthropology would be an applied one and would automatically be eschewed. Lévi-Strauss's attitude towards applied anthropology (of the right, and presumably also of the left) is cautiously categorical: 'je doute de sa portée scientifique'.[73] *Tristes Tropiques* is suffused by an implied anticolonialism, but it seems to express the wounded narcissism of the ethnographer rather than a political activism. Its confidential disclosures reveal nothing of the impatient wish to intervene that is characteristic of *TM*:

> Une juste appréciation des immenses conquêtes de l'Occident ne m'empêche pas de percevoir l'étrange paradoxe qui lui a fait créer les ethnographes au moment même où il entreprenait la destruction de l'objet des études qu'il leur reconnaît; ni de prendre conscience du rôle d'alibi que nous sommes contraints de jouer. Alibi seulement? Peut-être aussi, précaution sage d'une civilisation qui nous mesure les cobayes et nous les prête un instant avant de les manger, dans l'espoir malgré tout, que nos méthodes pourront un jour l'aider à comprendre les difficultés nouvelles qu'elle découvre en son sein.[74]

The ethnographer, in order to be the last expert witness of cultural difference, acquires techniques of objectification that cut him off from his society of origin and from the society of his fieldwork. Nowhere is he at home, except in the abstract framework of the vanishing differentiation. The two items published by Lévi-Strauss in *TM* during this period – 'Le Père Noël supplicié' and 'Les vivants et les morts' (the latter from *Tristes Tropiques*) – are both concerned with rituals of intercession between the living and the dead. The ethnographer, like Genet and the shaman, crosses two categories and is a stranger to both: 'Il ne circule pas entre le pays des sauvages et celui des civilisés: dans quelque sens qu'il aille, il retourne d'entre les morts.'[75] Lévi-Strauss's dual identification (of Mauss with Moses in 1950, of himself with Lazarus in 1955) derives from a remorse – that of the Western world *vis-à-vis* the cultures that it is destroying – which is allowed an eloquence only in the *journal intime*. It yields a conclusion which would resemble that of Leiris were it not for a nuance of impotence: 'C'est la société seule à laquelle nous appartenons que nous sommes en position de transformer sans risquer de la détruire.'[76]

From the Sartrean point of view, the melancholy paradox is that the structuralist anthropology is committed inasmuch as it will not allow political options to inform its research. Its commitment to preserve its object of study *from* change diminishes its commitment *to* change. Its claims to scientific objectivity within a conventional academic framework are reinforced correspondingly. For Lévi-Strauss, salvation lies in antithesis; his work can therefore be absorbed into the synthetic anthropology only as a moment heralding an *Aufhebung* unwelcomed by him.

Pouillon's assessment of 'L'œuvre de Claude Lévi-Strauss' comes tentatively to the same conclusion. It is broadly sympathetic to the quest for structural universals because it sees them as potential underwriters of the principle of comprehensibility postulated by the synthetic anthropology. Lefort, says Pouillon, was led to oppose structure to lived experience by his failure to grasp the notion of model: 'Or, cette notion est instrumentale et non ontologique: le modèle est non pas l'objet de la compréhension, mais son moyen.'[77] On the other hand, although prepared to concede the relevance of linguistics, Pouillon is unwilling to see all social phenomena as expressions of unconscious laws. He refuses the consequence, which is the 'subordination de l'histoire à l'analyse synchronique des structures'[78] and which leaves no room for 'la saisie d'une temporalité, d'un mouvement proprement historique qui, précisément en tant que mouvement, se donnerait à lui-même sa signification'.[79]

Close to both Sartre and Lévi-Strauss, Pouillon cannot easily rule out the possibility that the two might move their theories closer to each other. He therefore poses the central problem in a way that endorses Sartre's commitment to existential Marxism and invites Lévi-Strauss to keep pace:

La question de savoir comment unir analyse structurale et analyse historique, comment concevoir en même temps un ordre synchronique et un ordre diachronique, reste donc ouverte. Ce problème se pose au marxisme dans des termes formellement analogues. Le marxisme voit en effet dans l'histoire l'expression dynamique d'une structure sociale absolument générale – les rapports entre classes – et en même temps un mouvement autonome qui se donne sa propre signification. On met l'accent tantôt sur un aspect, tantôt sur l'autre, on ne veut renoncer – et on a sans doute raison – ni à l'un ni à l'autre. Le fait est que leur synthèse n'est pas vraiment réalisée. (C'est bien pourquoi il est absurde de vouloir 'dépasser' ou 'repenser' le marxisme: il s'agit de le développer.) C'est pourquoi on attend avec intérêt l'essai annoncé par Lévi-Strauss sous le titre *Ethnologie et Marxisme*.[80]

Pouillon is fortunate that Sartre and Lévi-Strauss did not take at its face value Lefort's formulation of their incompatibility in 1951. He is fortunate, too, that Mauss's concept of reciprocity suits both so well that a semblance of agreement is sustained until the question of history comes to the fore. History in this context means Algeria, and Pouillon's labours of mediation will henceforward be undertaken in unconducive circumstances. It is difficult to promote theoretical convergence when structural anthropology steers clear of analyses of colonialism and when the synthetic anthropology has so little time for the study of isolated, homeostatic communities.[81]

3

ALGERIA: INTELLECTUAL
RIVALRIES IN TIME OF WAR

The third period runs from September 1956 to September 1963 and is bounded by the assessment of Lévi-Strauss by Pouillon, which I have just discussed, and another, conducted this time by the Sartrean philosopher Pierre Verstraeten. Between the two dates come the anti-Stalinist commitment, which is renewed after the Soviet invasion of Hungary, the continuing movement of Pontalis towards Lacan, the death of Merleau-Ponty and, most important of all, the Algerian War. Great tension is generated by the contrast between Sartre's clamorous anti-colonialism and the troubled silence of structuralism in respect of events in North Africa. It is possible to identify three moments in the relationship between the two anthropological ventures: Sartre's attack on academic anthropology, his progressive rethinking of the synthetic anthropology and the subsequent structuralist riposte. In this chapter I propose to examine each of these moments.

By way of introduction, however, I shall comment briefly on the profile of *TM* in this period. Its interest in politics and the *sciences humaines* holds steady, something which is to be expected given the context outlined above and given that its Director throws himself during these years into the extraordinarily intense labour required by his *Critique de la raison dialectique*. Literature, equally unsurprisingly, suffers a further slight decline in terms of the quantitative measures of its presence, as I indicate in Appendix 3.

As far as the editorial team is concerned, the picture is also one of gradual change within a reasonably stable framework. In 1956, *TM* is run by Sartre, Cau, Lanzmann and Péju: Jeanson, the *gérant*, soon elects to devote his energies to the Algerian Revolution and is replaced in January 1957 by Michelle Léglise. Cau also withdraws early on and from 1959 no Editorial Board is named, responsibility resting with Sartre as Director and with Péju as General Secretary.

This arrangement continues until February 1961, when once again a large group of editorial personnel is listed on the front cover. Long-standing collaborators – Beauvoir, Bost, Lanzmann, Péju, Pontalis and Pouillon – are joined by two newcomers, André Gorz and Bernard Pingaud. In December 1961, this group becomes a *direction collective* based on the following division of labour: Lanzmann, Péju and Sartre (political affairs), Beauvoir and Pingaud (literature), Gorz (economics), Bost (the arts), and Pontalis and Pouillon (the human sciences).

No major policy considerations figure in this rearrangement. It is due rather to personality clashes and to administrative problems. These come to a head in June 1962 with the summary dismissal of Péju and the co-option of Jeanson. The latter move is motivated by a wish publicly to acknowledge Jeanson's underground activities during the years of armed combat and by the demand that other militants should enjoy complete amnesty. No clear reason is given for Péju's sacking, however, and this is somewhat surprising in view of his record of thirty articles and eight years as editor and as General Secretary. Aggrieved, he alleges by letter that the Directorate, by associating his name with that of Jeanson, has given the impression that he has been insufficiently committed to the Algerian cause; in fact, he claims, he is being victimised by a timorous Editorial Board for his excessive activism.

The letter elicits a long response from Sartre which is an interesting Directorial record of the life of the review in the period. He makes it clear that Péju carried little political weight and invites historians to bear in mind that 'Merleau-Ponty fut notre guide pendant cinq ans – Péju pas même une heure'.[1] There was neither partnership of Péju and Sartre nor autocratic Directorial control: 'En fait, nous étions quatre. Quatre "politiques"? ... Quatre *intellectuels* qui réfléchissaient sur les événements politiques et tentaient de s'orienter, tant bien que mal, au milieu des problèmes les plus difficiles de ce temps; par ordre alphabétique: Lanzmann, Péju, Pouillon et moi. Nous prenions nos décisions ensemble, après discussion.'[2] The real reasons for Péju's dismissal, says Sartre, were breach of faith, erratic editorial conduct and serious maladministration. Olivier Todd, who was close to *TM* during these years, notes that Sartre himself was not a good administrator and that without Beauvoir, 'qui lisait presque tous les manuscrits, rien ne se serait fait'.[3] The Péju episode was more stormy than it was significant. The editorial change with the greatest long-term importance – the recruitment of Gorz – had already taken place.

Sartre and academic anthropology

The specialist anthropologists who figure in *TM* in this period are Georges Condominas, Robert Jaulin, Lévi-Strauss, Métraux, Pouillon and Lucien Sebag. Here I shall look at the contributions of all but Lévi-Strauss and Sebag, whose work is more usefully mentioned at a later stage. Of the remainder, it is best to consider first the material supplied by Métraux, the friend and colleague of Leiris and of Lévi-Strauss. In June 1957, the review features the sixth chapter of his study of *Le Vaudou haïtien*. The product of great erudition and of considerable fieldwork, the book surveys the origins and the contemporary social framework of the voodoo cults, establishing a context for the detailed discussion of magic, ritual, the complexities of the pantheon and the phenomena of possession. The sixth chapter, 'Vaudou et christianisme', while not providing a sociological theory of religious syncretism, examines the interlocking of Catholicism and the African Fon religions at the levels of iconography and liturgy. It also deals with the counter-productivity of Christian opposition to voodoo. In general, Métraux's attitude is one of sympathy with the cult and with its adepts: although voodoo imposes financial burdens on an already impoverished people, it affords them psychological security, group solidarity and aesthetic satisfaction.

Both *Le Vaudou haïtien* and the later work on *Les Incas* are subsequently reviewed by Pouillon in the February/March 1959 and the May 1962 issues and receive praise for the scrupulous way in which different orders of data are marshalled and evaluated. Métraux is essentially a learned and respected ethnographer with few theoretical pretensions. This emerges very clearly from the set of obituary notices published in *L'Homme* shortly after his suicide in 1963. For Leiris, who had known him since 1934 and had worked for him at UNESCO, Métraux was one of those who, with their mutual friend Georges Bataille, taught 'une violente ardeur à vivre jointe à une conscience impitoyable de ce qu'il y a là de dérisoire'.[4]

The same issue of *L'Homme* carries Métraux's profession of faith: 'Je tiens à dire que d'autres civilisations que la nôtre ont pu, infiniment mieux que nous ne l'avons fait, résoudre les problèmes qui se posent à l'homme. C'est, je crois, cette idée, réellement fondamentale, qui m'a inspiré ma carrière d'ethnographe: j'ai voulu conserver le souvenir, ou l'image, de ces petites civili-sations.'[5] He was in fact so successful that the inhabitants of Easter Island regarded him, and not themselves, as the repository of their cultural heritage. The motivation is obviously very close to the meticulous melancholy of *Tristes Tropiques*, and it is not surprising that Lévi-Strauss should mourn the passing of the man who knew so much of what will never be known again: 'Avec lui, des tribus entières, des civilisations vénérables, s'oblitèrent et disparaissent de la surface de la terre.'[6] Lévi-Strauss concludes: 'Ce qui aggrave encore notre désolation, c'est de penser qu'il n'aurait peut-être pas surestimé la mort s'il n'avait injustement sous-estimé son œuvre, et qu'il nous a quittés sur ce double malentendu.'[7]

TM subsequently pays its own tribute by publishing in September 1966 an essay which dates from 1928 – 'L'anthropophagie rituelle des Tupinamba'. (It is later included in the posthumous collection of studies produced by Gallimard in 1967, *Religions et magies indiennes d'Amérique du Sud*.) Here Métraux's analysis shows him to be well within the French anthropological tradition: following Mauss, he sees cannibalism as an expression of vengeance which is itself described as a mode of reciprocity. It also follows in the line of those commentaries made by explorers of Brazil – Jean de Léry, André Thevet, Hans Staden – which are reviewed by Lévi-Strauss in *Tristes Tropiques*. As far as *TM* is concerned, Métraux is located in a triangular relationship with Leiris, to whom he gave encouragement in the 1930s, and Lévi-Strauss, for whom he was instrumental in finding work in New York during the Second World War. Their respect for their senior is duly communicated to Pouillon.

Reviews of Métraux's work, together with assessments of Verrier Elwin's *The Muria and their Ghotul* (August 1959) and of Dan Chuka Talayesva's memoir *Sun Chief* (May/June 1959), represent the sum of Pouillon's anthropological contributions to *TM* during the period. This lack of prominence, which contrasts with his editorial activity, is explained by two factors: first, his involvement, as a secretary at the Assemblée Nationale, in the parliamentary crises occasioned by the war in Algeria; secondly, his absence on fieldwork expeditions in Chad from July to October 1958 and from February to May 1963.

I indicated at the close of the preceding chapter the importance of Pouillon's position: it is he who stands between Sartre and Lévi-Strauss, calling for the integration of the diachronic intuitions of the former and the synchronic analyses of the latter. In his review of *Le Vaudou haïtien*, for example, he formulates a view of the phenomenon of possession which requires that the synthetic anthropology incorporate the insights into social reality brought by structuralism. Addressing his comments at the same time to Leiris's work on *La Possession et ses aspects théâtraux chez les Ethiopiens de Gondar*,[8] he notes the parallels between the Haitian *loa* and the Ethiopian *zar* and goes on to reject simulation and psychopathology as factors of explanation. Possession is, in his view, a cultural practice which gives to the individual the opportunity of referring certain modes of behaviour to external models; it contrasts with the Western tendency to use characterological types to account for different varieties of experience.

At times this account of possession appears very Sartrean:

Ce n'est pas l'inconscience qui est recherchée, c'est l'irresponsabilité [...] Toute action suivie peut être considérée comme un rôle que l'on tient en se conformant à des canons psychologiques appris et ensuite oubliés mais toujours efficaces. Après tout, il n'y a pas de sentiments 'naturels' [...],[9] on apprend à les éprouver et à les manifester, il y a toujours en eux une part de jeu et de mauvaise foi. Nous sommes tous comme le garçon de café qui joue à être garçon de café, dont parle Sartre dans *L'Etre et le néant*.[10]

By contrast with Sartre, however, Pouillon makes *mauvaise foi* constitutive of the individual's social experience and identity, to the extent that the spontaneous is a mode of expressing what has been learned. Although he neither invokes the writings of Lévi-Strauss on shamanism and on possession, nor speaks of accession to a symbolic order as a precondition of experience, the effect of his argument is to draw the Sartrean phenomenology towards structuralism and away from Sartre, or at least away from the ontology of *L'Etre et le néant*. The foregrounding of the interpenetration of the spontaneous and the acquired is an attempt to lay 'le fondement d'une analyse à la fois logique et historique (c'est-à-dire, si la psyché est une histoire, vraiment psychologique) de la conduite humaine'.[11]

On the other hand, it is a measure of the sociological substance Sartre has already taken on board that Pouillon's article reads like a commentary on *Les Mots*. Individuals are said to develop in the context of norms and models which pre-exist and permeate them and which condition the way in which they think of themselves:

Ce qui est en moi n'est pas uniquement de moi, cela est vrai du possédé et du non-possédé. Où est alors la différence? Dans l'attitude à l'égard de cet étranger si proche, dans le choix que l'on fait entre l'effort pour l'intérioriser, le reprendre à son compte et, au contraire, l'acceptation insolente ou modeste de son extériorité.[12]

The option of spiritual possession is therefore not open to all, but is culture-dependent. In Pouillon's view, it tends to correlate, by way of compensation, with material poverty; material well-being, on the other hand, permits the development of psychology as a science and as an alternative to the forms of religious experience studied by Leiris and Métraux.

Hitherto, the tension between synthetic and structuralist anthropologies has been manifested in the varying degree of autonomy accorded to the individual: while the synthetic has asserted the freedom of the person to confer meaning on the constraints of his or her situation (e.g. Genet, Sade), the structuralist has insisted that meaning is itself constrained by the society as a cultural system. Pouillon's efforts are devoted to excavating the common ground, with a view to producing a model of social organisation which would accommodate both points of view. His position is clarified in his review of Talayesva's *Sun Chief*, the autobiography of the Hopi Indian which *TM* would have published had it not been thought that the selection of extracts would damage the fabric of the text. The book is judged to be illuminating: it reveals nothing of Hopi culture that anthropologists did not already know, but describes a lived situation in a way that is beyond the reach of the most imaginative fieldworker; what has been acquired appears as natural and what has been constrained appears as a range of options. It allows Pouillon to conclude that

les coutumes sont les règles d'un jeu qui permet bien des parties individuelles, ou, plutôt, un langage qui laisse chacun dire ce qu'il veut, parce que, comme tout langage, il est, outre un vocabulaire que l'ethnologue peut apprendre par lui-même mais qu'il aurait tort d'imaginer absolument contraignant, une syntaxe dont seul l'usager peut manifester la souplesse.[13]

Sun Chief thus places the synchronic understanding of the anthropologist in a developmental perspective. It describes cultural acquisition from within, for the benefit of those who come to the culture as foreigners. It is the complementarity of the two modes of cognition that, in Pouillon's opinion, renders anthropology viable. Talayesva's testimony is thus opportune: because it can be used to validate academic anthropology, it can also be used to secure the latter's endorsement by the synthetic. It is inopportune, however, in that it reaches *TM* in 1959, a year in which the chances of peaceful disciplinary coexistence are slim: Pouillon does not carry enough weight to reverse the divisive effects of the war in Algeria and professional ethnographers are allowed only a very low profile.

Two who do make an appearance are Georges Condominas and

Robert Jaulin; both, like Métraux, are relatively untouched by the intellectual rivalries which are energising *TM*. Condominas is the less significant – because of the date of his contribution, which is July 1962 and therefore well after the most critical period of the war, and because the extract from his book *De l'exotique au quotidien, Sar Luk, Viêt-Nam central*[14] is badly chosen. Once again, it is a personal journal rather than a formal fieldwork report,[15] but rather than featuring the discussion of the sufferings of the Vietnamese *montagnard* people under French colonial rule or their harassment by the Diem regime, *TM* merely carries a simple description of a Mnong Gar festival.

Jaulin's presence is almost as fleeting and is limited to two extracts, in September 1957 and November 1959, from his book *La Mort sara*. A number of factors make of this text a work compatible with anthropological material previously published by the review. In particular, it touches on certain themes already broached in 'Le Père Noël supplicié' and in *Tristes Tropiques* and sets out to illustrate a principle which Lévi-Strauss had himself formulated: 'la représentation qu'une société se fait du rapport entre les vivants et les morts se réduit à un effort pour cacher, embellir ou justifier, sur le plan de la pensée religieuse, les relations réelles qui prévalent entre les vivants'.[16] Jaulin's analysis of the tribe's constituent exogamic components makes the exchange of women logically dependent on the correlation of the male–female opposition among the living with the endogamous relationship which binds the male dead to the female tribal land. His various hypotheses all derive from the central function ascribed to the initiation rites; these set in train a process of symbolic death and rebirth which effectively transfers the male child from a female world of infancy to the male world of adulthood, and without which the patrilocal exogamous groups could not be perpetuated.

The book does not consciously anticipate Jaulin's later work on ethnocide.[17] Its title directs the reader's attention to the role of death, actual and symbolic, within the cultural system of the Sara, and not to the death of the system itself. The study does not, however, lack political and historical interest, for it is unable to present the Sara experience as a homeostatic organisation divorced from its international context. Far from being a classical anthropological monograph, it falls – like *Tristes Tropiques*, Balandier's *Afrique ambiguë* and Condominas's *De l'exotique au quotidien* – somewhere between traditional ethnography, sociology of cultural change and journal of a voyage of discovery. Jaulin's African adventure joins the others in the category of anthropology for the *grand public*.

The generic indeterminacy comes from the fact that Jaulin forces participant observation to its extreme by insisting on his own initiation into Sara manhood. The procedures involve him in discipline and tribulation which he is able to document from within the secrecy of the institution. It must be said that this intrusion attests to a buccaneering mentality which does not marry well with Leiris's exemplary view of the political and ethical implications of ethnography. Jaulin's course of action nonetheless generates knowledge by heightening the tensions between the tribal fathers, the neighbouring tribes, the parallel local administration appointed from the capital, the 'modernist' bourgeoisie, the anti-colonialist forces, and institutions like the Church. *TM*'s readers, sensitised by events in Algeria, are likely to appreciate the irony of an ethnographer who, seeking to penetrate to the heart of a 'primitive' culture, cannot help discovering and sharpening all the contradictions inherent in a rapidly changing situation.

Unwittingly, Jaulin raises the question which much later he will turn into a vigorous assertion – that of the non-viability of ethnography. His position becomes increasingly distant from that of Pouillon, who remains steadfastly committed to what is shortly to become his own professional activity. No more needs to be said of Jaulin at this juncture – his influence is really very marginal – and in any case it is Sartre who, in the short term, dominates *TM*'s dealings with academic anthropology.

The review's attention to developments in the French colonies is at its most intense in this period. Between August 1956 and September 1963, two out of every three issues contain relevant material – not just on Algeria, but also on Morocco, the Ivory Coast, Martinique and Guadeloupe. Between 1959 and 1961, however, it is dominated by the Algerian crisis. It is essential to look closely at this material, for it has serious implications for ethnography.

For an account of the line adopted by *TM* throughout the French government's conflicts with the FLN (Front de Libération Nationale) and with the military authorities in Algiers, it is best to defer to Burnier's study. I shall simply observe that the review engages in persistent attempts to galvanise the French left, both in calls for negotiation with the FLN and for resistance to the return of de Gaulle. This programme involves presentations of the policies of the Algerian nationalists, together with denunciations of the torture practised by the French forces; Georges Mattéi's 'Jours kabyles' (July 1957) is a good example of the latter. As a result, there is frequent confiscation of whole issues in Algeria as well as, less often, in the metropolis.

Special mention must be made of the activities of Jeanson, who, after his withdrawal in 1957, establishes a clandestine network to assist the FLN in France. Public contact between him and the review is restored by the supportive testimonies made at his trial by Sartre, Lanzmann and Pouillon in 1960. The *TM* team, however, is already mobilised in 1959: 'Simone de Beauvoir prêtera sa voiture et son appartement [...]Bernard Pingaud, Marcel Péju, Claude Lanzmann abritent des Algériens; Michel Leiris verse de l'argent.'[18] *TM* is also instrumental in publicising Maurice Blanchot's 'Manifeste des 121', as it became known – the 'Déclaration sur le droit à l'insoumission dans la guerre d'Algérie' – and although the text is refused by the printers, the full list of signatories appears in the August/September 1960 issue. It contains a large number of regular and occasional contributors, as well as the following anthropologists: Condominas, Hubert Damisch, Simone Dreyfus, Jaulin, Leiris and Pouillon. Fernande Schulmann adds her name on behalf of Métraux, who is prevented from signing by his position as an official of UNESCO.

The principal contributors who supply analysis and commentary are, from the metropolis, Claude Bourdet, Claude Estier, Gorz, Gisèle Halimi, Jeanson, Albert-Paul Lentin, Maurice Maschino, Péju, Jean Rous and Daniel Vergès. From Algeria come the first-hand accounts, notably by Saadia and Lakhdar, of aspects of the society in crisis – conscription, emigration, prostitution and so on. Two writers stand out from all the others: Albert Memmi and Frantz Fanon. Both are spokesmen of the colonised, both have the backing of Sartre and both highlight the inadequacies of academic sociology and anthropology.

The tension between Western European academics and Third World intellectuals emerges clearly in a piece by Jacqueline Delange, an anthropologist and colleague of Leiris, in April 1957. She reports for *TM* on the 1956 Paris Congress of *Présence africaine*, a congress called to follow up the 1955 Bandung Conference of non-aligned nations and to facilitate a cultural stock-taking by black African writers. Delange's position is that of Leiris and of Sartre, namely support for *négritude* and repudiation of the colonisers' representations of the colonised. When she learns, primarily from the Haitian, Paul, that anthropology is held responsible for these representations, her reaction is one of shock: 'Voilà une condamnation, un enterrement, un peu rapides d'une science qui prétendait avoir la vocation (et profondément, et depuis sa naissance) du relativisme culturel.'[19] It is thanks to anthropology, she says, that 'la dépendance Race–Civilisation se disloque, que les cultures méconnues se revalorisent, que les cultures soufflées se dégonflent et que les dimensions authentiques se définissent. Les étapes du développement de l'ethnologie sont autant d'avancées vers un élargissement des connaissances et vers la libération des formes étouffées.'[20] It is as if Delange's profession of disciplinary innocence at once reinforces anthropology's claims to higher cognitive competence and confirms the worst suspicions of the colonised. Certainly her indignation affords an insight into why this particular problem is so rarely at the forefront of academic preoccupations.

It is Memmi who is the first since Tran Duc Thao to attempt a formalisation of the interdependence of group perceptions in the colonial situation; he does so in his *Portrait du colonisé*, of which *TM* publishes an extract in April 1957. He is concerned to emphasise the dynamic nature of this interdependence and the role of confirmation and reinforcement in the vicious circle of antagonisms. Predictably, he sees the independence of the colony as the only solution. In many ways, he is typical of a certain moment in the growth of the synthetic anthropology – that marked by *Saint Genet* and by *Le Diable et le Bon Dieu*. There is the same rejection of essentialist definitions, the same insistence on inter-group perceptions and their evolution in specific social contexts, the same tendency to express the local inadequacy of moral values: of the *colonisateur de bonne volonté*, for example, it is said that, though he may refuse evil, he can never attain good, 'car le seul choix qui lui soit permis n'est pas entre le bien et le mal, il est entre le mal et le malaise'.[21]

Sartre's preface to Memmi's book, published in the issue of July/August 1957, endorses this compatibility. Sartre has nevertheless moved on from his 1951 positions and has since proposed the view that colonialism is not primarily the sum of individual and group intentions and representations, but a system of economic, social and political interactions that cannot but proceed to its own destruction. He now considers that the representations studied by Memmi are ideological in the sense that they express social relations which are conditioned by the socio-economic order of the colony: 'J'ai toujours pensé que les idées se dessinent dans les choses et qu'elles sont déjà dans l'homme, quand il les réveille et les exprime pour s'expliquer sa situation.' And he adds: 'Toute la différence entre nous vient peut-être de ce qu'il voit une situation là où je vois un système.'[22]

A little startled, Memmi replies to this apparent economism in an article published late in 1957: 'On nous a reproché d'avoir donné à la relation psychologique et culturelle une importance trop considérable. Nous lui avons donné son importance, qui est considérable en effet.'[23] He goes on to outline a sociology of colonialism in some detail; it is a sociology that clearly does not yet exist, and its absence is an indictment of French academia and, in particular, of Balandier. The gulf between the predicament of colonised peoples and an adequate understanding of it is subsequently widened by Fanon and celebrated dramatically by Sartre, as I now hope to show.

Dominating all Sartre's writings on the Algerian War, whether in *TM*, in *L'Express* or elsewhere, is the thought that Frenchmen have become torturers. For him, this is the return of nausea and the rediscovery of the self as Other – not at the ontological level, but socially, politically and morally. He may now seem to revert, traumatised, to the ethical categories only shortly before deemed unviable, but in fact the concepts of good and evil are now expressed in terms of *humain* and *inhumain*; the latter are both more forceful and better able to designate the effects of the systematisation of individual conduct in the context of a radically divided group. Just as colonialism was declared a system, so now is torture: it is an institutionalised practice which thrives in the context of guerrilla warfare and into which individuals are drawn and dehumanised.

It is no surprise that *TM* should open its pages to Fanon, Martiniquan psychiatrist and member of the Provisional Revolutionary Government of Algeria. An extract from *L'An V de la révolution algérienne* appears in May/June 1959, and in February/March 1960 Maschino gives the book a very warm reception. The relationship of Fanon and Sartre is in fact notable for its reciprocity. Back in 1952 Fanon's great debt to the *Réflexions sur la question juive* had been repaid with constructive critique of 'Orphée noir', in which Sartre was taken to task for failing to distinguish between different black communities and for allowing *négritude* to be swamped in the currents of the Hegelian dialectic. 'Jean-Paul Sartre, dans cette étude', lamented Fanon, 'a détruit l'enthousiasme noir.'[24]

It is in May 1961 that *TM* features Fanon's most influential work, the essay entitled 'De la violence' and later to become the first chapter of *Les Damnés de la terre*. This article restates the now familiar analysis: colonialism is an act of violence to which counter-violence is the only and inevitable answer. What is fascinating in the present context is that, although it comes from the heart of the political and military struggle, the article nonetheless makes use of the *sciences humaines* which hitherto have managed to look at colonial reality only from the outside.

In the first place, Fanon is a psychiatrist. His basic postulate is that the counter-violence of the colonised is an index of health: it represents the reappropriation of the libido which is suppressed by oppression and diverted into superstition, mysticism, party political reformism, the desire for assimilation, and inter-tribal conflict. Bringing his psychiatric experience to bear on mysticism, however, he moves, like Sartre, onto the territory of the anthropologist. His comments on black African religious practices are worth quoting in full:

Sur un autre versant, nous verrons l'affectivité du colonisé s'épuiser en danses plus ou moins extatiques. C'est pourquoi une étude du monde colonial doit obligatoirement s'attacher à la compréhension du phénomène de la danse et de la possession. La relaxation du colonisé, c'est précisément cette orgie musculaire au cours de laquelle l'agressivité la plus aiguë, la violence la plus immédiate se trouvent canalisées, transformées, escamotées [. . .] A heures fixes, à dates fixes, hommes et femmes se retrouvent en un lieu donné et, sous l'œil grave de la tribu, se lancent dans une pantomime d'allure désordonnée mais en réalité très systématisée où, par des voies multiples, dénégations de la tête, courbure de la colonne, rejet en arrière de tout le corps, se déchiffre à livre ouvert l'effort grandiose d'une collectivité pour s'exorciser, s'affranchir, se dire. Tout est permis [. . .] dans le cercle.

Un pas de plus et nous tombons en pleine possession. Au vrai, ce sont des séances de possession–dépossession qui sont organisées: vampirisme, possession par les djinns, par les zombies, par Legba, le dieu illustre du Vaudou. Ces effritements de la personnalité, ces dédoublements, ces dissolutions, remplissent une fonction économique primordiale dans la stabilité du monde colonisé. A l'aller, les hommes et les femmes étaient impatients, piétinants, 'sur les nerfs'. Au retour, c'est le calme qui revient au village, la paix, l'immobilité.

On assistera au cours de la lutte de libération à une désaffection singulière pour ces pratiques. Le dos au mur, le couteau sur la gorge ou, pour être plus précis, l'electrode sur les parties génitales, le colonisé va être sommé de ne plus se raconter d'histoires.[25]

Although in *Les Damnés de la terre* Fanon partially substantiates the alibi of Western anthropology offered by Delange,[26] the

passage quoted above nevertheless constitutes its radical incrimi-
nation. It is reasonable to infer from it that even when anthropologists have striven to contextualise observed behaviour within the
framework of colonialism, ethnographic fieldwork has nonetheless
been informed by the assumption that the tendency of colonial rule
is to corrupt indigenous cultures by *weakening* them. The converse,
says Fanon, is more likely to be true: certain cultural practices are
reinforced by colonialism to the point of caricature and psychosis.

Fanon does not mount any concerted attack on anthropology –
he gives the strong impression that more pressing tasks await him.
It is certainly the case, however, that no anthropologist has ever
suggested in *TM* that there existed in each colony a transmutation
of political and economic impotence into cultural hyperactivity.
Typically, the position is that of Delange, whose reference to
'formes étouffées' prefers a model of cultural impoverishment
based on atrophy rather than on hypertrophy. It is true that
Pouillon, in his review of the work of Leiris and Métraux, correlates rites of possession with material dispossession, but he does not
carry the argument as far as Fanon does.

In fact, it is the synthetic anthropology in the person of Sartre
which has most closely approached the positions of the revolutionary psychiatrist. In the Salle Wagram in 1956, Sartre recognised
that the effect of Western occupation is to create 'natives' quite
dissimilar to the indigenous populations of pre-colonial days. When
asked by Fanon to supply a preface to *Les Damnés de la terre*, all he
has to do therefore is to pick up the threads of his own argument
and to develop it in the deeper anger of 1962. This yields passages
like the following:

Ce qui était autrefois le fait religieux dans sa simplicité, une certaine
communication du fidèle avec le sacré, ils [les colonisés] en font une arme
contre le désespoir et l'humiliation: les zars, les loas, les Saints de la
Sainterie descendent en eux, gouvernent leur violence et la gaspillent en
transes jusqu'à l'épuisement. En même temps ces hauts personnages les
protègent: cela veut dire que les colonisés se défendent de l'aliénation
coloniale en renchérissant sur l'aliénation religieuse. Avec cet unique
résultat, au bout du compte, qu'ils cumulent les deux aliénations et que
chacune se renforce par l'autre [. . .] L'indigénat est une névrose introduite
et maintenue par le colon chez les colonisés *avec leur consentement*.[27]

No statement better illustrates the Sartrean view that resentment,
in the Nietzschean sense of the damming-up of aggressive
responses, may be expressed as a consenting to be possessed. It is
an idea that can be traced from the *Esquisse d'une théorie des*

émotions through 'L'engagement de Mallarmé' and *Les Mots* to *L'Idiot de la famille*; as it develops, it gathers ethnographic reference.

But there is more in this preface than mere confirmation of Fanon's views. There is confirmation of him as a person, together with the correlative recognition by Sartre of himself as a member of the colonising society. In effect, the preface is Sartre's afterword, as violent, as paroxystic and as mutilating as Fanon's message. He writes his way through a dialectic which moves as follows. The discovery of the torture practised by the French army is the discovery of French inhumanity. Fanon's book meanwhile reveals the humanisation of the colonised by their adoption of measures of counter-violence. The French cultural self is then perceived to be other than what it was thought to be and is reconstructed on the lines of the image previously entertained of the Other. As a result, the violence hitherto confined to the colony is reimported into the metropolis in the form of OAS activity, and the metropolitan population, now ruled by the charisma of a *grand sorcier* with no political programme, is primitivised.[28]

Alluding to Leiris's ethnography, just as he had done in *Saint Genet* to describe Genet's possession by the collective representation of him, Sartre now leads his compatriots to the point at which they must make their own the opinion that was previously held by them *of* the colonised:

Où sont les sauvages, à présent? Où est la barbarie? Rien ne manque, pas même le tam-tam; les klaxons rythment 'Algérie Française' pendant que les Européens font brûler vifs des Musulmans [. . .] A notre tour, pas à pas, nous faisons le chemin qui mène à l'indigénat. Mais pour devenir indigènes tout à fait, il faudrait que notre sol fût occupé par les anciens colonisés et que nous crevions de faim. Ce ne sera pas: non, c'est le colonialisme déchu qui nous possède, c'est lui qui nous chevauchera bientôt, gâteux et superbe; le voilà, notre zar, notre loa.[29]

Sartre, like Fanon, writes from within the cycle of violence, as a party to the group conflicts and interactions that are the object of the synthetic anthropology. In doing so, he is bound to call into question the terms of reference of academic anthropology; not only does he imply that it has studied collective alienations without either combating them or conceptualising them as such, he also denies its detachment and objectivity. The synthetic venture, meanwhile, presses home its claim to be the anthropology of liberation; it requires that the French fight on the side of those whose counter-violence is a reassertion of the human in the face of the inhuman, for only then will 'finira le temps des sorciers et des fétiches'.[30]

Despite this assault on the French conscience, Pouillon's review of *Les Damnés de la terre* in April 1962 makes no effort to discuss the position of academic anthropology in respect of the wars of decolonisation. Pouillon merely notes that he finds nothing in Fanon with which he disagrees. He observes, in a manner consistent with the ongoing anti-Stalinism of *TM*, that it will be profitable to debate the relevance of the Algerian revolution to other contexts. Here he anticipates an aspect of the synthetic anthropology that will assume great importance as the decade progresses, notably in the work of Régis Debray. His own intellectual position of dual loyalty to Lévi-Strauss and to Sartre, meanwhile, is rendered less comfortable still by the extent to which the liberation struggles come to occupy the theoretical space opened up by the *Critique de la raison dialectique*.[31] The fact that Lévi-Strauss will eventually be drawn into discussion of the *Critique* is intimately related to academic anthropology's war-time loss of credibility. I shall return to this line of inquiry in due course.

Before doing so, however, I would like to pause briefly at adjacent areas of *TM*'s activity, turning first to literature. A salient feature of the period is the predominance of non-French writers over the French, by a ratio of about 2 to 1. This represents a reversal of the situation as it was in the early days. As much as a turning-away from the French literary developments of the fifties and early sixties, it obviously reflects the political concerns of the moment. Following the Soviet invasion of Hungary in 1956, it gives considerable space to the poets and novelists of the Eastern bloc countries. From Hungary itself comes material by, among others, Tibor Dery, Gyula Illyes, Attila Joszef and Lajos Kassak; from Yugoslavia the work of Miroslav Krleja and others; from Poland, promoted in the first instance by Péju, texts by Jerzy Andrzejewski, Kazimierz Brandys, Jan Kott, Slowmir Mrozek, to name only the most prominent; and from the USSR, the work of writers such as Mikhail Sholokhov, Alexander Solzhenitsyn and Andrey Vosnesensky. *TM* also tends to favour literature of Latin American origin and the literature of Western European countries with a strong Marxist tradition. Nothing, then, from Britain or the USA (with the exception of a short story by John Updike), but rather names such as the following: Jorge Luis Borges (Argentina), Jorge Amado (Brazil), Alejo Carpentier and Virgilio Piñera (Cuba), Miguel Angel Asturias (Guatemala), Elvio Romero (Paraguay), Juan Goytisolo and Jorge Semprun (Spain), and Italo Calvino, Carlo Emilio Gadda, Carlo Levi, Alberto Mondadori, Eugenio Montale, Elsa Morante and Cesare Pavese (all Italian).

One specific textual practice – autobiography – merits discussion here, because it is absolutely central to the synthetic anthropology. It is only later that *TM* will carry the ongoing work of Leiris and Sartre, that is to say *Fibrilles* and *Les Mots* (the composition of which dates back to 1954); in this period, however, it features Henri Lefebvre's *La Somme et le reste*, Violette Leduc's *La Bâtarde*, as well as substantial portions of the first three volumes of Beauvoir's memoirs. *La Force des choses* is particularly interesting because it is one of the two partial histories of the review (the other being Sartre's obituary for Merleau-Ponty); it is a work of cultural history rather than an existential self-analysis, a labour of retrospection rather than of introspection, a reminder that as *TM* enters the sixties editorial control passes largely into the hands of the second generation.

More significant, therefore, both because the author is to be a greater editorial force than Beauvoir and because his work is less a reference text and much more a substantive exercise in existential reflexivity, is the appearance in October 1957 and March 1958 of *Le Traître* by André Gorz. Gorz first met Sartre in Switzerland in 1946 and spent the immediate post-war years pondering the problems of the existentialist ethic, only to run into the same impasse as Sartre himself, namely the uncertainty as to whether writing and action constitute a mutually inclusive or exclusive pair, and the inability ever to dissolve this tension in unambiguous ethical formulations. As a result, his *Fondements pour une morale* see the light of day only in 1977,[32] Gorz having decided that a work of existential self-analysis (*Le Traître*) was more urgently needed. This provisional abandonment of the project of the ethic places *Le Traître* within the perspectives of *Saint Genet*. The antecedent is appropriate given the fact that Gorz can identify his *projet fondamental* – a desire for nullity and for total and unconditional self-creation – only on the basis of an objective exclusion from human community. In Gorz's case the exclusion is racial rather than legal, national rather than institutional (and he has perhaps more in common with Memmi in this respect): an Austrian half-Jew resident in Switzerland, he determines to make himself into a Frenchman *ab nihilo*. At many levels, therefore, he is the product of his own betrayal, notably in the sense that his very desire to exist without forebears is a guarantee that he will be receptive to the massive influence of

Sartre. He identifies, in other words, with Sartre's repudiation of identifications.

Le Traître resembles *Saint Genet* inasmuch as it follows the movement of ambivalence and makes of paradox the only source of continuity, problematising the subject in the textual space created for its deproblematisation. It is, as Pontalis said of Leiris's autobiography, cyclothymic: its organisation is dictated by an oscillation between doubt and hope, an oscillation which derives in turn from the fact that lucidity and delusion can never be said with certainty not to reinforce each other. The book nonetheless reaches a positive conclusion, for 'les certitudes se gagnent et restent révocables',[33] and a process of recurrent retotalisation enables the author to conjugate points of view of himself until he can risk a reasonably confident postulation of a *je* sufficiently unified to conduct its business in the world. Broadly speaking, the Gorz *pour-soi* displays itself in the now familiar manner: it lacks total self-confidence, it takes meaning and existence to be coterminous, and it seeks out possibilities of reciprocity that are usually actualised in writing.

Gorz's book ends, then, with a validation of writing, having liquidated 'les choix-complexes d'être qui s'opposent *et* à la prise de conscience de l'aliénation objective dont ils sont complices, *et* à la réalisation totale de l'homme dans le faire total'.[34] A triumph of subject over determinations, of human over inhuman, this is at least how Sartre's preface presents it.[35] His notes, entitled – with an anti-behaviourist flourish – 'Des rats et des hommes', celebrate the textual drama out of which, at the last, emerges an author; order is born of chaos, in his view, by an effort of totalisation and by the struggle of a voice to 'donner un sens *par des paroles* aux paroles qui viennent de lui échapper'.[36]

The unification of a subject in complete control of its predications – this, for Sartre, is the criterion of disalienation. For Lacan, it is the product of repression. In the context of this contrast, *Le Traître* is a useful point of reference, being one of the few occasions on which Sartre addresses himself to an obviously open and performative text. He is not willing to admit to the existence of an original linguistic polymorphism which is necessarily overridden by accession to the symbolic order; instead, he conceives of an already unified subject whose well-integrated intentions and meanings are vampirised by others. For Sartre, it is polyvocity that suppresses univocity, rather than the other way round. Hence the respect for Gorz, who reconquered what was stolen from him.

Once again, Sartre's thoughts turn to possession. Once again, ethnographic reference is brought in, this time to echo the preface to Fanon in its denunciation of Western savagery. The passage is worth quoting *in extenso*: it is redrafted from the essay 'L'engagement de Mallarmé', overshadows the composition of *Les Mots* and anticipates the analysis of the child Flaubert. The topic is the theft of subject identity by the social group:

Il paraît en effet, qu'on trouve encore sur terre des sauvages assez stupides pour voir dans leurs nouveaux-nés des ancêtres réincarnés. On agite au-dessus du nourrisson les armes et les colliers des vieux morts; qu'il fasse un mouvement, tout le monde se récrie: le grand-oncle est ressuscité. Ce vieillard va téter, conchier sous lui la paille, on l'appellera par son nom; les survivants de sa génération prendront plaisir à voir leur camarade de chasse et de guerre agiter ses jambes et s'égosiller; dès qu'il saura parler, ils lui inculqueront les souvenirs du défunt, un dressage sévère lui restituera son ancien caractère, on lui rappellera qu'*il* était coléreux, cruel ou magnanime, il en restera convaincu, malgré les démentis de l'expérience. Quelle barbarie: on prend un môme bien vivant, on le coud dans la peau d'un mort, il étouffera dans cette enfance sénile sans autre occupation que de reproduire exactement les gestes avunculaires, sans autre espoir que d'empoisonner après sa mort des enfances futures. Faut-il s'étonner après cela qu'il parle de lui-même avec les plus grandes précautions, à mi-voix, souvent à la troisième personne; ce malheureux n'ignore pas qu'il est son propre grand-oncle.

Ces aborigènes arriérés, on les trouve aux îles Fidji, à Tahiti, en Nouvelle-Guinée, à Vienne, à Paris, à Rome, partout où il y a des hommes: on les appelle des parents. Longtemps avant notre naissance, avant même de nous avoir conçu, les nôtres ont défini notre personnage. On a dit de nous: 'Il', des années avant que nous puissions dire '*je*'. Nous avons existé d'abord *comme des objets absolus*. A travers notre famille, la société nous assignait une situation, un être, un ensemble de rôles; les contradictions de l'histoire et les luttes sociales déterminent d'avance le caractère et le destin des générations à venir.[37]

For Sartre, what is elementary in the structures of kinship is their colonialism; reflexivity therefore involves exorcism. Does this mean that *TM* henceforth throws all its energies into promoting those writers who have proved their ability to exorcise – the poets of *négritude*? Now that the forebears have been unmasked – 'les voilà nus, les *Autres*, les Zars, les loas, les anges noirs, les fils de Caïn, tous nos parasites'[38] – does this signal a return to those exemplary poets who managed to liberate their own cultural ancestors? The short answer is not at all: *TM* now agrees with Fanon in believing the time of *négritude* to be past. The argument is spelt out by the black American Alan Albert, who in May 1962 asserts that *négritude* plays into the hands of the white racialists. Fanon also observes something of which the Editorial Board must have been aware – that of the original group of poets both Senghor and Rabémananjara have chosen to support France against Algeria at the United Nations. The August/September 1960 issue announces a special edition devoted to black Africa; it never appears and it is therefore difficult to say exactly what editorial line would have been taken and how the academic Africanist would have fared in it.

TM's preferences go instead to the literature of and surrounding the Algerian revolution. Militant poetry is published under pseudonyms; twice (in May 1957 and in July 1962) space is given over to Kateb Yacine's attempts to fuse mythology and actuality into a matrix from which a new national culture might emerge. The review also publishes poems by Albert-Paul Lentin which parody the attitudes of the *pied noir* community. Then there are the contributions of French metropolitans: Maurice Maschino's decision to avoid conscription, taken well before the 'Manifeste des 121' ('Le Refus' (October 1958)), and Olivier Todd's account in *Une Demi-campagne* (September and October 1957) of his tour of duty in Morocco in 1956. When Todd's book reappears as *Les Paumés* in 1973, a new preface by Sartre shows how Moroccan nationalism was the direct result of French abuse of the territory's status of protectorate. Sartre also traces the way in which the conscripts' boredom in 1956 developed into the violent racialism later mobilised in Algeria.

The most complex and best known literary work of the period is Sartre's play *Les Séquestrés d'Altona* (October and November 1959). It is easy to see why contemporary readings of it are informed as much by the Algerian conflict as by the theoretical apparatus of the *Critique de la raison dialectique*. It is a play of counter-productivities in which the instituted group – family, business corporation or army – renders all of the characters strangers to themselves and to each other. It demonstrates how, in societies based on the negation of positive reciprocity, the fulfilment of individual intentions yields a surplus which is appropriated and then fed back into the system as a systematic and dramatic irony. 'La France, autrefois, c'était un nom de pays', says Sartre in his preface to Fanon, 'prenons garde que ce ne soit, en 1961, le nom d'une névrose'.[39] Both *Les Séquestrés d'Altona* and *Les Damnés de la terre* contain case histories of torturers. Both subvert ethnographic discourse: while France is *névrosée*, Frantz (Gerlach, not

Fanon) is possessed.[40] It is understandable, given the invocation of Lévi-Strauss in *Saint Genet*, that Michel Contat[41] should see in Frantz, the sequestered torturer, a variety of the shaman, whose role it is to embody the contradictions of his society. On the other hand, in order to dispel the slightest hint of structuralism, it is perhaps better to invoke the spiritually possessed and materially dispossessed informants of Leiris and Métraux, whose company Sartre has been so assiduously cultivating.

At this juncture, I would like to introduce another reference – Brecht. Like most Parisians, Sartre had become familiar with his work in the late fifties, appreciating his anti-capitalism but begging to differ on matters of dramatic theory. It is interesting to see Sartre bring Brecht into contact with his own ongoing meditations on the epistemology of anthropology: 'L'idéal du théâtre brechtien, ce serait que le public fût comme un groupe d'ethnographes rencontrant tout à coup une peuplade sauvage. S'approchant et se disant soudain, dans la stupeur: ces sauvages, c'est nous.'[42] This may be an adequate refamiliarisation in the case of those tribes located outside the spheres of influence of repressive colonial regimes, tribes whose illusory difference can be dispelled in the name of a common humanity. It is clearly not appropriate for those 'natives' who have been economically and culturally vampirised by the ethnographers' compatriots and who paradoxically have acceded, in counter-violence, to the humanity that the colonisers have abdicated. Here the moments of recognition no longer abolish difference but confirm its polar change. Sartre has reiterated his view sufficiently: the French will remain savages for as long as they insist that the Algerians remain French; their civilising mission is their greatest illusion. Since it is the absence of possession which is illusory, a revolutionary metropolitan theatre, seeking to influence the course of the Algerian War, is obliged to deploy theatrical illusion in such a way as to make its spectators conscious of the experiences of possession, collusion and shame. *Les Séquestrés d'Altona* is thus anti-Brechtian in the same way that Leiris's *L'Afrique fantôme* is anti-Maussian.

It is not surprising that one of Sartre's few 'ethnographic' experiences took place in the theatre. In his Sorbonne lecture of 29 March 1960, in which he again discusses Brecht, he draws on his recent journey to Havana and describes an evening in the Cuban National Theatre, where he witnessed a programme of African religious dances. Spanish Catholicism had energetically suppressed the tribal religions; these, as a result, had survived virtually intact and had not evolved into syncretic forms like Haitian voodoo. In post-revolutionary Cuba, they could finally be brought into the theatre as a public spectacle. Thanks to Castro, therefore, Sartre was able to watch two groups of blacks, one on the stage, the other in the auditorium, neither distinguishable from the other in terms of theatrical or hieratic competence. He became fascinated by the shifting thresholds of representation and participation, with dances and trances taking place on both sides of the footlights. A single group of black Cubans, divided only by theatre architecture and convention, was encountering its existence as image and learning self-recognition. Sartre, meanwhile, deprived of the common cultural experience that made participation possible, did not dance. Instead, he became the ethnographer watching others accede to otherness, to ethnography and to solidarity. His point of view was primarily one of objectivity – he could understand what he saw by placing it in the appropriate socio-historical perspective. At the same time, although to a lesser degree, he could comprehend and appreciate the spectacle as the image of a religious impulse which he might conceivably share. This is how Sartre describes his modes of observation, and it is a reminder that by this time he has worked out the correct mix of *Erklären* and *Verstehen* in 'Questions de méthode'.

Before I move on to discuss this retheorisation of the synthetic anthropology, however, I intend to survey briefly the aspects of *TM*'s production supervised by Sartre's most able lieutenant, Gorz. I have already noted that events in Hungary stiffen the anti-Stalinist resolve of the editorial team. The key text in this respect is Sartre's essay 'Le fantôme de Staline' (November and December 1956, January 1957). Its *double refus* (of Stalinism and of capitalism) reinforces *TM*'s anti-colonialism by clearly specifying the dominant forms of oppression to be found in international relations. Sartre refuses to accept the Stalinian premiss of the inevitability of the Third World War. He also rejects the policies that proceed from it: the centralisation of the world revolutionary movement in Moscow, the extreme authoritarianism of Communist parties, and the mechanical application of the Soviet model of 'socialism in one country' to every society undertaking a struggle for its liberation.

After 1956, therefore, *TM*'s programme, directed principally by Sartre and by Gorz, becomes one of support for revolutionary movements which are theoretically and practically appropriate to local conditions. Intellectual freedom within these movements is seen as the *sine qua non* of their efficacy, since a dogmatic approach is likely to be politically suicidal. At the same time, the review begins to give a higher profile to Togliatti and to the Italian Communists; their influence is deemed potentially powerful in one particular area to which *TM* gives supreme importance – the destalinisation of the PCF.

'Le fantôme de Staline' incorporates a detailed analysis of the events in Budapest in 1956, as well as a history of Stalinism, which it sees as the product of the disjunction between the centralised economic plan and the distribution of material need in the Eastern bloc. It anticipates the *Critique* insofar as it is interested in the effects of scarcity; Sartre holds firm in his belief that when these have been eradicated, counter-productivity will be minimised and a formal ethic will become feasible for the first time. The construction of socialism is an attested human purpose and is therefore a legitimate part of his object of study: 'ce sont des hommes en marche qui se groupent et s'entraînent les uns les autres, qui s'organisent et changent en s'organisant, qui sont faits pour l'histoire et qui la font; leurs actions se fondent sur leurs besoins et leurs besoins sont aussi vrais qu'eux-mêmes'.[43] On the other hand, socialism is the project which requires his anthropology to be synthetic, that is to say, to transform itself and its conditions of existence. This means, to pick a precise example, that a colonial liberation movement has by no means the same (synthetic) anthropological status as a colonial religious system, for the former is both the object of study and the necessary means of study, while the latter is merely the object. Sartre writes:

l'édification socialiste *est privilégiée en ceci* qu'on doit, pour la comprendre, épouser son mouvement et adopter ses objectifs; en un mot, on juge de ce qu'elle fait au nom de ce qu'elle veut, de ses moyens au nom de sa fin, tandis qu'on apprécie toutes les autres entreprises sur ce qu'elles ignorent, sur ce qu'elles négligent ou sur ce qu'elles refusent.[44]

It is obvious, even if implicit, that the synthetic anthropology is renewing its claims for moral and political superiority over its academic counterpart. The tension is raised in the knowledge that the Sartrean venture is prepared to participate in global transformation, whereas classical anthropology may well be destroyed by it, either by being radicalised beyond recognition, or by indulging in suicidal immobilism, or simply by seeing its object of study placed by various means beyond its reach. I should stress that, in the course of this survey, I am gathering evidence to show that, when Lévi-Strauss finally moves against Sartre, it is because he perceives him to be a threat. Sartre never actually mounts a sustained attack on Lévi-Strauss, but even so the final *tourniquet* of his ethnographic train of thought is easy enough to formulate: structuralist anthropology, a reactionary force in a crisis-ridden country, is possessed by its own *loas* and its *zars*; it is therefore the task of the synthetic anthropology to undertake a revolutionary exorcism.

Exorcism, however, does not rule out the possibility of partial recuperation; both, in principle, are moments of the synthesising work of the Sartrean project. And in fact, 'Le fantôme de Staline' does display a degree of compatibility with classical anthropology. On two occasions,[45] once in reference to the attitude of the USSR towards China, and once in connection with the policies of the PCF, Sartre characterises Stalinism as a practice originally determined by need, but which hardens into a 'retractile' posture and becomes incapable of generosity and exchange, even when these are politically and economically feasible. This brings him right into the territory of Mauss and raises the question of whether Mauss's successors are able to supply models of societies based on material sufficiency. In the heat of the Algerian moment, Sartre sometimes forgets that Lévi-Strauss has already done so, and a number of years elapse before the Sartre–Gorz tandem has recourse instead to the work of the radical American anthropologist Marshall Sahlins.

In the late 1950s, *TM*'s relations with the social sciences take another turn with the attention given to radical American sociology. Five years previously, Crozier had hailed C. Wright Mills's *White Collar* as the 'plus extraordinaire feu d'artifice intellectuel de l'Amérique de ces dernières années',[46] locating it 'au confluent des recherches culturalistes et de l'analyse sociologique marxiste'.[47] Accordingly, in May and June 1957, *TM* follows up with extracts from *The Power Elite*. These are accompanied by other texts, notably those of Riesman, Glazer and Denney (*The Lonely Crowd* (May 1957)), A. C. Spectorsky (*The Exurbanites* (May 1957 and October 1958)) and William Whyte (*The Organisation Man*, (October to December 1958)). Wright Mills, particularly, is held in great esteem: learning of his death in 1962, *TM* notes that 'il était le seul grand sociologue américain qui, refusant le conformisme, les mythes et le scientisme ambiants, considérait son travail comme un métier d'homme [. . .] La connaissance, pour lui, ne se distinguait pas de l'action. Il était aux prises avec la société qu'il décrivait, et il l'a décrite à partir d'une exigence radicale.'[48]

A second category of sociological material is that dealing with the position of women; it is the closest that the review has yet come to providing a proper follow-up to *Le Deuxième Sexe*, now ten years old. Gorz's special issue on the distribution of wealth (September/October 1962) includes research by Geneviève Rocard ('Sur le travail des femmes') and by Andrée Michel ('Quelques budgets de familles parisiennes'). Michel also supplies an article on contraception in March 1961.

It is also worth mentioning certain examples of the early work of Pierre Bourdieu, a sociologist who will be drawn much more towards structuralism, but who will later be of relevance to *TM* by virtue of his studies of the education system. In this third period, however, his activity is at the interfaces of sociology, ethnography and colonialism. His analysis of 'Les relations entre les sexes dans la société paysanne' (August 1962) shows how the old peasant kinship system in rural Béarn is being transformed by urban development and how unmarriageable male peasants internalise the village representation of them as ignorant and archaic. This phenomenological approach is also used in a study of 'Les sous-prolétaires algériens' (December 1962). This is an article of a type still too rare in *TM* – a fieldwork investigation of the consequences of colonialism. It traces the destruction of the traditional peasant culture and its replacement by a lumpenproletariat. Bourdieu examines the attitudes of this group, its experience of social reality as incoherent and its recourse to a magical belief in the power of the *piston*. He notes how it makes of its poverty a component of its identity: 'Comme le racisme, le misérabilisme est un essential-isme.'[49]

The assumption of editorial responsibility by Gorz in 1961 makes it particularly unhelpful to attempt any separation between economics, sociology and politics. Prior to his arrival *TM* lacked co-ordination in these areas, even though it published the work of writers with a similar interest in critiques of both Marxist orthodoxy and modern capitalism: Henri Lefebvre, for example, or Serge Mallet (of whom it is later discovered that he 'donnait dans la collaboration de classes [et] se ralliait à cet économisme qui était la tarte à la crème du régime',[50] but who nonetheless should go on record as the only commentator who dared to think that de Gaulle might give Algeria its independence).

After 1961, Gorz introduces articles on the nature of neo-capitalism and on the Sino-Soviet rift and features analyses by economists, trade union activists, Party intellectuals and sociologists. Names such as Giorgio Amendola, Pierre Belleville, Maurice

Dobb, Lucio Magri and Bruno Trentin become increasingly familiar. With Gorz's 'Gaullisme et néo-colonialisme' (March 1961), *TM* produces for the first time a formal study of the Algerian economy. More important in the long term are his analyses of consumer society which complement Sartre's theoretical work by producing a new definition of poverty:

L'essence de la pauvreté, c'est d'avoir à subir comme inaccessibles, comme refusées, les possibilités et richesses que la société a instituées comme sa réalité dominante, comme sa norme: c'est d'être privé du seul titre humain qui a cours dans cette société [. . .] Ce qui importe, c'est que l'ensemble des possibilités normatives qui sont refusées à un salarié moyen n'a cessé d'augmenter et avec elles sa pauvreté.[51]

Gorz also offers a brief sequel to *Le Traître* entitled 'Le vieillissement' (December 1961, January 1962). In it, he examines childhood, adolescence and maturity in terms of the expectations imposed on the individual by the group. These reflections lead him to political considerations which show how well he is able to predict the evolution of French society and how well placed, as a result, *TM* will be to intervene. Gorz distinguishes between the young people faced with urgent tasks of social reconstruction (in 1945, for example) and those required to manage a system inherited from the previous generation. The fact that 'la courbe démographique qui préétablit depuis trente-cinq ans que la jeunesse est le destin que les vieux vous font subir, annonce que demain la vieillesse sera le destin imposé par les jeunes aux vieux',[52] leads him to give a high priority to an understanding of the French education system and of the revolutionary potential of 'ces émigrés de l'intérieur qui sont les étudiants pauvres'.[53]

All in all, it is a prophetic coda to the existential self-analysis. It heralds the work of the situationists Debord and Vaneigem which in turn helps to prepare student opinion for the events of May 1968. Its approach is soundly synthetic and Gorz does not miss the chance to bring up to date Sartre's early existentialist admonitions of Mauriac with anti-Lévi-Straussian strictures of his own: 'Tout sens s'évanouit au regard qui prétend tout voir en survol (regard de Dieu, de l'ethnographe–géologue).'[54] It is a comment to be added to the dossier.

The first redefinition of the synthetic anthropology

Between 1945 and 1956, Sartre's priorities underwent considerable change. In particular, the literary ethic of the earliest years disappeared, while more general ethical considerations were moved down the agenda pending the construction of their political pre-requisite, socialism. Now, in the late 1950s, anti-Stalinism and anti-colonialism are invested with even greater energy, some of which is expressed as anti-structuralism. The shift of emphasis is clearly visible in *TM* and even more so in Sartre's own reading, primarily in the promotion of the historiography which is necessary to his triple purpose. Only a detailed study of history, after all, can lead to an understanding of Stalinism and of colonialism, and only a properly researched diachronic perspective can offer an adequate counter to the arguments of structuralism. This is why *TM* con-tinues its serialisation of Guillemin's *Les Origines de la Commune* and embarks on that of Isaac Deutscher's biography of Trotsky. Significant, too, is the extremely warm review given in December 1961 to Michel Foucault's *Histoire de la folie* by the anti-colonialist psychoanalyst Octave Mannoni. As for the reading that informs Sartre's *Critique* – the works of Marc Bloch, Fernand Braudel and Georges Lefebvre – it indicates to what extent historiography has been a neglected discipline.

Soon, however, there is a rush into diachrony, and the fact that 'Questions de méthode' owes much to Henri Lefebvre, one of the co-ordinators of the Marxist forum *Arguments*, shows just how hard Sartre has to run to catch up. 'Questions de méthode' appears in *TM* in September and October 1957 and, with the addition of a brief conclusion, is then used as the preamble to the *Critique de la raison dialectique* in 1960. The two conjoined segments are designed to provide an answer to the following question: 'Avons-nous aujourd'hui les moyens de constituer une anthropologie structurelle et historique?'[55] The introduction of these new specifi-cations should not, however, be taken as the repudiation of the epistemological principles espoused in 1945. The inherence of the observer in the observed, for example, continues to be acknowl-edged, and this is why Sartre's urgent interest in the diachronic is expressed in terms of his own diachrony. His movement towards Marxism, embodied in 'Matérialisme et révolution', 'Les commun-istes et la paix' and 'Le fantôme de Staline', brings with it the recognition that existentialism was but an ideology. This makes of 'Questions de méthode' an interesting autobiographical fragment, and what is ostensibly a work of methodology should therefore also be read – with *Les Mots*, the *Carnets de la drôle de guerre*, the preface to Nizan's *Aden Arabie* and the obituary notice for Merleau-Ponty – as the intellectual and political history of the synthetic anthropologist.

Sartre is thus obliged to review the broad lines of his development: the initial rejection of bourgeois humanism, the desire for a philosophy of the concrete, and the receptivity to theories that acknowledge the existence of discrete human groups (and here he cites the Lévy-Bruhlian concept of *mentalité primitive*,[56] a reference that will later be used against him by Lévi-Strauss). He recalls how he came out of the war convinced of the necessity of Marxism, only to discover that its growth had been arrested. The brief period of fellow-travelling served only to confirm that Stalinism represents everything that the synthetic anthropology strives to subvert: 'Le principe euristique; "chercher le tout à travers les parties" est devenu cette pratique terroriste: "liquider la particularité".'[57] Between the right- and left-wing ignorances there is thus still room for an existentialism, one capable of leavening Marxism by insisting on the inseparability of knowledge and existence and of learning and *praxis*. This is the opportunity for Sartre to begin to elaborate the concept of *totalisation*: again, not a new specification, but a rewriting of one of the principles that has always obtained – the rule that 'le *dévoilement* d'une situation se fait dans et par la *praxis* qui la change'.[58]

The second section of 'Questions de méthode' deals with the academic disciplines that the synthetic anthropology will be obliged to mobilise in its quest for active intelligibility. Sartre identifies the 'Marxist' vices of schematisation and *apriorisme* in the work of Lukács, Garaudy and Guérin (although finding redeeming features in the historiography of the last-named) and compares them all unfavourably with Marx's *Eighteenth Brumaire*, which in his view achieves a 'synthèse difficile de l'intention et du résultat'[59] in its examination of specific persons in specific social groups. Particularity is what Sartre seeks to protect from the global generalisations of vulgar Marxism: Paul Valéry was a lower middle-class intellectual, but not all lower middle-class intellectuals are Paul Valéry, and Sartre refuses to endorse Engels's invocation of chance as the explanation of the gap between the two propositions. Accordingly, he points out the value of psychoanalysis and sociology as mediating disciplines. Psychoanalysis first, because it supplies the intelligibility of the family and of childhood, the importance of which Sartre acknowledges with all the virulence of his preface to Gorz's *Traître*. Thus, a study of *Madame Bovary*, for example, would not attempt to correlate the text immediately with the social structures, but would examine the way in which the structures were experienced by Flaubert in his formative years. Only with the help of psychoanalysis, says Sartre, can this be achieved. His argument is

nonetheless weak in two respects: it does not explain what becomes
of existential psychoanalysis, and it too easily accepts that the
Freudian variety is unencumbered by a theoretical base incompatible with Marxism. It is no wonder that Sartre's use of psychoanalysis in *L'Idiot de la famille* proves highly idiosyncratic.

The second mediatory discipline is sociology. Sartre sees its
integration into Marxism as just as unproblematic. He looks briefly
at the American sociologists Lewin and Kardiner and at the
culturalism which Merleau-Ponty had intended to feature more
prominently in *TM*. It is interesting to see him show such appreciation of Kardiner's ethnographic work on Marquesan culture and
to see him adduce Lévi-Strauss's *Structures élémentaires de la
parenté* to make up for its shortcomings: because Kardiner lacks an
understanding of kinship structures as an economic practice of
reciprocity, he tends to psychologise the results of the scarcity of
women. Once again, however, Sartre's synthetic momentum
carries him beyond the academicism of Lévi-Strauss:

Le sociologue, en fait, est objet de l'Histoire: la sociologie des 'primitifs'
s'établit sur la base d'un rapport plus profond qui peut être, par exemple,
le colonialisme: l'enquête est un rapport vivant entre des hommes (c'est ce
rapport même dans sa totalité qu'a tenté de décrire Leiris dans son
admirable *L'Afrique fantôme*).[60]

The mobilisation of psychoanalysis and sociology in an organised
labour of totalisation – *la méthode progressive-régressive* – this is
the focus of the third part of 'Questions de méthode'. The two
disciplines are called upon to inform the theorisation of the
dialectical interaction of existential project and material reality.
Marxism can only benefit from a demonstration that the link
between the material and its perceived modifiability is non-
mechanical, and this is the task that Sartre sets himself.

The first two sections of 'Questions de méthode' have shown that
anthropological phenomena, cultural artefacts, for example,
signify at a number of distinct levels: in terms of the relations of
production in a given community, and in terms of the producer's
aspirations, childhood history, attitude towards death and so on.
As the products of the *projets* of artists, they are moreover
conditioned by the technical resources available at the time, as well
as by the relation of the artist to intermediate cultural groups and
the socio-economic classes. The heterogeneity of these different
orders of signification does not lend itself to monolinear causal
description. Sartre therefore recommends that the investigation

proceed from the cultural artefact to the person of its producer, and thence to the socio-economic determinants which shaped the producer's childhood. This regressive moment of the study, moving from the concrete into increasing abstraction, would analytically identify the discrete levels of signification. A second, progressive moment of research would then be required, in which the *projet* of the artist would be revealed as the force synthesising all these different orders of factors and making of them a lived experience.

Sartre gives every indication that the acid test of the method will be the 'longue et difficile'[61] study of Flaubert, of which he presents an outline. The method might well also have been used in the study of Tintoretto, a fragment of which appears in the review in November 1957, but any such use implies a labour of such magnitude that it is likely that the Italian painter was dropped in favour of the French writer. This would accord with the expectation of *TM*'s readers, well used to the election of writers as the object of synthetic study. For although, as I have noted, 'Questions de méthode' does not favour the term, it is undoubtedly a programme of existential psychoanalysis that is being promoted here. The essential difference between the Flaubert enterprise and *Baudelaire*, for example, is the incorporation of the mediatory disciplines: these, given the cavalier manner in which they have been deemed to have little theoretical substance, are bound to be deployed exceedingly eclectically. The diphasic method is designed to handle additional complexity, not to make major concessions to determinism.

All this makes of the Sartrean anthropology what it has always been – a quest for intelligibility based on the assumptions that all that signifies is human and that all that is human is significant. The regressive–progressive method articulates, rather than juxtaposes, the *Erklären* and the *Verstehen* of Jaspers, the second always transcending the first. It is diachronic inasmuch as it promises access through empathy to another person's temporalisation. It is therefore still not quite clear how 'Questions de méthode' provides the groundwork for a historical anthropology that is also *structurelle*. To clarify this question, I suggest that it is useful to separate the 1957 text from its own conclusion, as well as from the *Critique* and from the preface to both texts, all of which are dated 1960. It then becomes apparent that the 1957 essay is primarily anti-Stalinist and has no overwhelming interest in putting on record its objections to structuralism, despite the final footnote, which seems to be addressed to the Barthes of *Mythologies*. By 1960, however, thanks to the FLN, the emphasis has shifted distinctly from the former to the latter preoccupation, and this is why I propose to tackle the *structurel/structural* problem – the second moment of redefinition – only after having reviewed *TM*'s coverage of psychoanalysis and linguistics. As far as *TM* is concerned, 'Questions de méthode' ends in October 1957 with the completion of the section dealing with *la méthode progressive-régressive*. Its continuation, although announced for the following month, is suspended due to 'les nécessités de l'édition'[62] and is replaced by material on Tintoretto, 'Le Séquestré de Venise'.

As for the reactions to 'Questions de méthode', they are not substantial. There is the article by the Polish Marxist Adam Schaff, 'Sur le marxisme et sur l'existentialisme' (August/September 1960); this, however, is not addressed to the *TM* text but to its draft predecessor which appeared in the Polish review *Tworczosc* in 1957. Schaff asserts the incompatibility of Marxism and existentialism, but ascribes the success of the latter in Poland to the failure of Marxism to deal with problems of moral responsibility. It is an anti-Stalinist piece designed primarily for domestic consumption. It suits *TM*'s purposes to publish it, but it cannot be said that the theoretical debate is carried a long way further forward.

More significant are the contributions of Pouillon. In the issues immediately prior to and following the publication of 'Questions de méthode', he reviews Desanti's *Introduction à la philosophie* and Goldmann's *Le Dieu caché*. That both he and Sartre should simultaneously approve the work of Desanti and Goldmann and comment on their complementary character[63] shows that their positions remain close and that, were it not for the Algerian War, those of Lévi-Strauss and Sartre might be perceived as partially reconcilable. Desanti, Goldmann and Sartre all proceed on the assumption that ideology is not a direct effect of a socio-economic infrastructure. This assumption, incidentally, with its concomitant anti-Stalinism, brings Goldmann into *TM*. Between 1957 and 1962 he contributes nine articles (some of which are later included in the volume entitled *Recherches dialectiques*) and is mainly intent on picking up the line of Lukácsian thought that did not survive the pressures of Stalinism. Pouillon approves of this direction: 'Il ne s'agit pas de déduire l'idéologie du social, il s'agit de les articuler et d'assurer ainsi entre eux une liaison plus étroite que celle qu'imposerait en apparence un déterminisme causal, et évidemment plus intelligible.'[64]

All important, of course, is the mode of articulation, and its complexity is evident inasmuch as it is dependent on the forever problematic interaction of synchronic and diachronic principles of organisation. The task of describing this complexity seems to Pouillon to be most urgent, just as it had seemed in 1956, although by now he is able to add a rider to his position:

Il n'est pas certain, en effet, que les deux intégrations – l'intégration sociale et l'intégration historique, ou, si l'on veut, l'intégration dans une totalité synchronique et l'intégration dans une totalité diachronique – aboutissent à des résultats concordants. La signification d'une œuvre quand on la considère comme exprimant la vision du monde propre à un groupe social, n'est pas forcément la même que celle qu'elle prend, quand on la situe dans une série idéologico-historique de visions du monde.'[65]

It begins to look as though Pouillon, in his search for reconciliation, is prepared to settle for a more modest assertion of complementarity. The idea that it is possible to produce equally valid but quite discrete bodies of knowledge in respect of the same object of study does not marry easily with the confident supra-disciplinarity of the synthetic anthropology. His cautiousness in 1957 should therefore be read as welcoming the mutation of the Sartrean venture into an *anthropologie historique* and as having reservations as to whether it can ever become *historique et structurelle*. He does not entirely rule out the possibility, of course, because he knows that the *Critique* is on the way. Moreover, as I have said, by 1960 other developments have occurred which draw the problem of the *structurel* into the foreground. Some of these – the Algerian – I have already surveyed; the others I shall deal with in the next section.

The second moment of redefinition and the structuralist riposte

After the sudden death of Merleau-Ponty on 4 May 1961, *TM* pays tribute with a special double issue 'personnellement dirigé par Sartre'.[66] In view of this exercise of total editorial responsibility, it is instructive to look briefly at the composition of the memorial number.

Pride of place is given to Merleau-Ponty's last published article, 'L'œil et l'esprit', which had just appeared in *Art de France*. The subsequent testimonies, many of which comment specifically on this final formulation of his thought, appear to have been commissioned by Sartre according to the predictable criteria of friendship with Merleau-Ponty, professional association with him and an ability to evaluate his contributions to philosophy. Lefort, for example, who will later edit the unpublished works, gives his own estimation, as do Jean Hyppolite, Alphonse de Waelhens and Jean Wahl. Fittingly, in what is a collection of *travaux de deuil*, but also as an acknowledgement of Merleau-Ponty's interest in psychoanalysis, Sartre secures the participation of Pontalis and, for the first and only time in *TM*, Jacques Lacan. All these articles form a relatively homogeneous group, since Hyppolite and Waelhens know psychoanalysis as well as Pontalis and Lacan know phenomenology. They are supplemented by Sartre's own 'Merleau-Ponty vivant', the most personal and the most political of the tributes and a partial editorial history of *TM*.

Even with due allowance made for the pressures of time and space, it is pertinent to note the absence of certain names: of Beauvoir, virtually a life-long colleague of Merleau-Ponty, and, of course, of Lévi-Strauss. It is curious that this long-standing friend, colleague at the Collège de France, leading representative of a discipline highly regarded by Merleau-Ponty and object of a warm appraisal in the recently published *Signes*, should not be represented in the tributes offered by a review to which he is by no means a complete outsider. Whatever the circumstantial reasons for this absence, there is no doubting Lévi-Strauss's desire to mark his respect, for *La Pensée sauvage*, when it appears in 1962, is dedicated to Merleau-Ponty. Its preface shows that Lévi-Strauss is not unaware of the constructions that might be placed on this decision:

De ce que le nom de Maurice Merleau-Ponty figure en première page d'un livre dont les dernières sont réservées à la discussion d'un ouvrage de Sartre, nul ne saurait inférer que j'ai voulu les opposer l'un à l'autre. Ceux qui nous ont approchés, Merleau-Ponty et moi, au cours des récentes années, connaissent quelques-unes des raisons pour lesquelles il allait de soi que ce livre, qui developpe librement certains thèmes de mon enseignement au Collège de France, lui fût dédié.[67]

Ironically, what Lévi-Strauss seeks to avoid is actually a powerful organisational principle of the memorial issue of *TM*, that is to say the juxtaposition of Merleau-Ponty and Sartre. Hyppolite is a good example, meticulously comparing and contrasting the two phenomenologies in the hope that the tensions between them will one day be resolved. Not only is the same procedure employed in the contributions of Sartre himself, of Pontalis and of Lacan, but it had already been a feature of the thinking of Merleau-Ponty and Sartre in the preceding years – in Sartre's preface to Nizan's *Aden Arabie* and in Merleau-Ponty's preface to *Signes*. Sartre, pushing his strong anti-Stalinist line, had proclaimed the bankruptcy of the French Left and had held himself responsible for it, having failed to reproduce Nizan's anger and commitment in the immediate post-war years. His retrospection in 1960 was much more bitter than three years previously in 'Questions de méthode' – largely as a result of the return of de Gaulle. The preface resembles the preface given to Gorz's *Le Traître*: there is the same violent hostility to parentage (Nizan 'possessed' by his father), as well as the faith, to which Gorz will shortly give greater substance, in the political potential of students. The constellation of texts suggests that Sartre now views Gorz as the historical successor to Merleau-Ponty as the political editor of the review, and at the same time sees in him a second manifestation of Nizan.

Merleau-Ponty, noting in *Signes* that Sartre tended to incriminate himself rather than others, regretted that his ex-colleague should resort to Oedipal utopianism. In attempting to account for this, he went on to propose two contrasting models of childhood, and while I assume that he had never read the manuscript of *Les Mots*, he nevertheless displayed acute awareness of Sartre's urge to exorcise all the inhabitants of his past:

Certains sont fascinés par leur enfance, elle les possède, elle les tient enchantés dans un ordre de possibles privilégiés. D'autres sont par elle rejetés vers la vie adulte, ils se croient sans passé, aussi près de tous les possibles. Sartre était de la seconde espèce. Il n'était donc pas facile d'être son ami. La distance qu'il mettait entre lui-même et ses données le séparait aussi de ce que les autres ont à vivre [. . .] En lui-même et dans les autres, il avait à apprendre que nul n'est sans racines, et que le parti pris de n'en pas avoir est une autre manière de les avouer.[68]

Passages such as this illustrate the extent to which Sartre's 'Merleau-Ponty vivant' is a continuation as well as a recapitulation of the long series of conversations, articles and silences exchanged by the two men over some thirty years. In 1961, Sartre's view of childhood seems to have mellowed somewhat; taking his cue from the remark quoted above, he sets out to chronicle the difficult friendship and to ascribe a key role in the divergence of the two phenomenologies to the closeness of the bond linking Merleau-Ponty to his mother. His friend's childhood is introduced here, not simply as a factor of difference, but as a positive advantage, since it established existential roots of such strength that Merleau-Ponty was unable to lapse into the *pensée de survol*.

Sartre's obituary notice is thus built on a juxtaposition featured in Merleau-Ponty's reply to the preface to *Aden Arabie*. As it surveys their friendship in the context of the political policy of *TM*, moreover, it transforms a simple juxtaposition into what is in both senses a moving complementarity. It does so in two ways: not only because the political trajectory of the one is the mirror image of that of the other, but also because Sartre succeeds, unwittingly, in giving further life to Merleau-Ponty's preface by writing an obituary to which remarks previously directed at his own preface to Nizan apply equally well: 'ce qui donne au récit de Sartre sa mélancolie, c'est qu'on y voit les deux amis apprendre lentement des choses ce que dès le début ils auraient pu apprendre l'un de l'autre'.[69]

Sartre's review of the post-war period is less despairing than the preface to *Aden Arabie*; it seems that due note is taken of Merleau-Ponty's judgement that 'il n'est pas vrai qu'à aucun moment nous ayons été maîtres des choses, ni que, ayant devant nous des problèmes clairs, nous ayons tout gâché par futilité'.[70] What Sartre really learns, of course, are the sense of historicity and the acknowledgement of the power of origins which permit him to write what is, as it were, a diachronic obituary. These he lacked in the 1940s, however much he believed the contrary at the time. Now, however, he realises that while Merleau-Ponty was discovering the shifting of meaning and purpose in the flux of political events, he himself, as a result – paradoxically – of his voluntarism, was more concerned with socio-political constants. 'En ne cherchant que ses permanences', he says, 'je souhaitais à mon insu que nous devinssions les ethnographes de la société française.'[71] The critique of Roquentin in *Les Mots* is thus paralleled in the Merleau-Ponty obituary by the critique of an apparent identification with Oreste.

The use of the term *ethnographe* is a good indication of the negative connotation that it now carries: it suggests not so much the study of a social formation from an avowedly non-participatory point of view, but rather the refusal to place the synchronic in its proper diachronic perspective, a refusal which condemns the ethnographer to a negligent participation. In a remark made to Madeleine Chapsal in 1960 – 'les ethnographes *décrivent*: les écrivains ne peuvent plus décrire: ils prennent parti'[72] – Sartre appears to rehearse the familiar existentialist notion of commitment; in fact, he is introducing it into the newly important diachronic context. The anti-structuralist obituary of Merleau-Ponty merely carries this a stage further – into the familial territory of *Les Mots*.

Merleau-Ponty's 'L'œil et l'esprit', which, says Sartre, 'dit tout pourvu qu'on sache le déchiffrer',[73] begins with a critique of the physical and social sciences, portraying them as sets of technical operations naively modelled on the Cartesian concept of perception; they abstract perceiver from corporeal location and investigate the positionality of objects without acknowledging the metaphysical problem of their being-there. In this context, suggests Merleau-Ponty, the task of philosophy becomes yet more urgent: it is to study perception, in an effort to determine how far it constitutes the primordial event which physically integrates the subject and the world. Preferring, as it were, Tintoretto to Flaubert, he wonders whether it is the study of painting that will best meet his philosophical needs. Perhaps the work of the painter, with its equal dependence on the manual and the visual, will afford a valuable insight into the mutual implication of body and world: 'Puisque les choses et mon corps sont faits de la même étoffe, il faut que sa vision se fasse de quelque manière en elles, ou encore que leur visibilité manifeste se double en lui d'une visibilité secrète.'[74]

Sartre admires both the intellectual power and the emotional force of Merleau-Ponty's last work. He refers to his 'dialectique décapitée'[75] and considers that his questioning of existence and being, of self and other, of necessity and contingency, became, at least after the death of his mother, so saturated by the implications, inherences and reversibilities of the terms of each pair, that stability was never great enough for moments of thesis, antithesis and synthesis to be identified with clarity. Nevertheless, Sartre goes on:

Je dirais volontiers, si le mot ne lui semblait douteux pour avoir trop servi, qu'il a su retrouver la dialectique interne du questionneur et du questionné et qu'il l'a conduite jusqu'à la question fondamentale que nous évitons par toutes nos prétendues réponses [...] Pour Merleau, l'universalité n'est jamais universelle, sauf pour la pensée de survol: elle naît selon la chair; chair de notre chair, elle garde, à son degré le plus subtil, notre singularité. Telle est la monition que l'anthropologie – analyse ou marxisme – ne devrait plus oublier.[76]

A quick glance at *Situations IV* is enough to reveal that Sartre is the master of polemical obituaries, and 'Merleau-Ponty vivant' is no exception. It acknowledges Merleau-Ponty's contribution to the dissolution of Sartrean voluntarism, but instead of foregrounding the structuralism to which he was increasingly drawn, it appeals to his intuition of historicity as a way of endorsing 'Questions de méthode'. In it, too, the absence of Lévi-Strauss is obtrusive. It is difficult to resist the observation that the relationship between the living and the dead editors of *TM* expresses the wish of the living to legitimise the exclusion of structuralist anthropology and to redraw the intellectual map in time of anti-colonialist war.

Lacan, on the other hand, is acknowledged: psychoanalysis, after all, is part of the post-1957 methodological apparatus. Both he and Pontalis are therefore invited to mourn Merleau-Ponty. As far as Lacan is concerned, there is considerable sympathy for Merleau-Ponty's aims as a philosopher. But while Lacan approves of the desire to liberate philosophy from the Cartesian tradition of the unified subject, he does not consider that the break has been successfully made. Nor does he think that the concept of intention has been fully abandoned. He criticises the views of sexuality proposed by both Merleau-Ponty and Sartre, finding in the former a masochistic formulation and in the latter a sadistic one, the description of which, even as sadism, he finds quite inadequate ('il n'est pas vrai que la voie vers la satisfaction normale du désir se retrouve de l'échec inhérent à la préparation du supplice'[77] – this in reference to the analyses in *L'Etre et le néant*). What is lacking in the two existentialist philosophies, in his opinion, is an understanding of fantasy; without it, asks Lacan, how can they hope to grasp the importance of fetishism and of the castration complex?

Les deux se conjurent pourtant pour nous sommer de faire face à la fonction du signifiant de l'organe toujours signalé comme tel par son occultation dans le simulacre humain, – et l'incidence qui résulte du phallus en cette fonction dans l'accès au désir tant de la femme que de l'homme, pour être maintenant vulgarisée, ne peut pas être négligée comme déviant ce qu'on peut bien appeler en effet l'être sexué du corps. Si le signifiant de l'être sexué peut être ainsi méconnu dans le phénomène, c'est pour sa position doublement celée dans le fantasme, soit de ne s'indiquer que là où il n'agit pas et de n'agir que de son manque. C'est en quoi la psychanalyse doit faire sa preuve d'un avancement dans l'accès au signifiant, et tel qu'il puisse revenir sur sa phénoménologie même.[78]

Lacan brings to readers of the review a reasonably succinct statement of his basic premisses. Asserting that the *signifiant* is 'exigé comme syntaxe d'avant le sujet pour l'avènement de ce sujet non pas seulement en tant qu'il parle mais en ce qu'il dit',[79] he allows his debt to Saussure to reveal how much closer he was to Merleau-Ponty than to Sartre. Lacan's article is, however, terse rather than carefully expository, and his ideas, far less familiar to readers of *TM* than those of Lévi-Strauss, require a programme of support organised by Pontalis. The latter's article on Merleau-Ponty is but a part of this programme.

Pontalis recalls that Merleau-Ponty's *Structure du comportement* sought to 'disjoindre les découvertes de la psychanalyse d'une idéologie objectiviste et retrouver le *sens* de mécanismes psychologiques incontestables que pervertissent les notions causales de la métapsychologie'.[80] This enterprise, he notes, involved a readiness to doubt the homogeneity of consciousness, and while neither the *Structure du comportement* nor the *Phénoménologie de la perception* solved the problem, at least the emphasis in the latter 'est toujours mis sur le mouvement par lequel l'homme reprend une situation qui constitue déjà son propre sens et non comme chez le Sartre de *L'Etre et le néant* sur le pouvoir de la liberté'.[81]

As Pontalis tracks Merleau-Ponty's work from the 1940s into the 1950s, he is able once more to distinguish him from Sartre; for the latter he reserves strictures of the type that Lacan seems prepared to address to both. One example of this (and continuing evidence that Pontalis is prepared to use *TM* to contest the work of Sartre) is his view of the Sartrean concept of the imaginary: 'Au "vide" de l'imaginaire correspond pour Sartre la plénitude du réel qu'il paraît réduire à ce qui s'observe et s'apprend; ce postulat réaliste le fait passer sous silence – au moins à ce moment de sa pensée – la structuration du réel par l'imaginaire.'[82] Merleau-Ponty, on the other hand, is said to be much less dualistic and to be prepared to find a place for the unconscious in his theory of perception. Pontalis, however, doubts that he was capable of completing his task without seriously mutilating psychoanalysis. Merleau-Ponty, in his opinion, was so concerned to avoid 'demonology', that he injected into his readings of Freud's case-histories a degree of polyvalence likely to render any dream unanalysable.

It is noticeable that Pontalis has no comment to offer on 'Questions de méthode'.[83] Instead, a curious situation now develops in *TM* in which psychoanalysis, deemed by Sartre to be harmless and useful, so threatens to dominate the review that it has to be symbolically expelled at the end of the 1960s. Pontalis is the key figure in this labour of subversion and I shall now turn to the related fields of linguistics and psychoanalysis in order to measure the terrain that he manages to occupy.

In terms of quantity of material, linguistics is insignificant. Georges Mounin's discussion of 'Communication humaine et communication non-linguistique animale' (January 1960) is, in the context of *TM*, anomalous; one thing that Sartre and Lévi-Strauss have in common is the strength of their human frontier with the animal. There is only one other contribution by a linguist, but it has major historical importance: in January 1962, the review carries the French translation of Roman Jakobson's famous paper on aphasia.

In 'Deux aspects du langage et deux types d'aphasie', Jakobson takes from structuralist phonology the general principles of linguistic production – selection from paradigm and combination into syntagm – and assimilates them to the rhetorical figures of metaphor and metonymy respectively. Like much of his work, the article is resolutely interfacial, not only postulating models of selectional and combinatory aphasia to supplement the sensory and motor types recognised by psychiatry, but also suggesting the extension of his typology to psychoanalysis (the mechanisms of the dreamwork), to anthropology (Frazer's taxonomy of magic) and to literary criticism (the theory of genres). It is worthy of note that an influence which reached Lévi-Strauss during his war-time residence in New York surfaces in *TM* only twenty years later. In 1962, its contact with the synthetic anthropology is antithetical, and the terms in which it is presented show clearly that publication is undertaken on the initiative of Pontalis. The introduction cites Lévi-Strauss as evidence of the fecundity of structuralist linguistics and places even greater emphasis on the Lacanian integration of Freud and Saussure. It ends with a statement which, while no longer grossly provocative in itself, is nonetheless little short of astonishing when seen as editorial material in *TM*: 'S'il est vrai qu'il n'est pas un petit morceau de réel qui ne soit pris dans les rets des différents "langages" – ou systèmes signifiants –, la linguistique n'apparaît plus seulement comme une discipline pilote par sa méthode mais *princeps* par son objet.'[84]

1962: the year of Algerian independence and the appearance of Jakobson in *TM*! It is as if the return of de Gaulle, the *grand sorcier*, facilitates the intellectual hegemony of that other great magician Jacques Lacan. Pontalis's position as spokesman for the opposition cannot yet, however, be regarded as completely clear-cut, simply because Sartre seems unaware of how far the supposedly anodine Freudian theory has become dependent on the structuralism that binds Jakobson to Saussure, Lévi-Strauss and Lacan. Psychoanalysis is still theoretically *récupérable*: this, after all, is the period in which Sartre composes his screenplay for the John Huston film *Freud: the Secret Passion* and in which he even asks Pontalis to psychoanalyse him. To this extent, it is not surprising that *TM* should be open to analysts of different persuasions; indeed, the degree of disagreement within the profession is itself the focus of interest.

The editorial work, nonetheless, is undertaken by Pontalis. Sartre's involvement is non-existent: 'Questions de méthode' makes passing reference to Lagache; the Sorbonne lecture of 1960 mentions Lacan's theorisation of the mirror phase but is more interested by Serge Lebovici's work on psychodrama at the Institut de Psychanalyse. His attitude is distant and eclectic, and the psychiatry of Fanon is clearly regarded as much more important.

Pontalis, meanwhile, brings in articles from the conservative and medical Société Psychanalytique de Paris (Racamier returns briefly in September 1957, and there are contributions from Christian David and Daniel Widlocher in 1962) and from the intellectually more adventurous Société Française de Psychanalyse. The latter camp, to which Pontalis belongs, enjoys greater representation. Among the Lacanian names are the following: Françoise Dolto, interviewed twice by Pontalis – on Helen Keller (December 1961) and on motherhood (January 1963); Jean Laplanche, whose *Hölderlin et la question du père* is reviewed by Jean Beaufret in July 1962; Octave Mannoni, who, in addition to discussing Butor on Baudelaire (May 1961), Koestler (November 1961) and Mallarmé (November 1962), investigates in March 1962 the need for interpretation in literature. Pontalis himself explores the same territory in studies of Henry James in March 1958 and December 1962.

Pontalis's prime concern, however, is with the organisation and status of psychoanalysis as a discipline and as a therapeutic practice. When Serge Moscovici's study of *La Psychanalyse, son image et son public* is reviewed by Claude Faucheux in January 1961, he is quick to add his own comments under the title of 'Homo psychanalyticus'. He puts on record the same misgivings that Lévi-Strauss had felt in 1949 (and which Pasche, now on the other side of the divide, had attempted to allay), namely that 'la psychanalyse est en train de devenir quelque chose comme un mythe collectif'.[85] He obviously regards this mythification as disastrous, at least when psychoanalysts come to subscribe to their own myth, objectifying their knowledge and burying their working relationship with analysands under sets of normative and mechanistic concepts.

Much of Pontalis's work in *TM* can be seen as an attempt to minimise this danger by investigating the status of psychoanalytical knowledge. Evidence of this premium set on theory is provided by the publication in August 1961 of 'L'inconscient: une étude psychanalytique' by Laplanche and Serge Leclaire. This paper offers a succinct account of the ideas of Lacan, predating by one month the latter's note on Merleau-Ponty, and predating also the article by

Jakobson which, for *TM*'s readers, it might have done better to follow. Both the paper itself and André Green's reply in July 1962 are highly technical; so much so that they prompt from Pontalis a justification of such intensely theoretical work.

Much of the Laplanche–Leclaire–Green discussion is concerned with the question of whether the unconscious is best described in topographical or in economic terms. The first frame of reference has the obvious advantage, in terms of Pontalis's drive for hegemony within *TM*, of allowing psychoanalysis to reclaim the *mauvaise foi* that Sartre had long ago deployed against the Freudian unconscious:

Chez un Sartre, par exemple, la critique de l'inconscient psychanalytique méconnaît son hétérogénéité radicale, en ramenant les contenus inconscients aux franges et aux implications méconnues d'une intentionnalité actuelle, soit, en termes freudiens, à la limite entre conscient et préconscient. Les questions ainsi posées (mauvaise foi, réticence consciente, méconnaissance-pathologie du champ de conscience, etc.) ne perdent pas leur intérêt si nous les caractérisons de marginales par rapport au champ proprement psychanalytique, elles se situent au niveau de cette deuxième censure que Freud place à la limite du préconscient et de la conscience, mais dont il n'a guère amorcé la description.[86]

Laplanche and Leclaire then move on to the Saussurean dimension of Lacan's reworking of Freud – the fixing and unfixing of signifiers in the process of repression. Here the intellectual boundaries in question are to be found within psychoanalysis rather than between psychoanalysis and philosophy, and the usefulness of *TM* as a relatively non-aligned forum becomes apparent. Laplanche and Leclaire belong to the SFP, while Green is a member of the SPP.[87] Pontalis is well placed to mediate between the Lacanians and the establishment; his note on 'La lecture de Freud' (July 1962) justifies the theoretical debate in a number of ways. Circumstantially, first of all, since the availability and reliability of Freud's texts in French is poor, and every recourse to the original is thus a sensible safeguard against distortion. Secondly, says Pontalis, the return to source is a way of combating the decay of psychoanalytic terminology resulting from institutionalisation and mythification. Thirdly, he remains convinced that therapeutic practice must never be divorced from theoretical inquiry. Fourthly, in an appropriately synthetic manner, he maintains that psychoanalysis is permanently psychoanalysable inasmuch as it owes all to a symbolic father, without whose authority the professional analyst could not be constituted as subject. This last consideration shows how far

Pontalis is from Sartre, despite the admission of psychoanalysis into the methodological armoury of the synthetic anthropology. Reflexivity is something that Sartre continues to deny to Freudian theory[88] and dependence on linguistics is not a feature that is likely to cause him to modify his view.

It is apparent that in this third period, as far as the content of *TM* is concerned, the attack on the Sartrean positions is led by Pontalis, who is much less of a mediator than Pouillon. Curiously enough, Algeria has the paradoxical effect of moving Lévi-Strauss down *TM*'s agenda; the periodic sniping by Sartre and Gorz merely confirms that during a colonial war the bankruptcy of structuralist anthropology seems more or less to go without saying. Lévi-Strauss, for his part, despite having lent himself to a degree of recuperation by Beauvoir in *Le Deuxième Sexe*, is by no means as passive in relation to Sartre. To devote one academic session to the study of the *Critique de la raison dialectique* is to reveal a wish to get to grips with the arguments of the antagonist. The fact that he, too, has also claimed to be working within a Marxist framework and that he has repeatedly endeavoured to situate his work *vis-à-vis* diachronic study, albeit in an unco-ordinated manner, suggests that he is bound to venture a response.

The time has now come, therefore, to consider the period 1960–2, when the two anthropologies, the *structurale* and the *structurelle et historique*, having for so long operated adjacent to one another in *TM*, are now forced by their own movements of self-definition to take stock of each other. Three bodies of work are of particular relevance: first, the publications of Lévi-Strauss that appear between 1956 and 1960, particularly those that are featured in the review; secondly, Sartre's *Critique*; thirdly, Lévi-Strauss's *La Pensée sauvage*.

The work in the first category is of fairly narrow specialist interest, for the most part. One article with a provocative title is the 1956 tribute to Jakobson, 'Structure et dialectique'. It deals with the relation of myth and ritual and suggests that their contact is not one of mechanical causality in either direction, but that it is dialectical – by which Lévi-Strauss means that each is a structural transformation of the other. It becomes quite apparent that the basis of the dialectic is taken to be the formal permutability of structural elements, something which is evidently incompatible with the Sartrean view and likely to impose a heavier burden on Pouillon.

In March 1961 *TM* presents to a wider public the account of 'La geste d'Asdiwal' that had already been published by the Ecole Pratique des Hautes Etudes. This detailed study of a body of North Pacific Amerindian myth is perhaps best viewed as a preamble to the vast four-volume *Mythologiques*, a *magnum opus* which emerges in the sixties and in the seventies and of which there is no trace in *TM*. In 'La geste d'Asdiwal', Lévi-Strauss's investigations of social organisation, kinship structures, magic, art and ritual are brought to bear on a set of myths; these he succeeds in describing in terms of their structural characteristics. The dialectical relation of myth to reality remains purely formal, the myth being like a collective dream, a mode of access to the unconscious categories that inform the reality. Necessarily, there is no diachronic frame for the analysis, nothing that really explicates what Lévi-Strauss refers to as 'le propre des mythes [. . .] d'évoquer un passé aboli, et de l'appliquer comme une grille sur la dimension du présent, afin d'y déchiffrer un sens où coïncident les deux faces – l'historique et la structurelle – qu'oppose à l'homme sa propre réalité'[89] – except insofar as the past is constructed in imagination.

It is revealing that Lévi-Strauss should deploy the very terms of the new dual specification. They appear in his inaugural lecture at the Collège de France on 5 January 1960, three months prior to the publication of the *Critique*. Although it does not appear in *TM*, this lecture is worth examining because it attempts to defend anthropology in terms of the conceptual opposition that Sartre used in 'Questions de méthode' – that of understanding (causal explanation) and comprehension (recognition of human purpose). Lévi-Strauss now declares that his professional activity 'consiste – au lieu d'opposer l'explication causale et la compréhension – à se découvrir un objet qui soit à la fois objectivement très loin et subjectivement très concret, et dont l'explication causale puisse se fonder sur cette compréhension qui n'est pour nous qu'une forme supplémentaire de preuve'.[90] This would appear to be much closer to the Jaspersian view of *Erklären* and *Verstehen*.

Far, then, from being confined to understanding, the ethnographer is said to learn from his or her subjective experience of the society under investigation, this experience subsequently taking on a confirmatory function. Lévi-Strauss gives notice, in other words, that his mode of intellection is not to be assigned to the lesser of the two categories but that it incorporates both. His inaugural lecture, fittingly, lays claim to methodological sufficiency and academic dignity; it is committed to the preservation of a 'pure anthropology' – the study in a small, relatively independent discipline of a relatively independent object, that is small, homeostatic, distant, 'cold' and threatened societies. At the same time, aware that he is under attack on two fronts, he dwells momentarily on the relation of anthropology to colonialism: his discipline is, he says, a belated act of remorse, a gesture of fraternity intended to atone for the violence and the exploitation.

It is as if the Lévi-Straussian gesture elicits Sartrean action, for it is into this apologetic context that Sartre introduces his *Critique* and attempts to 'donner un fondement politique à l'anthropologie'.[91] At the same time, he supplies an italicised conclusion to 'Questions de méthode' in which he restates the aims of his projected anthropology. The regressive–progressive method outlined in 1957 is now attached to a *Critique* consisting of two volumes, the first structural and the second historical. The first will operate at a certain level of abstraction, and because Sartre considers this to be one of the negative features of structuralism, he feels the need to justify himself. He does so by a discussion of terminology: *projet*, he says, may appear to denote a concept and to be part of a theoretical apparatus, but as denotation it is also a project of signification. Ever eager to show how reflexivity goes beyond linguistics, he gives himself due synthetic status as a speaking subject: the *Critique* will be formulated by one whose utterances impinge irremediably on the object of study and whose discourse can handle the concept of totalisation only by being aware that it is itself a process of totalisation. He concludes as follows:

L'anthropologie ne méritera son nom que si elle substitue à l'étude des objets humains celle des différents processus du devenir-objet. Son rôle est de fonder son *savoir* sur le *non-savoir* rationnel et compréhensif, c'est-à-dire que la totalisation historique ne sera possible que si l'anthropologie se comprend au lieu de s'ignorer.[92]

Synthesis and reflexivity remain therefore at a premium, at least as far as Sartre's intentions go. To what point they might have been pushed is difficult to assess, given the continuing absence of the second volume.[93] In 1976, he allows the *New Left Review* to extract from the available 500 pages a discussion of Stalin and Trotsky in the inter-war period.[94] The passage concerned is a rethinking of an aspect of 'Le fantôme de Staline', the development of the programme of 'socialism in one country', in the light of the theses and descriptions of the first volume of the *Critique*. It sets out to show that the programme was not only a massive reaction to external political and military pressure, but also the product of the symbiosis of Stalin's and Trotsky's perceptions of each other. I have mentioned that the preamble to the *Critique* identifies the dialectical course of history with its investigation by the historian–anthropologist. Sartre had doubtless planned to supplement his account of Stalinism with a review of his own changing attitude towards it. It is fair to assume, as *New Left Review* does, that events – May 1968 and the Soviet invasion of Czechoslovakia – overtook him and that his totalisations could not be documented in the desired manner.

The second volume was intended to substantiate the very anti-structuralist assertion that 'il y a *une* histoire avec *une* vérité et *une* intelligibilité'.[95] The first volume is required to provide, in terms of a typology of interpersonal and inter-group relations, the basis for this single historical intelligibility – and thus to save history from chaos. It represents an act of faith in the dialectic. The direction being followed is precisely the opposite, at a different level, of that of Lévi-Strauss, for whom, as *Tristes Tropiques* showed, it is the existence of the single intelligibility, in the shape of the global monoculture, which constitutes catastrophe.

The first volume is structural, rather than historical, in the sense that it seeks to describe the different modes of interpenetration of various sets of totalisations: of the individual in contact with inert matter, with self and with others, and of these totalisations in a macro-social context. Different anthropological categories are set up as a result: series, collectives, groups-in-fusion, pledged groups, institutions and classes. These are then all investigated from the point of view of the extent to which they derive from, facilitate or inhibit individual *praxis*, that is to say the exercise of freedom, as work, in response to material need. *Praxis* may, as a result of scarcity, be betrayed by its consequences; it is these two factors taken together – *praxis* and counter-productivity – which found a set of concepts capable of accounting for both the intelligibility of history and its apparent unintelligibility.

This is not the place to debate at length the validity of the *Critique*. Sartre, in any case, gives no extracts to *TM*; this may be due to its difficulty, to the frantic manner of its composition, or to its unsuitability for segmentation (although a fragment was published in a review called *Voies nouvelles* in June 1958). There is no doubt that *Les Séquestrés d'Altona* lent itself much better to serialisation, particularly at a time when so much space was given over to Algeria. The non-appearance of the *Critique* in *TM* is a trivial matter, however, and an anti-structuralist labour of such magnitude cannot pass without comment, for, whatever its ambition in respect of Marxism, it displays a real determination to incorporate and to redirect the anthropology of Lévi-Strauss. The diphasic methodology of the two volumes is synchronic–diachronic rather than regressive–progressive; it thus facilitates the incorporation of poorly defended academic ethnography into the strongly running dialectic.

Annexation is what Sartre has in mind, and this is why the allusion to denotation is indeed a *projet*; by way of Barthes's *Mythologies*, presumably, he identifies it as an outsider that can be picked off with ease. Similarly, he dabbles once more with the signifier and the signified (as tool and artisan, and as product and producer). He even follows Lévi-Strauss into the analysis of the linguistic sign as object of exchange – but, characteristically, the sign transacted by the communities of the *Critique* is '*A la Bastille!*' As if to deny now that Lévi-Strauss's societies – the 'cold' civilisations with minimal historical change – fall outside the regime of material scarcity within which he establishes his dialectical descriptions, he makes a point of selecting examples from *Les Structures élémentaires de la parenté*. It is assumed, although not made explicit, that societies which seem to have resolved problems of material scarcity by whatever means (demographic control, geographical mobility, production techniques) have done so temporarily and locally in a universal context that threatens to undermine them. For Sartre, scarcity and history are coextensive: to be without either is to be without both, but it is also to be doomed to both in the long term.

The bid is thus made for Lévi-Strauss's structuralism. Humanity and inert matter replace culture and nature, synchrony finds its rightful place within diachrony, and the synthetic anthropology moves onto the terrain of kinship studies, religion and law. Not only this, but the 'cold' societies are denied continued insulation so that the Sartrean expedition might go where the Lévi-Straussian cannot – into analyses of racialism and colonialism.

In these latter areas, Sartre remains consistent: he refutes interpretations based on economistic and sociologistic premises, showing instead how a 'projet d'exploiter'[96] is undertaken by individuals serialised in certain conditions. Serialisation, he observes, is a dialectical reality (when each is rendered other to the other as well as to the self), which academic sociology has never been able to conceptualise. Specifically, the positivist social sciences have never assigned proper importance to the role of the third party in monitoring and mediating all relations between the individual and the group. This touches on one of the basic principles of the *Critique*, the element that provides the dynamic of group formation and which has huge relevance to political organisation. It explains why Fanon 'avait été passionné par la *Critique de la raison dialectique*, en particulier par les analyses sur la fraternité-terreur',[97] and why it is Fanon who makes the first feedback from the *Critique* into *TM* in his essay on violence.

But it is here also that Lévi-Strauss is directly implicated. With his mediating third party, Sartre returns to the Maussian sources of *Les Structures élémentaires de la parenté* and to the issues raised by Lefort at the end of *TM*'s first period. At that time, the problem was whether the obligations (to give, to receive and to give in return), schematised in the *Essai sur le don*, were more appropriately described in phenomenological or in structuralist terms. Sartre now proceeds beyond Lefort's position in order the better to challenge Lévi-Strauss. In institutions such as the *potlatch*, the act of giving is indeed designed to obligate the other, as Lefort has observed, but the reciprocation now requires ratification by the third party.

The importance of this new agent is to shift the scheme of things away from binarism and towards a dynamic ternary model much more consistent with the Hegelian dialectic. The third party, having ratified reciprocity, is excluded from it, and, in the regime of scarcity, is compelled to enter a similar sequence of transactions. No longer, therefore, can the anthropologist envisage discrete or parallel chains of exchange; on the contrary, the deals taking place in the course of time intertwine and prejudice each other. *Praxis* now tends towards counter-productivity, and the practico-inert emerges as a factor which necessarily informs all those who struggle against it.

What Lévi-Strauss describes as a kinship structure is therefore, in terms of the experience of the members of the marriage system, a 'réciprocité complexe de créances et de dettes',[98] a *praxis* of obligatory donations and receipts; each member is bound to participate if the group is to survive. When the community successfully withstands the threat of scarcity, says Sartre, it is thanks to its consciousness of the necessity to do so. Each member is pledged to a certain pattern of solidarity: it is a *de facto* pledge that is entered into at birth and later freely and responsibly assumed on the occasion of the *rites de passage* into adulthood. At the end of this agonistic dialogue, Sartre thanks Lévi-Strauss – for having shown how structure is intelligible as organised *praxis*.

At the same time, Lévi-Strauss is rebuked for having misapprehended the structure as structure, in exteriority, and for not having been able to comprehend the totalisations of the marriageable kin concerned. The ethnographer, maintains Sartre, constructs as objectivity what is in reality irreducible human experience; he likewise marvels at the capacity of the 'native' for abstract thought (from a position of ethnocentric superiority) without realising that abstract thought is constrained by concrete reality (by the experience of having to marry 'X'). The 'native', on the other hand, knows better; when he traces in the sand a diagram of his kinship system, he is deliberately reducing synthetic comprehension to objective representation – for the benefit of the epistemologically handicapped ethnographer! The irony in this debate operates at the expense of Lévi-Strauss. It is no accident that it is held back in the *Critique* to constitute, as it were, the endgame. In the closing pages of the existing first volume, when Sartre seeks to stress how much the concept of scarcity saves his Hegelian description of conflict from idealism, he picks up the Saussurean analogy of the chess-game, only to deploy it in an anti-structuralist manner and to show how reciprocity and comprehension imply each other.

In the end, then, it is the concept of reciprocity – so ill-defined by Sartre and by Lévi-Strauss hitherto, but on which both have been so dependent that at times each has misunderstood the proximity of the other – which now marks out the divergences and permits the subordination of the Lévi-Straussian apparatus to the Sartrean. In the end, it is the synthetic and not the structuralist anthropology which is better equipped to anthropologise the rivalry between them; Sartre's general view – that '*justement pour cela*, nous devons comprendre que la lutte comme réciprocité est fonction de la réciprocité de compréhension'[99] – is specifically applicable to the intellectual field in which he pursues his totalising ambitions.

Before moving on to see how comprehensive Lévi-Strauss's riposte is, it is worth looking closer at the reciprocity purveyed by the *Critique*. It is clearly not a moral value; rather, it is ontological – the necessity of mutual comprehension. In this sense, it is not the converse of conflict, but its empathetic prerequisite. Competition for what is materially scarce presupposes the synthetic grasp, by each, of the projects of the other. Reciprocity is now postulated *a priori* in order to permit a taxonomy of the forms that it may take – positive, negative, antagonistic, mediated, collective, and so on. It is a matrix generating all forms of human interaction from collision to collusion. Specifically, reciprocity underwrites the notion of the individual as the prime unit of sociality and awaits ethicalisation at a time when the appropriate material conditions have been secured. It suggests a return to the implied ontology which pre-existed *L'Etre et le néant* and in which antipathy was conditional upon empathy; one effect of this is that, as in the *Esquisse d'une théorie des émotions*, magic, too, is wrested from the grasp of the ethnographers.

In what seems increasingly like a battle for legitimate kinship with Mauss, Sartre denies Lévi-Strauss the right to speak con-clusively of reciprocity – for this right belongs not to those who understand and explain, but to those who comprehend. Beau-voir notes, unsurprisingly, that the *Critique* was 'étrillée par la droite, par les communistes et par les ethnographes'.[100] Sure enough, Gurvitch writes that Sartre 'ne s'occupe que d'un monde social imaginaire, entièrement engendré par la raison dialectique toute-puissante, camouflant une philosophie précon-çue'.[101] But it is, of course, Lévi-Strauss who offers the greatest resistance.

The eighth chapter of *La Pensée sauvage*, 'Le temps retrouvé', appears in *TM* in April 1962; the ninth, 'Histoire et dialectique', is a response to the *Critique* and does not appear in the review. It is important to recall that the book is itself a sequel to *Le Totémisme aujourd'hui*, which announces that totemism is a figment of the Western imagination designed to segregate the 'primitive' from the 'civilised' societies. This is important, because it rehearses a reproach to be addressed to Sartre.

The main body of *La Pensée sauvage* need not be discussed here, save to say that the free-range thought manifested in mythology is shown to be, in each particular society, a logical system. The system does not seek to explain natural phenomena, but uses them as signifiers in a powerful cultural code; it constitutes a set of terms of reference employed to classify and to signify, internally coherent and infinitely extendable, capable of both extreme particularisation and extreme generalisation, and amenable to Saussurean description.

Lévi-Strauss in any case summarises his principal findings in the chapter that he gives to *TM*, but not before having revealed a second motivation for his work, that of contributing to a Marxist theory of ideology. For 'wild thought', in his view, is wild in the sense that it is not cultivated in order to yield scientific know-ledge; it is not wild in the sense of being independent of a socio-economic infrastructure. It must be said that *La Pensée sauvage* seems to inscribe itself within Marxism more as an act of protocol than as a programme of research, for it does not investigate the articulation of infrastructure and superstructure, nor does it move towards a Marxist analysis of 'primitive' modes of production.

The eighth chapter, 'Le temps retrouvé', probes other aspects of 'wild thought'. Turning once more to the problem of the shaman's magic and/or trickery, Lévi-Strauss revises the opinion contained in his first contribution to *TM* ('Le sorcier et sa magie'). Previously, he had contrasted magic and trickery; now he drops the distinction as ethnocentric, a move which serves his purpose as the protector of 'wild thought' and paves the way for the accusations to be levelled against Sartre. He is also interested in the link between religion and magic, arguing against Comte – who set them in evolutionary sequence – that they are synchronically complementary. His third point, however, is the most important: he invokes myths of origins to demonstrate that his apparently static societies acknowledge history, even if they only document it mythically. It is wrong, he concludes, to say that structuralist anthropology excludes consideration of history.

One wonders whether mythic representations express actual structure rather than the ghost of structure past. The question can never be answered with certainty, but at least it reveals to Lévi-Strauss a depth of local historical consciousness probably resulting from the tension between demographic instability and the solidity of the totemic classification. This makes of structure, he says, something like a waterborne palace, constantly disassembling and recomposing in the flow of the river. Event and structure thus go hand in hand: some societies, however – the totemic – see themselves as structure; others, like our own, see themselves as event and become evolutionist. This is perhaps an incautious observation: not only is it a phenomenological one with which Sartre would agree, but it invites the retort that the ethnographer has no obligation to sanction the relatively ahistorical prejudices of the peoples under scrutiny.

The final chapter of *La Pensée sauvage*, 'Histoire et dialectique', the fruit of seminars at the Ecole Pratique des Hautes Etudes in which Pouillon participated, is offered as 'un hommage indirect d'admiration et de respect'[102] to the author of the *Critique*. The indirect tribute is in fact the direct attack towards which Lévi-Strauss has been moving: *La Pensée sauvage* uses a certain amount of Sartrean vocabulary, such as *praxis*, synthesis and totalisation, but this, he says, is because he intends to establish whether or not 'wild thought' is dialectical.

The implication here is that the divergence is twofold: that there is disagreement over the meaning and the scope of the term 'dialectic' and that there are different assessments of the nature of 'wild thought'. The first point is easy to accept, although Lévi-Strauss complicates the issue by committing the error that he imputes to Sartre. Sartre is said not to know whether analytical reason is complementary or antagonistic to dialectical reason, whereas in fact it is clear from 'Questions de méthode' that the former is the antithetical moment of the latter. In any case, Lévi-Strauss shows that he has understood perfectly by rewriting the distinction in terms of *explication* and *compréhension*. Praising Sartre for his proficiency in the latter operation, he observes that 'le rôle de la raison dialectique est de mettre les sciences humaines en possession d'une réalité qu'elle est seule capable de leur fournir, mais que l'effort proprement scientifique consiste à décomposer, puis à recomposer suivant un autre plan'.[103]

The difference lies not so much in the definition as in the role. For Lévi-Strauss, unlike Sartre, the dialectic is to be integrated into the analytic. He does not mind being called an *esthète* or being accused of looking at human beings as if they were ants: 'nous croyons que le but dernier des sciences humaines n'est pas de constituer l'homme, mais de le dissoudre'.[104] Lévi-Strauss regards the *pensée de survol* as a scientifically productive illusion; for Sartre, its epistemological impossibility extends immediately to a moral unacceptability, except where it can be proved to be useful by being built into a methodology designed to maximise the non-detachment of the analyst.

The second issue – the nature of 'wild thought' – is more problematic because Sartre has never paid great attention to non-French peoples unaffected by French history. Lévi-Strauss notes the omission and imputes it to the Lévy-Bruhlian view of the pre-logical mentality. The accusation is grossly unfair, but it helps Lévi-Strauss conflate anti-structuralism and ethnocentricity.[105]

'Qui commence par s'installer dans les prétendues évidences du moi n'en sort plus';[106] such admonitions are by now familiar to readers of *TM*. Lévi-Strauss regards Sartre's overvaluation of *compréhension* and of diachrony as deriving from his Cartesian ego-based world-view; he considers that it shows a wilful ignorance of linguistics and of psychoanalysis and reveals how parochial his universalising ambitions are. All that has happened in twenty years of intellectual development, suggests Lévi-Strauss, is that the self–other dichotomy of *L'Etre et le néant* has been displaced and has become the opposition between peoples within history and peoples without it. An angry footnote complains that the price paid for 'l'illusion d'avoir surmonté l'insoluble antinomie (dans un tel système) entre le moi et l'autre, consiste dans l'assignation, par la conscience historique, de la fonction métaphysique aux Papous'.[107] Lévi-Strauss goes on: 'En réduisant ceux-ci à l'état de moyens, tout juste bons à satisfaire son appétit philosophique, la raison historique se livre à une sorte de cannibalisme intellectuel qui, aux yeux de l'ethnographe, est beaucoup plus révoltant que l'autre.' This, then, is the crux of the argument: that Sartre, 'qui prétend fonder une anthropologie, coupe sa société des autres sociétés'[108] and that 'il faut beaucoup d'égocentrisme et de naïveté pour croire que l'homme est tout entier réfugié dans un seul des modes historiques ou géographiques de son être, alors que la vérité de l'homme réside dans le système de leurs différences et de leurs communes propriétés'.[109]

As I have said, however, Sartre nowhere discourses at length on the so-called *sociétés sans histoire*. He never implies that non-accession to history is non-accession to humanity. The fact is that in self-defence Lévi-Strauss has jumped to extreme conclusions. Sartre uses the term 'société sans Histoire',[110] so embarrassing to a Marxist–structuralist anthropology, only in a conventional way and as an explicit borrowing from professional ethnographic usage. Whether he uses it innocently or in order to embarrass, it is unreasonable to conclude that its presence attests to a wish to dehumanise the exotic peoples. In any case, and this Lévi-Strauss fails to mention, Sartre is perfectly happy to take the 'hot–cold' distinction at its face value.[111]

The final section of *La Pensée sauvage* is as much informed by Lévi-Strauss's discomfort *vis-à-vis* Marxism as it is by Sartre's ignorance of linguistics and psychoanalysis. 'Histoire et dialectique' ends, for example, with an analysis of history as a mode of 'wild thought' and of historiography as its cultivated correlative. Yet again, Lévi-Strauss tries to situate his anthropology in relation to the discipline of history. This time he offers a simple complementarity of synchrony and diachrony which cannot disguise how much his discomfort has been increased by Sartre's decision to promote Marxism at the expense of structuralism. The upshot of the debate is that the two anthropologies continue to attempt to incorporate each other and to achieve compatibility with Marxism. Sartre and

Lévi-Strauss react against each other, clearly conscious of the extent to which their ambitions are shared: the redesignation of the synthetic anthropology as *structurelle* bears this out; so, too, does the tendency of Lévi-Strauss in *La Pensée sauvage* to favour *ethnologie* in place of *anthropologie*, a reversal of the option on which he had built his professional career, but still designed to mark out his own difference.

The fact remains that there exists a major gap between an outlook that is consciousness-based and one that is not. It is a gap that each party understands but which the Algerian context serves to maximise. The result is that Sartre can tolerate the concept of structure only as a configuration of *praxis* and *pratico-inerte* within the group, while Lévi-Strauss fails to explicate the relationship between *praxis* and structure. With the two anthropologies so near and yet so far apart, the similarities oblige each to remain uncompromising as far as the real divergences are concerned. The tensions, as is appropriate in war-time, rule out any possibility of co-operation between the adversaries: no attempt by Sartre to come to terms with linguistics and psychoanalysis; no attempt by Lévi-Strauss to theorise colonialism. Sartre nonetheless emerges fitter from the fray, because not only are his arguments more powerful in the historical context, but his grasp of the relatedness of many things leads him never to attack his enemies singly; he can thus do great damage by association – of structuralist determinism with Stalinist determinism, for example. Lévi-Strauss, meanwhile, already contemplating his own discipline in terms of its diminishing returns, is moved to defend those whom he perceives as doomed and thus overplays his hand. Sartre therefore has the luxury of the last generous word: 'Je suis loin de mépriser Lévi-Strauss – je le considère au contraire comme un très bon ethnographe – mais il a écrit des pages qui, selon moi, sont absurdes, sur la *Critique de la raison dialectique*. Mais je n'ai pas à le lui dire, pour quoi faire?'[112]

The two main protagonists drive the debate into deadlock. There are others, however, who continue to seek solutions. The first of these is Lucien Sebag, an ex-student of Métraux, who in 1962 is working on the mythology of the Pueblo Indians under the supervision of Lévi-Strauss. An article of his entitled 'Histoire et structure – idéologie et réalité' appears in *TM* in July 1962, two years after the publication of the *Critique* and three months after the eighth chapter of *La Pensée sauvage*. It is in fact a draft of the central third chapter of his work on *Marxisme et structuralisme*.[113] Although it does not explicitly extend the discussions (the *Critique* is mentioned only in footnotes), it nevertheless tackles the same central problems.

Sebag is a fascinating figure, for his wide-ranging preoccupations place him at the point of convergence of many of the currents running through *TM*. He is a specialist ethnographer, close to Lévi-Strauss and with a consequent interest in linguistics, as well as being in touch with Lacanian psychoanalysis. At the same time, he is an ex-PCF militant with solid anti-Stalinist convictions and, moreover, a philosopher by training, well versed in Hegel and Marx. Although there is no strong link with Sartrean phenomenology, priorities are shared in the sense that Sebag is committed to deriving revolutionary activity from a knowledge that is normative and capable of founding an ethic.

His particular wish is to explore the contributions that structuralism has made to the understanding of the relation of knowledge to reality. In this respect, he is able to take up some of the undeveloped aspects of *La Pensée sauvage*, notably the study of myth as ideology and the implications of this for the base–superstructure model. He is able to point out, for example, that the 'hot–cold' distinction had also been made by Marx, who went on to assign an epistemological superiority to industrial societies over pre-industrial societies – because of their capacity to identify ideology as the mask concealing the real. This leads Sebag to ask in which way structuralism might constructively question Marx's 'acte métaphysique audacieux'.[114]

He considers that, following Saussure, ideologies now have to be regarded as symbolic systems. Furthermore, their relations with each other, with reality and with the economic base may be studied only subsequent to the analysis of each system. The pre-eminence of the economy cannot therefore be assumed *a priori*. Recourse to Saussure also leads Sebag to problematise the relationship of subjectivity and ideology: 'Ce qui est en cause c'est le rapport de la subjectivité au signifiant en tant qu'elle le constitue, le rencontre ou s'y soumet.'[115] If ideology and discourse are coterminous, then, he goes on, Marx's view of the proletariat's unmediated access to truth can no longer be acceptable, and, indeed, there remains no reality that can be known prior to its construction in language, nor any extra-linguistic subjectivity capable of knowing it. So much, then, for the *Critique*: 'En aucun cas le pouvoir propre des sociétés, l'activité créatrice des groupes ne seront compris sur le modèle de la dialectique individuelle.'[116]

Having noted fairly early on the availability of two vantage points

– the historical, which seeks out causal continuity, and the structural, which sets out to discover discontinuities – and having, like Lévi-Strauss, postulated their complementarity, Sebag finds himself, the further he goes, validating the latter at the expense of the former. Unable to say in what methodological procedures the complementarity might be expressed, he thus observes the limitations of Sartre from a position limited by its dependence on Lévi-Strauss and Lacan. As he moves from the 1962 draft to the published work of 1964, he sees his chances of reaching an ethico-political programme diminishing. Having hoped for the adequation of knowledge to reality, he is forced to the conclusion that all *praxis* is in the last analysis founded in *méconnaissance*. The distance between his starting and finishing positions is thus substantial: beginning by requiring an intelligibility that would legitimate political activity, he ends by pressing the claims of a structuralist science that can understand the limits of intelligibility and by handing the problem back to the philosophers.

Sebag certainly fails to achieve the objectives of the synthetic anthropology. Instead, he voices the increasingly widespread view that not only must Marxist anthropology abandon the idea of determination by the economic base, but that it must also contribute to a reworked Marxism that would avoid evolutionism, linear causality and phenomenological attitudes towards the subject in history. In this he heralds the work of the PCF philosopher Louis Althusser, with which *TM* has to come to terms in its fourth period. I propose to step briefly outside the chronological boundaries that I have set to this chapter, not to deal with Althusser, but because Sebag's short-lived inquiry extends into the mid-sixties. *TM* publishes his 'Analyse des rêves d'une Indienne Guayaki' in June 1964 and a discussion of 'Le mythe: code et message' in March 1965. The latter appears by way of tribute in the month following his suicide and is accompanied by an obituary notice written by J.-P. and M.-C. Boons.

The thoughts on myth are extracted from the final chapter of *L'Invention du monde chez les Indiens Pueblos*,[117] the study of Keresan mythology undertaken under the supervision of Lévi-Strauss. The work is an orthodox structuralist analysis based on the following assumptions: that myth is a discourse drawing its content from its natural and human environment; that by using the same logic as presides over social organisation it is able to resolve symbolically certain contradictions inherent in the social reality; that it is an effect which goes on to acquire a determining power over human behaviour; finally, that its significance is wider than its context, since ultimately it derives from mental universals.

Sebag's view is that structuralist analysis shows how human cultures conceptualise their apartness from nature, that is to say the 'passage du continu au discontinu'.[118] The particular origin myths with which he deals, those of the Acoma Indians, are exemplary in this respect. Yet to the extent that the cultural order, once its organising principles have been revealed by structuralist analysis, is made contingent upon a certain attitude or posture adopted by the group in relation to its situation, the whole problem is once again opened up to investigations of existential choices. Sebag now seems to be coming round to the view that structuralist analysis is a prerequisite for an understanding of *praxis*: it 'permet toujours une reprise herméneutique qui n'était pas possible jusqu'alors'.[119]

It is not between Lévi-Strauss and Sartre that Sebag is trying to find a way, but between Lévi-Strauss and the Catholic philosopher Paul Ricœur; his comments are in answer to the special issue of *Esprit* (November 1963) devoted to *La Pensée sauvage*. The positions of Ricœur are in some respects similar to those of Sartre, however, and Sebag's mediation is thus relevant to the problems posed by structuralism to existential Marxism. The first source of tension with which he deals, for example, is the question of the implication or otherwise of the observer in the field of observation. When Ricœur gives priority to the myth of Adam in his study of the mythic origins of evil,[120] says Sebag, it is because he is prompted by an interest in his own conditioning; structuralism, on the other hand, cuts out as far as possible the subjectivity of the investigator. It does so, not on the basis of methodological, moral or political choice, but for obvious empirical reasons: his own position in relation to the Pueblo cannot be the same as that of Ricœur in relation to the Judaeo-Christian culture. The Ricœurian approach is an activity of reflection in which the spontaneous bond of individual with culture is taken as the object of study. Sebag sees this as part of the philosophical enterprise, one which has a political necessity, for its findings are required to inform strategy in ideological struggle; it is not, on the other hand, part and parcel of ethnographic fieldwork.

To Ricœur, who insists that Judaeo-Christian mythology has greater semantic consistency than do other systems, Sebag replies that he has misunderstood the concept of *bricolage*. Yet he does not deny that there is a qualitative difference, and ascribes it to the fact that certain mythologies have engendered philosophy when others have not. There is an evolutionism here that sets Sebag apart from Lévi-Strauss and brings him back towards the Marxist camp. It consists in a belief that philosophical revolutions have taken place in mythological cultures at the moment when 'la pensée s'est affranchie de la prégnance du lexique parce qu'elle n'a plus pour tâche de rendre compte de la diversité des êtres comme telle'.[121] It is essentially a change in signifying practice, for to a formal systematicity based on the arbitrariness of permutation is added motivated content: water, for example, ceases to be available for *bricolage* and to fit negatively or positively into a variety of binary oppositions; it now acquires a permanent significance which makes of it an elemental force of unity, operating beneath the apparent multiplicity for which mythology had to account.

Unfortunately, Sebag's account of the epistemic shifts, from myth to philosophy to science, is too brief to be clear. He suggests a historical shift from the expression in mythology of the diversity of the world to the thematisation of certain aspects of it; quite what socio-economic factors might correlate with this shift, and the manner in which it might take place, remain obscure. If it is true that myth demonstrates a lexical arbitrariness and an unconscious syntax which effectively decentres the speaking subject in its relation to a mythic discourse, and if it is true that in philosophies and sciences the arbitrariness and unconsciousness decrease, all of which no doubt remains to be confirmed, then Sebag is right to call for 'une morphologie des types de discours, fondée non pas sur des considérations extérieures à l'intellect mais sur les diverses combinaisons de leurs éléments constitutifs'.[122]

Sebag's position is that ideology should be studied as the sum of symbolic systems, and that these should be classified according to the space that they make available for the consciousness of the signifying subject. This view informs his fieldwork in South America in 1963 and 1964. After having been advised by Métraux, who had himself collected South Amerindian dreams in the thirties, Sebag spends several months with the Guayaki Indians in Paraguay, followed by several more, accompanied by Pierre Clastres, with the Ayore on the Paraguay–Bolivia border. Before his suicide in 1965, Sebag had little time to write up his research. An essay on shamanism in *L'Homme* and the analysis of the Guayaki dreams in *TM* are the only texts that he leaves. A total of one hundred dreams and their associations, collected over a period of two months, are presented in the latter article as a psychoanalytical insight into the way in which an individual's development is constrained by the cultural signifiers available. With considerable procedural caution and ethnographic contextualisation, Sebag maps the identity of a woman who, in a culture in which the female is relatively expendable, wishes to compensate her father, by production of a male child, for the guilt of having been born a woman. This problem of 'comment peut-on être une femme? – question que J. Lacan a désignée comme étant celle de l'hystérique'[123] is partially resolved by the transgression of cultural norms in her dreams.

Sebag takes the opportunity to show the advance he is making over American culturalist anthropology; Benedict and Mead were prepared to specify a cultural ethos, but were unable to conceptualise the relation of subject to symbolic order. He himself is much more in line with the Lévi-Strauss of 'L'efficacité symbolique', merging an original phonological polymorphism with an original sexual polymorphism taken from Freud. He writes:

l'individu marqué par un certain codage de ce qu'il est, continue à porter en lui ce que ce codage méconnaît ou refuse. Les sociétés en inscrivant les énergies individuelles dans des réseaux qui leur préexistent, donnent à cette énergie le pouvoir de devenir histoire; mais chaque individu, qui ne s'achève pourtant que dans sa rencontre avec de tels réseaux, est encore bien autre chose. Qu'est-ce à dire sinon que l'enfance n'est jamais révolue et que c'est à la confluence de l'enfant et de l'adulte, de la nature et d'un univers social particulier que se situent plusieurs activités qui, du jeu au rêve, nous font sans cesse passer du réel au possible.[124]

Underlying Sebag's writing is the belief that the understanding of the symbolic order as repressive opens up possibilities of ideological struggle; it is to be deeply regretted that someone who embodied the intellectual tensions of the sixties should not have survived beyond 1965.

From the Sartrean point of view, Sebag's profile is also one of promise unfulfilled. He does not tackle directly the incidence of transference in his dealings with the Guayaki girl; had he done so, and had he analysed his own dreams, and had he wondered, for example, whether all ethnography is counter-transferential, then he would have brought his work very close to Leiris's exemplary *L'Afrique fantôme*. Despite the title of *Marxisme et structuralisme*, moreover, he ends up by leaving the specifically economic a long way behind. Maurice Godelier, the economic anthropologist who comes into *TM* in the fourth period, acknowledges Sebag's work to be of 'importance majeure', but criticises it for having taken Lévi-Straussian anthropology in the wrong direction, towards 'un idéalisme de l'esprit humain'.[125]

Certainly Sebag did not have the status of official *TM* spokes-man, and in the absence of Pouillon the last Sartrean word on the Lévi-Strauss question goes to Pierre Verstraeten, 'jeune philoso-phe belge que Sartre considère comme l'un de ses rares "disciples" ayant assimilé sa pensée de manière créatrice'.[126] Verstraeten's long and complex article, 'Lévi-Strauss ou la tentation du néant' (July to September 1963), is far from hostile and aims at a philosophical recuperation of structuralist anthropology. (It is particularly badly printed; a long list of *errata* appears in November of the same year.)

Verstraeten begins by reviewing briefly the attitudes adopted in *TM vis-à-vis* Lévi-Strauss: of Beauvoir in 1949, of Lefort in 1951 and of Pouillon in 1956. It is the 1951 debate which concerns him most – in particular, the contrast between Lefort's purposive view of reciprocity and Lévi-Strauss's preference for the buried mechan-isms of the kinship system. For him, the contrast is one between a dialectical approach and a scientific one. Like Pouillon, he con-siders that each has need of the other if synchronic and diachronic perspectives are to be integrated and if *praxis* is to come to recognise its own discontinuities. But where Pouillon calls for more theoretical work, Verstraeten sets out to show that it has taken place – for does not Sartre's *Critique* account for the discontinuities with the concept of the *pratico-inerte*? Does it not represent 'la totalisation de ces deux niveaux au sein d'un monisme dialecti-que'?[127] He stresses the importance of the third party in mediating between the experience of continuity that accompanies specific acts of reciprocity and the structural features which, unbeknown to the individuals concerned, constitute their socio-economic context. He concludes that 'la totalité sociale doit se comprendre en même temps comme universalité dialectique dans la reconnaissance pra-tique des subjectivités, et comme universalité analytique dans la méconnaissance d'elle-même que nous enseigne l'objectivité sci-entifique'.[128]

From this point onwards, Verstraeten carries the fight to Lévi-Strauss. Criticising the correlation of kinship systems with language and arguing that the former are structural (expressions of group purpose) while the latter is serial, he strikes at the heart of the structuralist anthropology. The force of his argument is unfortu-nately weakened by a familiarity with linguistics which appears to be no greater than that of Lévi-Strauss and by an apparent tendency to regard Lévi-Strauss's deployment of the phonological model as a fully blown semantic theory:

Nous dirions que Lévi-Strauss confond *volontairement* les domaines de la séméiologie [*sic*] et ceux de la sémantique (ou de la linguistique) en appliquant *systématiquement* les principes de la sémantique à tout champ séméiologique. Tout le champ de l'intelligibilité est certes constitué de significations, mais tous les modes d'articulation ne correspondent pas à l'articulation linguistique, et, surtout, tous les champs de signification n'entretiennent pas *un rapport identique* au sujet.[129]

Linguistics, says Verstraeten, cannot dominate all the *sciences humaines*; it is limited to the investigation of *langue* and cannot handle linguistic *praxis – parole*. He, in any case, is more interested in showing how language is a crystallisation of *pratico-inerte* and how therefore philosophy is able to do what linguistics cannot, namely show the force of the imagination – the internalisation by consciousnesses of their externalisation by third parties – in the establishment of language and of other symbolic systems. He thus agrees with Sebag, but with acknowledgement to Althusser (of whom this is the first reference in *TM*), that the central problem is that a discourse which structures reality cannot at the same time account for its own appearance. Verstraeten deals with this problem in the following way: he suggests that the native speaker's probable unconsciousness of syntax derives from the fact that language, which is subsequently thought of as a means of solving existential problems, is itself the solution to an existential problem long forgotten. 'Autrement dit, l'Etre et le Néant, la liberté ou l'angoisse, ne se traduisent pas dans les mots: ils les rendent possibles dans le mouvement même où ils se rendent impossibles.'[130]

This last formulation explains the title of the article, the temptation of *le néant* being the logical recourse to ontology which Lévi-Strauss's positivism spurns. It contains, incidentally, not one, but two Sartrean titles and anticipates, by one issue of *TM* only, the serialisation of *Les Mots* with which the fourth period begins and which explores the ramifications of the ontological security afforded to Sartre by language. Thanks to Verstraeten, meanwhile, the synthetic anthropology for the first time expresses the wish to use the conceptual apparatus of the *Critique* to describe the accession of the subject to the symbolic order. Hence the warm welcome, extended rather suddenly, to the Lacanian theses of Laplanche and Leclaire: 'il est facile de concevoir que ce soit la même situation problématique qui à la fois rompt l'unité originaire, refoule cette unité comme manque à être fondamental, inconscient originaire, et en aliène le sens dans un signifiant particulier'.[131]

Once again, the Sartrean reaction is one of incorporation, and the *méconnaissance* of the subject in relation to language is now made a function of the imaginative activity that governs the interaction of subjectivities in regimes of perceived scarcity.

Just as every collective is a potential group, all *pratico-inerte* capable of a degree of dissolution in *praxis*, and every seriality a possible structure, so also the inadequation of linguistic knowledge with performance is not absolute. Unfortunately, Verstraeten does not offer any detailed insights into what this might mean, beyond the suggestion that the process of transference in psychoanalysis might be an instance of the transformation of language from seriality to structure. 'A nouveau', he recalls, 'nous recherchons une intuition qui offre comme thème d'intelligibilité le fonctionnement incon- scient du discours; nous devons résoudre le paradoxe de cerner une évidence intérieure et dialectique d'une intelligibilité extérieure et analytique, une conscience [d'] un savoir qui est l'index d'un savoir systématique échappant aux normes de la conscience.'[132] But at least Verstraeten is certain that the problem is a philosophical one and not an ethnographic one and that it will not be solved by retreat- ing, like Lévi-Strauss, into scientism and physicalism.

Lévi-Strauss is nonetheless praised for having demonstrated in *La Pensée sauvage* the variety and complexity of the ways in which different social groups conceptualise their origins. This, however, only goes to show, in Verstraeten's view, that the rationalities revealed are founded on existential choices; ontologisation of the problem discloses that 'ce qui fait être le signe en tant que signe n'est pas de l'ordre du signe'.[133] For lexical arbitrariness, then, read freedom. For binary opposition, read an expression of the contra- dictory relationship that consciousness entertains with being. At every stage, says Verstraeten, the analyses of Lévi-Strauss require relocation at the ontological level which they fail to acknowledge; in the last analysis, a culture is a '*problématique problématisée par ce dont elle est la solution*'.[134]

Verstraeten goes on to deal accordingly with sacrifice, totemism, shamanism, the art of the Caduveo, the sociology of the Bororó and the homeostatic quality of the 'cold' societies. As a result, 'wild thought' is read in terms of the ethic as 'l'*abdication* du projet de *faire* la liberté, de la *réaliser* en la confrontant à l'origine même de son pouvoir pour la libérer de son autonomie symbolique et lui donner l'effectivité de la praxis'.[135] Both the ethnographer and the 'cold' societies themselves are thus deemed to have fallen short of their responsibilities.

This, then, is the response of *TM* to *La Pensée sauvage*; it is substantial and more constructive than Sartre's own brusque observations. It is also the first sustained discussion within the review of the *Critique*. It shows a readiness for *rapprochement* with Lacanian positions in particular and looks forward to a fourth period in which the construction of subjectivities in ideology might be fruitfully researched.

4

THE CRITIQUE OF
ACADEMIC KNOWLEDGE

The fourth period of *TM*'s history covers the eight years between October 1963 and July 1971. Not only is it longer than the preceding period and equally eventful, but it moves beyond the scope of the political commentary by Burnier to which I have referred previously and which goes only as far as the mid-sixties. For these reasons I shall give it greater space. It is also the most complex period in the sense that what I shall loosely call the two competing sets of terms of reference – the Sartrean–Gorzian and the structuralist–psychoanalytical – reach a degree of animosity which radically changes the character of the review in the aftermath of 1968.

Broadly speaking, the two tendencies observed hitherto remain unreversed: there is a gradual decline in the number of literary articles and a more dramatic rise in the amount of political material (see Appendix 3). The composition of the Editorial Board is nevertheless stable and the *direction collective* set up in 1961 lasts (with the exception of the dismissal of Péju) until the departure of Jeanson, who in 1967 becomes too busy to continue. It is only at the end of the period that the Board suffers major upheaval with the resignations of Pingaud and Pontalis. On the other hand, the stability is perhaps more apparent than real. The occasional delay in publication is attributed to the *incurie* of the Board and in 1964 there is a determined attempt to recruit additional editorial staff. Beauvoir comments as follows:

Il y avait dans la revue une lacune que nous souhaitions combler. Absorbés par leurs travaux, les membres du comité n'avaient plus le temps de se livrer à cet exercice difficile et assez ingrat: rédiger des notes sur la littérature, l'art, les ouvrages d'histoire ou d'économie. Nous avons pensé que les jeunes seraient plus disponibles et qu'ils saisiraient peut-être avec plaisir cette occasion de s'exprimer.[1]

I shall indicate the importance of some of this new blood in the course of this chapter. For the moment, I note merely that the editors are obliged to make an effort to hold on to their readers, particularly those in the militant student movement.[2] This is one of the factors explaining the increased editorial influence of Gorz.[3]

I intend, however, to discuss the activities of Gorz only at the end of the chapter; this is because he is instrumental in causing the withdrawal of Pingaud and Pontalis and because his dominance results in part from Pouillon's failure to sustain his own programme of conciliation and mediation. I shall proceed by looking at the different academic disciplines represented in Pouillon's special issue on structuralism (November 1966) and turn subsequently to the anti-academic forces marshalled by Sartre and Gorz.

The continuing participation of Pouillon

I noted in the previous chapter that Lévi-Strauss's *Mythologiques* do not find their way into *TM*. In fact, he makes only one further contribution before all public contact between him and the review is discontinued. This final text is the preface to the second edition of *Les Structures élémentaires de la parenté*, given the title of 'Vingt ans après' by Pouillon.

The bulk of this essay, which appears in September 1967, is addressed to fellow specialists. It also contains, however, a reconsideration of the nature–culture opposition; it is a revision which has some significance, since it comes as a last word to *TM* and as a reiteration of the criticisms addressed to Sartre and to the Western world in general. No longer, suggests Lévi-Strauss, is nature a realm that is to be opposed to culture by virtue of the objective presence or absence of articulated language or of social rules. Instead, he shifts its validity to another level by making of the distinction an expression of *pensée sauvage* that has been taken up by scientific thought. In its wild form, in other words, it is a classificatory stance adopted by the human species in order to assert its difference from, and superiority over, other species. Moreover, he adds, it has not only wild and scientific forms, but a savage form as well. Acceptable in societies which use it to codify their proximity to nature, it becomes morally unacceptable when used by an industrial culture to naturalise, and thus to dehumanise, those cultures that are not so divorced from nature as itself.

As an attempt to defend the existence or the memory of the societies to which Lévi-Strauss is attached, and as an accusation of ethnocentrism directed against those who attack the structuralist anthropology, his remarks remain consistent with those in *La*

Pensée sauvage. They point once more to the views of Lévy-Bruhl which are felt to inform the *Critique de la raison dialectique*. At the same time they serve as a reminder that, whatever the divergences of Sartre and Lévi-Strauss, and indeed as an expression of these divergences, both men now tend to have recourse to the basic postulate that savagery begins at home.

More interesting still is the apparent possibility that with this reformulation of the nature–culture distinction, Lévi-Strauss has relocated his object of study in a nexus of intentional acts. If this were true, it would open up his field to dialectical investigation in the Sartrean manner – and indeed, by making of the binary opposition which underpins the wild symbolic systems an expression of their existential choice, he does seem to come very near to satisfying the conditions of ontologisation imposed on the structuralist anthropology by Verstraeten. It seems more likely, however, that the revision of his scientistic binarism is a response to the philosophical critique offered in the same year by Jacques Derrida in *L'Ecriture et la différence*. It is probable that the greater intellectual challenge is now felt to come from periodicals like *Tel Quel*, and this is a good indication of how the younger intelligentsia favours reviews with no Sartrean allegiance.

The preface to the second edition of *Les Structures élémentaires de la parenté* is thus the end of a collaboration extending over eighteen years. To learn whether and how Lévi-Strauss's reputation is maintained in *TM*, it is necessary to turn to Sartre, to Verstraeten and to Pouillon as those most likely to continue the debate bearing on his work. Surveying the review, however, is not profitable in this connection, at least as far as Sartre and Verstraeten are concerned: the latter makes no further contributions, while articles by the former are rare and relate either to Flaubert or to immediate political issues such as the war in Vietnam. It is in other periodicals[4] that Sartre, too, makes his views known, and while they show a familiarity with Lévi-Strauss's recent writings, they dismissively reiterate positions established in 1960.

On the other hand, as I have mentioned, Sartre plans a critique of positivist sociologies of ethics, with Lévy-Bruhl and Lévi-Strauss as prime targets. The address delivered in the Gramsci Institute in Rome in 1964 and published as 'Détermination et liberté'[5] gives an idea of his approach. Before turning to it, however, it is worth summarising the directions taken by the interest in ethics. The phenomenological ethic that was intended to proceed from *L'Etre et le néant*, even though it reached in draft form the proportions now visible in the *Cahiers pour une morale*, did not survive the increasingly strong desire to elaborate a materialist base for the ontology. This latter work, embodied in the *Critique*, was deemed before 1960 to be that which would demonstrate, thanks to its mapping of the practico-inert, the redundancy or the mystificatory function of idealist ethical systems. After 1960, however, when anti-structuralism has been added to the anti-capitalist and anti-Stalinist strains of earlier thinking, the *Critique* is deemed the sufficient precondition of a renewed consideration of ethics.

This time Sartre's attitude is much more descriptive than prescriptive – his priority is no longer to establish a moral code by universalising his own personal intuitions. He is driven instead to challenge the positivist positions which regard individual moral freedom as the mere expression of an ignorance of a complex determinism. Against this view, he locates the moral value at the point of intersection of social norm and individual course of action, in order precisely to safeguard the relative unpredictability of the individual's conformity or deviation.

Everything thus turns on the nature of the relationship of person to norm. Sartre's choice of example – exogamy – suggests that the struggle against positivism is to be waged against its contemporary manifestation, the structuralism of Lévi-Strauss. What Sartre calls the *'paradoxe éthique'*[6] thus harks back to the discussions of Talayesva's *Sun Chief* a few years earlier: the 'paradox' is that the structural norm constituted by a set of marriage rules, the object of anthropological knowledge, is experienced by those observing the rules not as structural constraint but as custom and as the object of possible transgression. The fact that choice and norm coincide to a high degree, particularly in stable societies, does not permit the identification of the one with the other. Once again Sartre insists that history cannot be reduced to structure, nor interiority to exteriority, nor praxis to process; the ethic, in fact, is that which marks where freedom begins and where the determining power of the structure ends. A familiar view, no doubt, but now stated in a way which anticipates the end of the decade: the individual has a future within the system, but the future also holds out the possibility of the overthrow of the system by concerted ethico-political action.

The appearance in *TM* of the second preface to *Les Structures élémentaires de la parenté* should therefore be viewed as evidence of a continuing undercurrent of tension. This tension is not massive and does not inhibit, for example, the friendly relations that continue to exist between Lévi-Strauss and Beauvoir.[7] Pouillon, however, embodies it more than anyone else does and on occasion it is a source of embarrassment. In April 1970, for instance, when Lévi-Strauss is subjected to heavy irony by Claude Courchay, he is obliged to intervene. The following is a good sample of Courchay's approach: 'Lévi-Strauss a raison. Le terrain, tout est là. Il y est allé, lui. C'était en 18 . . . non, en 1940.'[8] Significantly, this breach of the respect hitherto professed by all parties occurs in the month of Gorz's iconoclastic 'Détruire l'université' article and preludes the first major attack by professional anthropologists on the terms of reference of their own discipline. Pouillon, who does not see fit to resign along with Pingaud and Pontalis, is nevertheless moved to announce in May 1970 that 'la publication de cet article [i.e. that of Courchay], qui ne peut certes pas passer pour une mise en question de l'œuvre de Claude Lévi-Strauss, ne saurait démentir l'attention que les *TM* lui ont toujours portée'.[9] His loyalties remain as they have been for many years – dual. By way of illustration, I shall look briefly at his commentary on the Sartre–Lévi-Strauss debate, at his own ethnographic practice and at his editorial record in the period.

Pouillon's comments on Sartre and Lévi-Strauss in *L'Arc* in 1965, which, by the way, make no mention of Verstraeten, suggest that the way out of the incompatibility of the dialectical and structuralist positions is not to continue the sequence of attempts of each to subordinate the other, but for both to be subsumed in a new and broader framework at present beyond the reach of either. He notes that the problem is also expressed at the level of the relations between Western anthropology and the societies which it studies. The latter, known and transformed if not destroyed, are caught up in a process of universal totalisation, yet are studied as synchronic systems abstracted from the whole. He asks whether this is a viable procedure. Is the anthropologist permitted to discount the extent to which observation exposes the observed to modification? This is of course the fundamental question on which *TM* has based its critique of the *sciences humaines*. In 1965 Pouillon is still not prepared to answer it. He notes only that it informs the divergences. Abstraction of the object of study from the imperialist context leads to the discovery of theoretical links of structural permutability and ends in a quest for universal mental mechanisms. Refusal to abstract, on the other hand, requires that intelligibility be sought in a theory of praxis.

Although Pouillon rehearses once again the intermediate position, he seems in 1965 to lean slightly towards the side of Sartre. He rejects, for example, Lévi-Strauss's definition of the dialectic and he wonders whether it is not the notion of the *totalisation sans totalisateur*, which emerges at the end of the *Critique*, that will lead to an adequately decentred existential subject compatible with some aspects of structuralism. Basically, his contribution is typical of his work as a whole: impressively coherent, yet so wary of categorical assertion that it acquires an oscillatory character. At this juncture, moreover, it is easy for him to slip into an understandable and familiar posture – that of waiting for a second volume.

In a similar position is the Belgian anthropologist Luc de Heusch. Known in the earlier stages of his career as a Lévi-Straussian, he comes to adopt towards his colleague an attitude more characteristic of the early days of *TM*. In 'Réflexions ethnologiques sur la technique' (December 1963), he discusses *La Pensée sauvage* in conjunction with the passage in *Tristes Tropiques* which maintained that writing has contributed more to oppression than to enlightenment.[10] Heusch prefers writing to be regarded as a means of potential liberation and his comments accordingly have a Sartrean flavour. The article marks his sole appearance in *TM*, but he gives elsewhere his view of the Sartre–Lévi-Strauss debate. He supports Lévi-Strauss 'lorsqu'il affirme d'un point de vue général, et contre Sartre, que la nécessité logique préexiste, en tant que réalité naturelle de l'esprit, à la praxis qu'elle modèle';[11] at the same time, he agrees explicitly with Verstraeten that kinship structures cannot be derived from the phonological model. The latter is more appropriate to the analysis of mythology,[12] although Heusch would prefer to see it deployed in the framework of research into the diffusion of myths. His own position is thus located somewhere between the two intransigences, as follows:

Une synthèse de ces deux types d'anthropologie nous paraît cependant impossible dans l'état actuel des choses, car Sartre et Lévi-Strauss ont choisi deux horizons différents, en se tournant délibérément le dos. Ils apportent l'un et l'autre des outils conceptuels remarquables sur des plans différents, et ils ont tort l'un et l'autre de vouloir en étendre l'efficacité au niveau qu'ils abandonnent ou traitent avec une certaine négligence.[13]

The merit of Heusch is to show that Pouillon's bipolarity is shared by others in the profession and is not merely the product of his close friendship with two intellectual rivals. It raises the interesting question of whether Pouillon is able to sustain his dual allegiance *sur le terrain* in Chad. I propose therefore to glance at his essay on the Hajerai peoples,[14] even though it is published, not unsurprisingly, outside *TM*.

In two visits to Chad, Pouillon had investigated the political and religious power structures of a group of villages. Curiously, his study focuses on 'l'organisation de ces groupes avant la colonisation [...] Elle est rédigée au présent, mais, dans bien des cas, c'est du passé qu'il s'agit.'[15] Abstraction of the object of study, then, from the colonial context. This is surprising, no doubt, but history nevertheless is not wholly disregarded, for a key role is given to the pre-colonial contact of the Hajerai with neighbouring Arab kingdoms. Pouillon claims that study of this past contact yields a hypothesis capable of handling the realities of colonialism, but unfortunately he is not able to demonstrate his case.

Pouillon's fieldwork is in fact resolutely structuralist: it studies the social groups comparatively, showing that the different political systems are variants of a common structure that only comparison can reveal. Each village unit is made intelligible in terms of its neighbours; each configuration of political and religious hierarchies is shown to signify diacritically. Consideration of their origin myths leads Pouillon to his principal conclusion – that there is a strong correlation between the heterogeneity of the social group and the degree of separation of political and religious power structures. From this correlation he derives the hypothesis that each village unit evolved from an original homogeneity (with a fused politico-religious power structure) towards heterogeneity (with separation of political and religious powers). The fact that no two villages are organised in the same way tells him that all are at different stages of this linear development, a feature which he ascribes to the varying degree to which they have absorbed immigrant groups in the course of their history.

Pouillon is clearly seeking to combine the lessons of both Sartre and Lévi-Strauss, and his achievement consists in describing a model in which the transition from one structured social formation to its successor is the result of immigration, a factor which impinges on the social group from without and impels a reorganisation that otherwise would not have taken place. Certainly, this represents an attempt to orchestrate the two points of view: the emphasis, nevertheless, is on the static rather than on the dynamic, on the power structures as configuration rather than as active organisation and disorganisation. It is clear from Sartre's comments on Pouillon's work,[16] comments admittedly made in passing, that this emphasis is found to be displeasing. Pouillon is criticised for relegating history to a contingent and secondary role as the passive stimulus of structural change. However much structural analysis may nod in the direction of history, feels Sartre, it never gives praxis its due prominence; it studies isolated formations of the practico-inert while at the same time parading its own illusory self-sufficiency.

From this position of stalemate, Pouillon embarks on his last attempt to find a resolution. In November 1966 he edits and introduces a special issue devoted to structuralism; it carries articles by Marc Barbut, Pierre Bourdieu, Jacques Ehrmann, Maurice Godelier, A.-J. Greimas and Pierre Macherey. His own contribution is primarily a work of conciliatory definition, and it is interesting to see that his first move is to describe structuralism as a synthetic investigation of totalities by reference to the interdependence of their parts; he stresses, in other words, its anti-atomism which, because it is a characteristic shared with the Sartrean dialectic, 'indique une base commune sous une opposition si souvent et fortement marquée'.[17] He goes on, however, to offer the following view of structure:

La structure est essentiellement la syntaxe des transformations qui fait passer d'une variante à l'autre et c'est cette syntaxe qui rend compte de leur nombre limité, de l'exploitation restreinte des possibilités théoriques. Cette restriction éventuelle ne s'expliquera donc pas par des hasards de fait et l'histoire n'est pas abandonnée à une prétendue et incompréhensible contingence. Tels cas et non tels autres se réalisent en raison des règles structurales de leur coexistence ou de leur succession.[18]

Rendering history structurally intelligible, however, seems unlikely to persuade Sartre that praxis has been restored to its prime position.

Similarly, Pouillon's discussion of the adjectival rivalry set in train by the *Critique* merely appears to bridge the epistemological and methodological gap:

L'existence en français des deux adjectifs 'structurel' et 'structural' permet de montrer que ce dualisme n'est nullement une ambiguïté: une relation est 'structurelle' quand on la considère dans son rôle déterminant au sein d'une organisation donnée; la même relation est 'structurale' quand on la prend comme susceptible de se réaliser de plusieurs manières différentes et également déterminantes dans plusieurs organisations. 'Structural' renvoie à la structure comme syntaxe, 'structurel' renvoie à la structure comme réalité.[19]

Structuralism, insists Pouillon, is not reductive. It has wide applicability and is not limited to the study of stable consensual

organisations: 'pour reprendre le langage de Sartre, le structuralisme est par essence totalisant, et ce qu'il cherche à totaliser, ce ne
sont pas nécessairement des symétries, des récurrences, ce sont
aussi bien des oppositions et des déséquilibres, non pour les effacer
mais pour comprendre le lien qui les maintient'.[20] Not only can it
address itself to conflictual social systems, it can also examine
structural variations situated in relations of diachronic sequence as
well as in relations of actual or possible synchronic coexistence.
Above all, then, it reveals the logic of historical transformations.
Pouillon acknowledges that a theory of praxis is the prerequisite for
understanding the actualisation of this logic, but in his view this
simply serves to underline the indissociability of praxis and structure: 'On ne peut penser l'une sans l'autre, et leur opposition n'est
peut-être si radicale que pour être celle des *deux* faces d'une *même*
réalité.'[21] All of which goes to show, says Pouillon, how wrong
Sartre is to turn his back on structuralism precisely at the moment
when his theory of praxis has found a way of accommodating the
notion of structure.

Pouillon's own approach may be described as the converse: he
seeks a place for praxis within structuralism. It is to this end that he
produces the special number of *TM* in 1966. It stresses the
applications of structuralism in precisely the fields visited by
'Questions de méthode' and by the first volume of the *Critique* –
Marxism, literature, sociology and history. Significantly, there is no
place for psychoanalysis: this is because Pouillon's line of mediation excludes the assertions of consciential heterogeneity that
Lacan or Pontalis would undoubtedly bring. As he remarks in a
lecture in 1968: 'Il suffit qu'on ait formulé *une fois* l'hypothèse
d'une causalité inconsciente pour qu'on ne puisse plus *jamais* s'en
défaire, pour qu'on ne puisse plus en aucun cas affirmer l'indépendance de sa pensée.'[22]

It is to Pouillon's credit that his special issue tries to bring history
into contact with linguistics; not only have both disciplines received
less attention than they merit, but in addition they have generally
been assumed to be mutually exclusive. Before I look at Greimas's
contribution to this debate, however, I shall briefly review *TM*'s
activities elsewhere in these fields.

The incidence of historical articles is once again low and the
sector is once again dominated by Guillemin. Worthy of mention
also is the extraordinarily powerful reconstruction by Jean-
François Steiner of the history of the Treblinka extermination
camp. Like Sartre's *Réflexions sur la question juive*, but with the

added advantage of detailed documentation, it combats the myths on which anti-semitism feeds, in this case the belief that the Jews went passively to their deaths. Steiner's account of Jewish resistance, which appears in extract in February 1966, may be read, as Beauvoir suggests in her preface to the book,[23] as a study of serialisation and of group formation wholly consistent with the descriptions to be found in the *Critique*.

As far as linguistics is concerned, it finds itself with the lowest of profiles. The name of Noam Chomsky might suggest otherwise, but his attack on the rhetoric of US foreign policy (May 1967) is better placed under the rubrics of ethics and politics; *TM* is not sufficiently interested in his academic work to ask why it should be so easily divorced from his political writings. Likewise, when Mounin discusses 'la notion de situation en linguistique et en poésie' (December 1966), *TM* fails to take up the obviously helpful invitation to develop an interest in pragmatics.

Greimas's 'Structure et histoire' thus enters a debate from which linguists and historians have been absent and which has been left unresolved by the philosophers and anthropologists. As a linguist who wishes to bring structuralist method to semantics and to understand language as ideological superstructure, he thus widens the discussion. His aims obviously bring him into interested contact with Lévi-Strauss's theory of myth, which he believes can assist in the task of identifying minimal units of meaning. On the other hand, his desire not to lose sight of the diachronic potential of Saussurean linguistics ensures an interest in historical transformations and makes him a likely ally of Pouillon.

It seems at the outset, however, that what Greimas is attempting is not a consideration of structure and history as two complementary terms which have somehow to be articulated into a theory of social change, but the now familiar structuralist analysis of history. He begins by conflating the diachronic and the syntagmatic, such that history and story become homologous, not only as sequences of events and utterances, but also inasmuch as their perception by a structuralist observer hastens their detemporalisation. As he proceeds, the distinction between synchrony and diachrony thus becomes less and less sharp until, after a consideration of the historiography of Braudel, he reaches the same structure-centred question as Pouillon: 'comment rendre compte des transformations diachroniques qui se situent entre structures juxtaposées sur une même ligne de succession temporelle?'[24]

Not surprisingly, Greimas is obliged to take the line followed by

Pouillon in his fieldwork – namely, that a structure is characterised by the limitations imposed on its combinatory possibilities. Moreover, since every structure is constituted in history, he is forced to conclude that 'l'histoire, au lieu d'être une ouverture, comme on n'a cessé de la répéter, est au contraire une clôture; elle ferme la porte à de nouvelles significations contenues, comme virtualités, dans la structure dont elle relève: loin d'être un moteur, elle serait plutôt un frein'.[25] Equally unsurprisingly, given the way in which the question is posed, he decides to endorse Lévi-Strauss in a manner that seems intended to be anti-Sartrean: 'Sans renier l'histoire, comme certains le prétendent, ni surtout le comparatisme historique, sa recherche vise, en définitive, à les intégrer dans une typologie générale des structures de signification.'[26] Once again the main question for *TM* – the acknowledgement of radical praxis – is not pursued. The principal benefit accruing from Greimas's contribution is the reminder that the Sartrean project has avoided equally systematically any real engagement with linguistics.

Both Verstraeten and Sartre, however, are aware of the need to remedy this, and hence the discussion published in the *Revue d'esthétique* in 1965. Sartre offers his long-standing view of language as a set of signifying tools to be made use of by the subject and once more tries to bring Saussurean terminology into the ambit of dialectical reason, revealing ever more clearly that he might be more successful if he were more familiar with the object of incorporation. He is unsure of the difference between signified and referent and always tends to conflate the signifier with the speaking subject. Hence his insistent and somewhat anxious adherence to his established views: 'Je repousse [...] le structuralisme en tant qu'il est derrière moi: je n'ai rien derrière moi. Je pense qu'un homme est au milieu, ou, s'il a des choses derrière lui, il les intériorise.'[27] No priority of language over speaker, then, unless it be in terms of the socio-historical antecedents analysable as practico-inert; to prove his point, Sartre goes on to discuss his own neologistic practice.

Precisely the same sort of limiting anti-structuralism is deployed by *TM* in its discussion of Michel Foucault's *Les Mots et les choses*. Sartre himself sets the tone by referring to the work as a geology rather than as an archaeology;[28] *TM*'s readers know already from Gorz's critical opinion of Lévi-Strauss's intellectual history that the geological connotes a reactionary positivism and a rejection of the dialectic. In the review itself, however, the attack is taken up by

Michel Amiot with 'Le relativisme culturaliste de Michel Fou-
cault' (January 1967) and in the same issue Beauvoir's friend
Sylvie Le Bon follows suit with 'Un positiviste désespéré: Michel
Foucault'.

Amiot and Le Bon amass serious objections to *Les Mots et les
choses*: it lacks method, proof and clarity; it can account neither
for the identification of epistemes nor for their discontinuous
sequentiality; it is therefore neither a work of history nor a work
of epistemology; above all, it fails to found knowledge in praxis
and to consider the position of the observer *vis-à-vis* the structures
of knowledge under observation. In the view of *TM* it is thus a
peculiarly regressive work which falls well short of matching the
achievements of Bachelard. The promise of Foucault, announced
in earlier years by Octave Mannoni, is now deemed to be
unfulfilled; the judgement, it seems, is definitive, for his subsequent work on the history of particular institutional discourses is
sadly ignored.

The PCF theorist Louis Althusser, on the other hand, is felt to
be of a different order of importance. Amiot, for example, con-
fesses himself 'tenté de penser que Sartre, lui, sous-estime la distance qui sépare Althusser de Foucault'.[29] And indeed, although
Sartre tends to dismiss the two in the same breath, the same is not
true of *TM*, which publishes a number of thoughtful assessments
of Althusser's work, including one by Pouillon. I shall consider
these in connection with the economic anthropology brought into
the review by Maurice Godelier.

The appearance of Godelier requires explanation in terms of
the editorial line followed by Pouillon in respect of anthropology.
Pouillon's fieldwork, as well as negotiating between Lévi-Strauss
and Sartre, is also interesting insofar as it regards the political and
religious structures of the Hajerai as interdependent and refuses
to reduce the former to an expression of the latter. This represents
something of a departure from French anthropological tradition
and a step towards the development of political anthropology as a
discipline. One might expect Pouillon to orient *TM* in this direction: given his desire to find a place for praxis in structuralism, the
political would seem a more appropriate object of study than the
religious or the mythological. This, however, does not happen.
Although he is an Africanist, Pouillon brings to *TM* nothing of the
work of British political anthropologists. Neither does he maintain
contact with Heusch, who is in the process of moving from Lévi-
Straussian structuralism into political anthropology. It is true that

a number of contributions are made by Pierre Clastres, but these arrive late in the period and are disappointingly lightweight.

The man who has already taken the lead in the elaboration of political anthropology in France is of course Georges Balandier, erstwhile contributor to *TM*. By 1967 he is affirming elsewhere that the discipline studies all that is most dynamic in non-Westernised societies and that all such societies, whether or not they possess an organised State apparatus, are nevertheless characterised by political activity. It is worth pointing out in passing that the view he ascribes to Sartre[30] – that historical consciousness reaches the 'primitive' societies only as a result of colonisation – is not an accurate record. It is nonetheless a reminder that Sartre's position is ill-defined: 'primitive' societies have never been his major preoccupation, as I have noted before, but at least he has clearly criticised Pouillon for explaining Hajerai political change by purely exogenous factors. Sartre may, indeed, be seen as oscillating between two stances: on the one hand, he regards segmentary societies as self-regulating and consequently less interesting than unstable societies; on the other, he refuses to regard them as mechanically homeostatic since presumably the *projet d'exploiter* knows no cultural boundaries, but he has no access to ethnographic data capable of supporting his point of view. *TM*, although a forum rather than a team research venture, has an ideal opportunity to move into the obscure area of the political in 'primitive' societies and to test the phenomenological descriptions of group formation set out in the *Critique*. Unfortunately, Pouillon does not draw up or implement this programme.

Instead, in a move nonetheless consistent with its Marxism, the review moves towards the political by way of the economic. In May 1965, it features an article on 'La notion de "mode de production asiatique"'' by Godelier, who, with Claude Meillassoux and Emmanuel Terray, is identified as one of the principal practitioners of a new French Marxist anthropology. Then, in Pouillon's special issue, Godelier supplies a consideration of 'Système, structure et contradiction dans *Le Capital*'. Finally, there appears in October 1968 'La première société d'abondance'[31] by the American anthropologist Marshall Sahlins.

Sahlins's article is precisely of the type required by *TM*, combining the presentation of ethnographic data with a critique of academic anthropology. Using research undertaken by American cultural ecologists, he shows that the pre-neolithic societies of hunters and gatherers did not live permanently in a state of near starvation but in one of considerable affluence: the latter is measured in terms of the hours of labour required to satisfy the material needs of peoples whose subsistence depended on high mobility. Quantification of both leisure time and of the potential capacity to sustain higher levels of population show hunting and gathering to be an extremely efficient mode of life. If hunters and gatherers have traditionally been depicted as slaves to the quest for food, then it is because, says Sahlins, unrealistically high levels of material need have been ascribed to them by bourgeois anthropologists using business economy models. Both his demonstrations and his conclusions display a real Sartrean verve, particularly in the predisposition to sweeping reversals of accepted opinion. The polemical edge, however, cuts both ways, and two consequences proceed from his main thesis.

First, having shown that hunters and gatherers, even when pushed by colonialism into less favourable terrains, achieve full satisfaction of their needs and regard acquisitiveness as something not to be acquired, Sahlins is able to represent material need as a cultural variable and to counterpose the Australian aborigines and modern industrial society. Discussing the latter, with its institutionalisation of scarcity and its creation of artificial needs, he cites the analyses of Gorz and thus brings anthropology into contact with one of *TM*'s dominant themes in the period, the critique of consumerism.

Secondly, basing his economics on studies of production and consumption rather than on psychologistic notions of individual and communal need, Sahlins asserts his 'substantivism' and rejects the 'formalism' of the bourgeois anthropologists. He is followed by Godelier, who denounces 'le postulat métaphysique que les hommes sont condamnés par nature à l'insatisfaction de leurs besoins'.[32] What is interesting here, of course, are the implications for the *Critique*. It is clear that in it Sartre considers the threat of material scarcity to be universal; less clear is the extent to which empirically identifiable groups have been able to stave off its actualisation. In his assertion that 'il existe des sociétés arriérées qui souffrent, en un sens, plus que d'autres de la disette ou de la suppression saisonnières des ressources alimentaires et qui pourtant sont classées à juste titre par les ethnographes comme des sociétés sans histoire, fondées sur la répétition',[33] he seems to be labouring under the ethnocentric prejudice subsequently swept away by Sahlins. If it were to avoid accusations of formalism, therefore, the second volume of the *Critique* would have to feed back the theoretical genesis of human groups into spatially and temporally localisable societies, in such a way as to reverse the tendency of the first volume to apparent formalist universalisation. This would give Sartre a chance to go much more deeply into his concept of reciprocity, for its phenomenologisation has not so far endowed it with clear economic or political definition.

All this makes the appearance of Godelier in *TM* very welcome, for his Marxist economic anthropology offers a new perspective. He resumes the attack on Stalinism that the review has consistently waged and also deals with Marxism at a theoretical level, something which has always been rather rare in *TM* and which has placed contributors like Goldmann in a small category of their own. On the other hand, whereas the review has tended to explore how far structuralism is consistent with Sartrean Marxism, Godelier's approach is to ask how far Marxism is consistent with structuralism. At least this represents a salutary return to Marx and to Engels, authorities who had been obscured by the claims of both Sartre and Lévi-Strauss to be their rightful heirs.

Godelier's article on the Asiatic mode of production contains no critique of Stalinist anthropology such as is to be found in the work of Bastide.[34] Its main concern is to stress the hypothetical and non-dogmatic character of the writings of Marx and Engels on pre-capitalist modes of production. Godelier traces the various appearances of the Asiatic mode in the evolutionary schemata elaborated at different times by Marx and notes its omission from Engels's *Origins of the Family*. Based on a complex division of labour but also on the communal ownership of land, the Asiatic mode is typically regarded as the transitional form leading away from primitive communities towards societies based on exploitation. In the view of Godelier, Engels discarded the concept while under the influence of the evolutionist and ethnocentric Lewis Henry Morgan. This development, although unfortunate, at least showed the readiness of Marxism to incorporate the latest research. On the other hand, it provided Stalin with just the monolinear evolutionary schema that he needed to justify the political and economic programmes of the 1930s. Godelier concludes that Marxism must envisage the probability of multilinear evolutions and that the Asiatic mode of production is a useful concept, provided that it is not assumed inevitably to usher in forms of Oriental despotism. In November 1966 he is thus able to promise a 'Marx largement inconnu des marxistes'.[35]

The advent of Godelier assumes full significance when seen in the context of *TM*'s attitude to Althusser. Here it is necessary to digress. It will be recalled that Beauvoir records the recruitment of younger contributors in 1964: among them is Nicos Poulantzas, lecturer in the philosophy of law, who 'préparait d'importants ouvrages d'économie politique'.[36] The main focus of Poulantzas's early articles is the place of the State in Marxist theory: at the level of strategy his work is consistent with the contention embodied, as I shall show, in Gorz's revolutionary reformism and in Régis Debray's rejection of *golpismo* – namely, that the State apparatus is not at all neutral or capable of being taken over in an unproblematic manner. It is Gorz, indeed, as political editor, who creates the space for Poulantzas's examination of British Marxism in March 1966. A regular *chronique marxiste* is projected and designed to 'rassembler les moyens théoriques susceptibles d'éclairer l'histoire du marxisme [...] cette possibilité nous est donnée par le marxisme lui-même, seule théorie capable de se situer et de se critiquer selon ses propres principes'.[37] The rubric does not last long in name; its synthetic motivation, however, is easily recognisable. One of the best debates that it stimulates is the consideration of Althusser two months later.

Poulantzas begins by asserting the importance of Althusser as an innovatory theorist working within the PCF. The text under discussion is *Pour Marx* and Poulantzas is able to inform *TM* readers that the mechanical base–superstructure model of vulgar Marxism has been dropped in favour of the theory of the determination by the economic in the last instance. This is a view reminiscent of that of Lefort in 1951. It is also one that Godelier dwells on at length. It takes social structure to be a set of interacting and discrete instances or agencies (economic, political, ideological, theoretical), each enjoying relative autonomy from, and relative determination of, the others. This conception of social structure as a constellation of instances with variable force fields, held together by economic factors which are not necessarily located in a dominant economic instance, leads Althusser to affirm the existence of an epistemological break between Hegel and Marx. For Hegel, time was a unified linear continuum, in which any sectional cut would reveal the motivating spirit of the epoch concerned; Marx now becomes non-Hegelian insofar as his concept of history has to incorporate different time-scales, each relatively autonomous instance having its own evolutionary movement.

It is this heterochrony that most interests Poulantzas. Having already investigated the compatibility of the *Critique* with Marxism,[38] he is enthusiastic about the possibilities apparently offered by Althusser of finding a way through the history–structure impasse that has puzzled *TM* hitherto. What both Lévi-Strauss and Sartre fail to appreciate, suggests Poulantzas, is the degree of overdetermination at once separating, binding and ranking the discrete instances of social reality. Lévi-Strauss is nearer the mark in his correlation of different levels, but lacks a sense of their mutual implication; his social totality is simple in the sense that its synchrony is completely undifferentiated. Sartre, meanwhile, says Poulantzas, purveys a Hegelian temporality in which inaction between levels always reduces to the consequences of praxis. Closed synchrony on the one hand, open monolinear diachrony on the other – 'ces deux pensées', he wonders, 's'exclueront-elles réciproquement dans la mesure où elles seraient deux aspects d'une même problématique invariable?'[39] Poulantzas no doubt pushes Lévi-Strauss and Sartre further apart than they actually are, in order to make room for Althusser, but to a certain extent they are themselves to blame for this. That Sartre should begin to be thought of as simplistic in this way, in the absence of the second volume of the *Critique*, to some extent explains the complexity of his colossal study of Flaubert.

As Poulantzas's title ('Vers une théorie marxiste') implies, Althusser's work is considered promising. More than that cannot be said, since too many questions remain unanswered: the nature of his dependence on psychoanalysis, the validity of his distinction between science and ideology, the implications for political strategy, and so on. Robert Paris's contribution also has an explicit title – 'En deçà du marxisme': in his view, Althusserian Marxism cannot be understood outside the context of the policies of the PCF. Only a theorist interested in separating theory and practice and in neutralising the intellectuals, he says, would jettison the concept of praxis and regress so spectacularly to Kantian idealism. Paris probably reads the French situation in the light of events in Italy, where the impact of Gramsci had been dulled by such anti-Hegelians as Della Volpe.

At this point, Pouillon steps in to provide a third judgement. He agrees with Althusser that Marx does more than merely correct Hegel: Marx reapplies the Hegelian dialectic and gives it a new object – praxis. On the other hand, to oppose Marx to Hegel, as Althusser does, is to fall into the Hegelian trap; Althusser would have been better employed attempting to transcend the opposition of Sartre and Lévi-Strauss. As far as the *structure à dominante* and overdetermination are concerned, Pouillon looks forward to Godelier. In his view, Althusser persistently confuses the bourgeoisie–proletariat contradiction (within the relations of production) with the contradiction between relations of production and forces of production; this is important because it is the second that impels political change.

Despite the initial hopes that Althusser could break out of the history–structure impasse, *TM* adopts an increasingly hard line towards him. Sartre's interview in *L'Arc* in 1966 offers brief and negative comment. In general, his attitude is that anything which is anti-Hegelian must be pre-Hegelian, except, that is, his own antipathy to the *esprit de survol*. He therefore reduces Althusser to Descartes, while André Glucksmann, writing on 'Un structuralisme ventriloque' (March 1967), is no less dismissive and designates Kant as the major intellectual force behind *Lire le Capital*. After 1968, *TM* is quite sure that Althusser has nothing to offer. François George robustly reiterates Paris's accusations of Stalinism in June 1969; Sartre is more conciliatory in his discussions with *Il Manifesto* (January 1970), but this is because by then Althusser is deemed to be a man of the past and because everything that is remotely useful has been taken on board.

Of all the contributions that fall within the Althusserian problematic, there is no doubt that that of Godelier is the most interesting. 'Système, structure et contradiction dans *Le Capital*', the third article in Pouillon's special issue, compares Marx's work on capitalism with Lévi-Strauss's study of kinship systems and, in so doing, draws Lévi-Strauss back into Marxist acceptability. 'L'immense portée de la démonstration'[40] in *Les Structures élémentaires de la parenté*, he says, is based on its similarities with *Capital*, similarities hitherto unnoticed. In the first place, both works describe structures (economic or kinship) which are real but invisible to the members of the communities concerned. Secondly, both observe the principle that the structure under consideration must be studied in terms of its internal logic before any attempt is made to specify the logical conditions governing its appearance: the structural precedes the genetic, while both precede the diachronic study of actual economic and social formations. Marx, says Godelier, did not study the history of capitalism: he studied its structure, the relation of labour and capital, as well as, subsequently, the structural prerequisites for the development of capitalism. In the same way (and did he not dedicate his study to the Morgan beloved of Engels?) Lévi-Strauss analysed kinship systems and the logical possibilities of the transformation of one system into another. In general, Godelier's attitude towards Lévi-Strauss is one of great respect. He regrets, however, that the *Mythologiques* of later years have failed to fulfil the promise of the early work.[41]

On the other hand, Godelier makes no mention of Sartre. Absence of reference may be taken as absence of endorsement and the following quotation makes this clear. Godelier is commenting on the fact that, while initially the capitalist forces of production develop in a manner favourable to the system as a whole, a point is reached at which their development begins to prejudice the system and to initiate its transformation into a new and incompatible entity. He then remarks:

Cette contradiction est donc *inintentionnelle*. Elle est un résultat de l'action de tous les agents du système et du développement du système lui-même, mais elle n'a jamais été le projet d'aucune conscience, elle n'a été un but poursuivi par personne. Marx met donc en évidence l'existence *d'aspects du réel qui ne se réfèrent à aucune conscience et qui ne s'expliquent pas par la conscience.* C'est le mode de production lui-même, la mise en valeur du capital, qui crée ce résultat 'sans le savoir'.[42]

What is extraordinary is not that this is what Sartre wrote about colonialists in 1956 and that the French intellectual memory should be so short, but that the consciousness of the oppressed has been so completely edited out. Nothing illustrates more graphically the extent to which the previous ten years have 'cyberneticised' the Marxism which Sartre has striven to 'existentialise'.

However fascinating Godelier's views are on superstructural institutions performing infrastructural functions and on multilinear evolutionary models, however useful his contributions to the eradication of vulgar Marxism, it is nonetheless clear that his analyses lend themselves to the elaboration of technocratic positions and, as such, run counter to the political line of Gorz and Sartre. As far as Pouillon is concerned, the political situation that *TM* seeks to create does not ultimately correspond to the sort of editorial initiatives that he favours. Without ever being forced out of *TM* in the manner of Pingaud and Pontalis, he nevertheless becomes less effective during the militant 1960s. His moment of editorial crisis arrives in 1971 and I shall deal with it at the end of the chapter.

The brief tenure of Pingaud

In 1961 *TM*'s readers were probably surprised to see Bernard Pingaud join the team and take up a position alongside Beauvoir as joint literary editor, for only six years previously she had denounced him as a right-wing ideologue.[43] In the interim, however, he had been a colleague of Pouillon at the Assemblée Nationale and had been suspended from duties for having signed the 'Manifeste des 121' in 1960. From 1961 onwards, he successfully complemented Beauvoir and brought to *TM* a greater interest in poetry, in avant-garde literature and in the *nouveau roman* in particular. It is due in part to his efforts that the literary content of the review increases once more and that literature in translation loses its predominance. His editorship begins to wane from the middle of 1966, and as he becomes more interested in psychoanalysis, so he is increasingly identified with Pontalis. They eventually resign together in circumstances which I shall describe in the next section.

As far as the role of literature in *TM* is concerned, there are a number of points that need to be noted. The first is that, consistent with its loss of prestige after 1952 and with the penetration of the review by competing modes of thought, literature becomes an object of study amenable to theoretical approaches far removed from existential psychoanalysis. In Pouillon's special issue in 1966, for example, two articles highlight the availability of techniques deriving from the Lévi-Straussian study of myth: Jacques Ehrmann's 'Les structures de l'échange dans *Cinna*', which adopts them, and Pierre Macherey's 'L'analyse littéraire, tombeau des structures', which is hostile – although not for Sartrean reasons.

Ehrmann reads the Cornelian dilemmas as expressions of the transactions that bind the characters of the tragedy together. His own debt to Mauss and to Lévi-Strauss is visible in the descriptions of Cornelian dignity as *mana* and of the heroine as object of exchange. The close attention paid to the reciprocity imperative, however, does not carry him beyond an 'ethnographic' study of the *dramatis personae*. Moreover, his failure to extrapolate to other structural features of *Cinna* and to the ideological context of its creation plays into the hands of Macherey.

Although Macherey's name is usually associated with that of Althusser, his first article in *TM*, 'L'opéra ou l'art hors de soi' (written with François Regnault and published in August 1965) is more reminiscent of the work of Foucault. It sketches the history of opera as a venture of total symbolic social inclusion, much as Foucault's history of madness is a study of real social exclusion. Two further contributions, however, subsequently gain wider currency: 'Borges et le récit fictif' (January 1966) is included in *Pour une théorie de la production littéraire*, published by Maspero later in the same year; 'L'analyse littéraire, tombeau des structures', on the other hand, is taken from the Maspero volume, in which it appears dated November 1965, and after amendment is given to *TM* in November 1966.

Macherey's theoretical activity seeks to acquire scientific status from the Marxism within which it operates. His most significant move is to separate literature and ideology and to make of them discrete units within a given economic system. According to this view, the economy gives rise to, and is confirmed by, an appropriate ideology. The literary artefact, meanwhile, enjoys, not independence from, but relative autonomy within, both economic and ideological contexts. This autonomy is attributed by Macherey to the fact that ideology never enters literature unprocessed: already illusion (that is to say, systematic and non-reflexive misrecognition of reality), it is transformed by literature into a fiction that is not continuous with the illusion which previously it was. Macherey concludes that the fictionalisation of ideology assists in its identification and that fiction might thus be said to denounce ideology; literature, in his view, reverses the misrecognition process and in so doing affords the critic an understanding of how both the process and its reversal operate.

In November 1966, Macherey supplements this thesis with objections to the dominant forms of structuralist literary description, those of Barthes and Genette. The critic, he allows, has the right and even the duty to turn to linguistics for a theory of language, but not to transplant mechanically its conceptual models or to ignore the material conditions informing linguistic productivity. It cannot be said that this article founds a literary science in a convincing manner. Too much of Macherey's procedure and his debt to Lacan by way of Althusser remain unexplicated. Lacan, indeed, is the great 'unsaid' here, just as he is in *TM*'s discussions of Althusser. In any case, having had his say, Macherey departs and thereafter there is no literary criticism in *TM* that can be regarded as following his line. Indeed, there is very little of any kind. Were it not for *Les Mots* (and traces of *L'Idiot de la famille*, which I shall deal with in the Conclusion), Michel Rybalka's outline of an existential psychoanalysis of Boris Vian (January 1968) would represent a rehearsal of the dominant theoretical discourse of the immediate post-war years, which, for *TM*, would be completely incongruous and anachronistic.

But what of *Les Mots*? Sartre's autobiography appears in *TM* in

October and November 1963, at the very beginning of the fourth period, and its presence poses many questions. Is, for example, its status that of existential psychoanalysis? How far is it consistent with 'Questions de méthode'? How precisely does it relate to *L'Idiot de la famille*? What is its significance in terms of Freudianism? How far is it informed by academic anthropological discourse? How far does it represent a policy statement superseding those embodied in the 'Présentation' and in *Qu'est-ce que la littérature*? How far does it inhibit the literary editors of the review?

I have endeavoured to answer some of these questions elsewhere[44] and will merely observe here that *Les Mots* is indeed easy to read as a polemical intervention in the intertextual and interdisciplinary space mapped by *TM*. Specifically, it mobilises the fieldwork of Leiris and of Métraux in a radical attempt to eradicate what might be called Freudianism's familial monotheism. It uses anthropology, in other words, to fight an anti-colonialist struggle against the grandpaternal voice which Sartre hears echoing at the origins of all his motivations and which, by habitually 'thinking against himself', he constantly strives to shake off. *Les Mots* also enlists the Mauss of Lefort, rather than the Mauss of Lévi-Strauss, to track the inequitable reciprocities of Sartre's childhood years; in doing so, it shows that his resistance to Freud is not merely a symptom, but also an expression of the ethical and political terms of reference of the synthetic anthropology.

I say 'not merely a symptom', because it is evident from the *qui perd gagne* logic that governs *Les Mots* that Sartre is also prepared to concede implicitly a symptomatic element in his own theoretical position. (Pontalis is no doubt correct to accord to *Le Scénario Freud* a powerful influence on the composition of *Les Mots*.)[45] It is, after all, difficult to combat effectively what is unacknowledged, and Sartre's very anti-Freudianism requires concessions to Freud in order to be waged. This is why questions of methodology remain paramount and why the apparent absence of the technical trappings of existential psychoanalysis should not deceive.

In fact, *Les Mots is* an existential psychoanalysis, the work of a writer identifying his fundamental project, and is consistent with the premisses of 'Questions de méthode'. Of its two parts, 'Lire' and 'Ecrire', the second is the progressive moment that assumes and endeavours to transcend the determinations identified in the first. Process and reception, praxis and production, these are the successive moments of the story narrated. The switch is manifest in the changing function assigned to books: from an original status as

object of taboo (sacramental and phobic), they later lend themselves to manipulation as *choses–ustensiles* in the context of the
specific projects that *Les Mots* is organised to reveal.

These projects require only the briefest of mentions here: the
flight from the precariousness of life into the certainty of literary
glory and into the community of cultural saints; the confusion of
signs and referents; the overinvestment in the imaginary; the desire
to redeem by and in art both the self and the world. All this is
recorded succinctly by Sartre. It is more urgent here to consider the
third part of *Les Mots* – that is to say, the last six pages – in which
the projects are submitted to critical evaluation. This, after all, is
where Sartre's ethnography of the bourgeois family becomes
synthetic, where the analysand confronts the analyst and where the
transcendencies of the progressive moment (*écrire*) are themselves
transcended. It is in this section that *Les Mots* becomes irrevocably
distinct from an empirical socio-historical study of a *fin-de-siècle*
family and begins to approach the standards of reflexivity set by
Leiris.

What happens in *Les Mots* is that the regressive–progressive
method is brought to bear on the research worker himself, with the
result that each moment tends to invade the other. *Lire* investigates
the conditioning, while *écrire* follows the development of the person
within the *situation*. In the course of the investigation, however, it is
realised that the progressive moment reveals little progress, particularly as far as the persistence of the father-figure is concerned,
since the determinations and the constraints are much greater than
had at first appeared to be the case. As a result, the freedom of the
synthetic anthropologist comes to express itself as comprehension of
determinations rather than as detachment from them. Beyond comprehension, no further detachment is possible, except insofar as it
can generate the refusal to perpetuate the material and social conditions that presided over the genesis of the investigator.

Sartre writes his autobiography at a time when he is discovering
the weight of the past and the power of the practico-inert. He seems
to arrive at the knowledge of himself that Beauvoir possessed in
1946:

Sartre refuse de s'identifier avec son passé. Il reconnaît ses fautes avec une
sincérité déconcertante; il peut se décrire et se critiquer avec une stricte
impartialité. La vérité, c'est qu'il a déjà cessé de se reconnaître dans le
Sartre précédent dont il parle. Sa véritable identité existe dans l'avenir,
voilà pourquoi il n'éprouve aucune vanité au sujet de ce qu'il a accompli
dans le passé.[46]

The judgement is perhaps harder-headed than that imagined by Sartre for his hero Kean, whose beautiful exorcist Anna Damby finds 'si émouvant un homme qui lutte contre sa langue'.[47] In *Les Mots* what has been repressed returns and the past catches up with Sartre; so far is his purpose confounded that what ultimately emerges is a morality of ambiguity. Even as he learns more of why he always wished to be what he was not and not to be what he was, the knowledge radically threatens his venture. This is because the greater the degree of coincidence between analysand and analyst is, the greater the incidence of ambivalence and duplicity and the greater the interpenetration of regression and progression: 'nos intentions profondes sont des projets et des fuites inséparablement liés'.[48] Hence the cyclothymic rhythm which Pontalis had detected in Leiris's autobiography, too; hence Sartre's desperately literary farewell to literature.

I do not mean to suggest, however, that *Les Mots* proposes an ethic. The more synthetic it becomes, the less it is able to specify ethical universals – these, after all, are more appropriate to an analytic mentality prepared to write abstract rules and to bracket out of this process the inherence of the rule-writer. Seen in this light, it is clear that as long as the synthetic anthropology hankered after its first formal moral code it could not develop properly. It lacked the necessary reflexivity at source.

In respect of the new viability of the ethic in the 1960s, *Les Mots* stands alongside the *Critique* as one of the modes, reflexive rather than theoretical, of attaining the comprehension of the dynamics of sociality, on which the ethic depends. It is difficult not to conclude, for example, that Sartre's reflections on his childhood encouraged him to ponder the importance of baptism and initiation rites and to add the following rider to his own nostalgia for the *ens causa sui*: 'Naître, c'est se produire comme spécification du groupe et comme ensemble de fonctions (charges et pouvoirs, dettes et crédit, droit et devoir).'[49] To be born and to grow up is to engage in praxis, much of which appropriates and revivifies the practico-inert that constitutes the circumambient culture. Young Poulou is thus recalled, by the Sartre old enough to be his father, as a child suffering material affluence and psychological dispossession in a micro-social group permeated by the imperialist and revanchist ideologies of the society at large. His resentment takes the form of a spectacular generosity that is never to fade: 'L'une des qualités qui impressionnent tous ses amis, c'est l'immense générosité de Sartre. Il donne sans compter son argent, son temps et lui-même: il est toujours prêt à s'intéresser aux autres mais il ne veut rien en retour; il n'a besoin de personne.'[50] The phenomenology of this generosity is precisely that outlined by Lefort in 1951: generosity as violence and attempted subjugation. Its anti-structuralism is now enormously boosted by being worked through in the reflexivity of the synthetic anthropologist.

Les Mots, by recording an immoral genealogy, embodies a genealogy of moralism, together with the prospectively pre-ethical decision to abandon the latter. Mauss and the gift, deployed in the combat against psychoanalysis and structuralism, are also required to play their part in a programme of politicisation, as Sartre looks forward to a structural reciprocity that will permit non-violent generosity. There is therefore no ethic in *Les Mots*, only its precondition – the materialist critique of the moralist.

The *autocritique* affects literature inasmuch as it acknowledges a tendency to confuse 'l'art d'écrire et la générosité'.[51] In 1963, this appears as a partial repudiation of *Qu'est-ce que la littérature?*: Sartre's interest in literature remains, but is now subordinated to the construction of the society that will render morality possible. Gone is the view that literature is of itself *necessarily* committed or that it anticipates, in terms of writer–reader reciprocity, the society that is yet to be built. Sartre thus settles for an *engagement* purged of its illusions and its euphoria:

Longtemps j'ai pris ma plume pour une épée: à présent je connais notre impuissance. N'importe: je fais, je ferai des livres; il en faut; cela sert tout de même. La culture ne sauve rien ni personne, elle ne justifie pas. Mais c'est un produit de l'homme: il s'y projette, s'y reconnaît; seul, ce miroir critique lui offre son image.[52]

Les Mots is clearly not a piece of confessional literature; in the context of an absent ethic a *mea culpa* makes little sense and yields only an appearance of virtue and generosity which invites suspicion. Rather, *Les Mots* is a work of synthetic anthropology which systematically denies validity to confessions: it exorcises at the same time both delusion and guilt, a venture consistent with Freudian psychoanalysis but which is here to be perceived as anti-Freudian and as politically motivated. It confirms that *TM*'s evangelical mission is over and that the task of politicisation is well under way. The role ascribed to literature in the review will in due course be secondary and occasional; this shift of emphasis is brought about by the speed of political events as well as by changes in Editorial Board membership and policy.

It should be noted in passing that the autobiography's date of composition is not the same as that of its publication. Essentially, it is a work of the mid-fifties. Its slightly anachronistic character misled many of its readers. Like a number of Sartrean texts it promises a sequel but, as if to enshrine the paradoxes of reflexivity in the tortuousness of chronology, the autobiographical writing which follows it (the articles on Nizan and on Merleau-Ponty) is actually published before it, while the writing that precedes it (the *Carnets de la drôle de guerre*) is published posthumously.

The implications of *Les Mots* for Sartre, then, are easily stated: there is to be no decrease in political activity, but the attention given to literature will inevitably be reduced. This, on the face of it, has little significance for *TM*, for not since 1951 has it been able to call itself primarily a literary review. Sartre's position in 1966 is formulated in a very characteristic manner for the benefit of Pingaud: 'Pour lutter contre la faim, il faut changer le système politique et économique, et la littérature ne peut jouer dans ce combat qu'un rôle très secondaire.'[53] By this time, Sartre regularly counterposes physical starvation and literary satisfaction,[54] dispensing with the latter in favour of political action. He cannot expel it altogether, however, and the fact that he borrows Margaret Kennedy's title, *The Fool of the Family*, for his study of Flaubert raises interesting questions – for in the Kennedy novel a child dies of malnutrition.[55] The relative unimportance of literature is hugely important to Sartre: the tension that it generates conditions his view of the role of the intellectual and marks out the parameters of his reflexivity. For this reason, *L'Idiot de la famille* will be as great a test of the synthetic anthropologist as *Les Mots*.

His actions in the period under consideration, however, testify to his priorities. He makes no literary contributions to *TM* following *Les Mots*, with the exception of two draft sections of *L'Idiot de la famille* – and this as the result of persuasion by Pingaud. He reiterates his opposition to the *Tel Quel* group, which appears to him to have opted for a form of literary practice as non-communication and as non-revelation of the state of the world.[56] He refuses the Nobel Prize for Literature in 1964 in order, among other things, to preserve his position as an independent producer of literature in the Cold War context. His adaptation of Euripides's *The Trojan Women* is undertaken specifically to bring out its anti-imperialist content and its relevance to 1965. His most significant sponsorship is of the explicitly anti-capitalist literary works of Georges Michel.

Before considering the editorial contributions of Beauvoir and

Pingaud, it is worth returning to Sartre's 1965 discussion with Verstraeten, this time in connection with the long-standing distinction between prose and poetry. Sartre now takes the opportunity to recast it, with the help of the conceptual apparatus of the *Critique* and in reaction to the positions of the *Tel Quel* group. What emerges, broadly speaking, is a tripartite typology of writing, in which one median and two polar categories segment the spectrum of textual production. On the one hand, there is poetry – an infantile and narcissistic enterprise undertaken by an *écrivain*, an enterprise which Sartre calls retrospective inasmuch as it consists of abdication by the writer in the face of language as practico-inert. On the other, there is the prose of the philosopher – a mature programme of communication implying reciprocity with the reader and undertaken by an *écrivant*; this is a praxis that is necessarily prospective, oriented towards the future and towards transcendence of linguistic and other determinations. What lies between is literary prose, and although Sartre does not mention *Les Mots*, it clearly occupies this position, claiming a synthetic grasp of its own ambivalence. This discussion, however, takes place outside *TM*, and the only echo in the review is an article by Michel Beaujour (May/June 1968). This text reinforces Sartre's *autocritique* by revaluing the earlier attitudes towards Ponge. Beaujour's conclusion – 'nulle poésie n'est révolutionnaire'[57] – shows the extent to which Pingaud's editorship must have been problematic.

Yet it would be a mistake to think that Beauvoir lines up behind Sartre and that Pingaud's penchant for poetry progressively excludes him. Beauvoir's position, in fact, is more reminiscent of *Qu'est-ce que la littérature?* Literature retains for her its importance as a source of solidarity; in it, or through it, the particular is universalised as the imaginations of writer and reader commune. Of this 'lieu privilégié de l'intersubjectivité'[58] she supplies two excellent examples: *Une mort si douce* (May 1964) and *L'Age de discrétion* (May 1967). She, presumably, is responsible for the wide range of French and foreign prose writers featured by *TM*. Considerable space continues to be given to the anti-Stalinist authors working inside the Eastern bloc (Brandys, Gera, Kundera, Solzhenitsyn, Tvardovsky, Voinovich), to Latin Americans like Carlos Fuentes and to Italians such as Elsa Morante, Cesare Pavese and Leonardo Sciascia. Many of the names are personal acquaintances or at least reminders of travels undertaken in the period – the Japanese Tanizaki and Yoshie, for example. As for the French,

Alain Badiou and Maurice Pons make significant contributions, as do Annie Leclerc and Georges Pérec, two 'romanciers en herbe'.[59]

As far as Pingaud is concerned, it is true that between 1964 and 1969 *TM* carries a substantial amount of poetry. The list of poets is too long to reproduce *in extenso*: it contains 35 names, including that of Henri Corbin, the Guadeloupian whose work was first presented by Leiris in 1950. Pingaud's literary views, however, are not at all wholly incompatible with those of Sartre. His interest in psychoanalysis, structuralism and the *nouveau roman* does not preclude a concern for the political implications of writing. He takes fewer opportunities than does Pouillon to express his views directly, yet in the early sixties his position seems to be similar: it is one of loyalty to the Sartrean way of thinking, combined with a desire to complement it with structuralist intuitions.

Two texts, 'La main chaude' (July 1964) and the preface to a collection of essays published one year later,[60] reveal Pingaud's view of the activity of the writer. He follows Sartre closely: writing, for him, has two complementary movements – centripetal (that of the *écrivain*, artistic invention and the discovery of what is known but unformulated) and centrifugal (that of the *écrivant*, whose experience legitimises statements concerning the reality of the world). He goes on:

On a beaucoup reproché à Sartre d'avoir dit qu'aucune œuvre ne tenait devant la douleur d'autrui. C'est là pourtant une vérité évidente, et il n'est même pas besoin de parler de douleur, il suffit de parler d'existence. Ecrire est une façon d'exclure le monde, mais l'œuvre ne saurait s'affirmer face au monde que si le monde à son tour l'exclut, que s'il peut se passer d'elle.[61]

In the end, Pingaud's view is consistent with, although broader than, that implied by *Les Mots*, both in terms of definitions of literature and in terms of the policy of *TM*. The writer uses language to set at a distance the self that is constituted in language: success is measured not only by the extent to which language may then be used to intervene in the world, but also by the extent to which the writer learns that intervention must never be merely linguistic. Pingaud regards himself as, in Barthes's terms, both *écrivain* and *écrivant*, and, in Sartre's terms, as a producer of both *sens* and *signification*.

Why, then, does he resign from the Editorial Board in 1970? It is not because he can no longer tolerate sharing responsibility with Beauvoir, nor because he is too indulgent towards the *nouveau roman*. A 1964 comment is interesting:

L'esprit de parti n'est pas mon fort: je me sentirai toujours, à l'intérieur d'une cause, le traître de cette cause, le 'modéré', celui qui trouve qu'on exagère, que les problèmes ne sont pas si simples, qu'il y a du vrai dans les raisonnements de l'adversaire. Du moins ai-je jeté l'ancre quelque part et fait ce qu'il fallait pour me compromettre. Quand le doute me vient, il me suffit de regarder autour de moi pour savoir que ce camp est celui de la conscience et de la générosité.[62]

Prophetic words: perhaps Pingaud could foresee the days when his anchor would no longer hold. Ultimately, he leaves because his median position becomes increasingly difficult to sustain. The controversy with Sartre over 'L'homme au magnétophone' (April 1969) is a source of great tension; the resignation itself, however, comes as a result of Gorz's call to 'détruire l'université' in 1970.

In retrospect, Beauvoir sees the signs of disaffection coinciding with the events leading up to May 1968:

Quand dans les numéros 64 et 65 [*sic*; she is referring to the years] Kravetz et d'autres après lui réclamèrent 'la Sorbonne aux étudiants' et attaquèrent vivement les cours magistraux, Pontalis et Pingaud furent hostiles à ces thèses. Ils ne le manifestèrent pas mais en privé ils ne cachaient pas que certaines des positions prises par la revue les heurtaient.[63]

Sartre's subsequent judgement – that Pingaud had been 'politiquement hostile'[64] – endorses her view. It seems clear that Pingaud could not survive the rise in political temperature.

The departure of Pontalis

With the exception of another piece of hatchet-work by François George ('Lacan ou l'effet "yau de poêle"' in May and June 1979), *TM*'s interest in psychoanalysis ceases very suddenly in 1969; thirty articles give it a fairly high profile in the preceding six years, but when Pontalis goes it completely disappears from view. The change is abrupt, but should not be taken to mean that between 1963 and 1969 Pontalis's position was unproblematic. As in previous years, he remained the most anti-Sartrean of the editors and showed no desire to seek a theoretical *rapprochement*. Anthony Wilden notes that 'the journalistic furor in Paris which followed the publication of Lacan's *Ecrits* in 1966 resulted in the creation of a tendentious opposition between Sartre and Lacan';[65] Pontalis makes no attempt to dispel it. One explanation is that the tension between Lacan and Sartre was less than that within the French psychoanalytical movement itself. Many commentators were capable of discussing all that separated the two men, but this would have required a public display of their own attitude towards Lacan, something which might well have been difficult.

It is important to recall that 1963 was the year of the second schism. As early as 1953, opinions had been polarised by Lacan's objections to ego psychology and to the close association of psychoanalysis with the study of medicine, together with his belief that Freudian thought should resist all institutionalisation. This had led to the setting-up of the Société Française de Psychanalyse (SFP), independent of the Institut de Psychanalyse and of the International Psychoanalytical Association (IPA). All those who followed Lacan and Lagache into the SFP suffered a loss of professional status as teachers and as analysts.

Sherry Turkle's account of events[66] shows how the tensions of 1953 sharpened to produce the split of 1963. Those Lacanians who wished to operate as psychoanalysts under the aegis of the IPA could do so only on condition that they dissociated themselves from Lacan. Hence the winding-up of the SFP in 1963 and the emergence of two new bodies: Lacan's Ecole Freudienne de Paris (excluded from the IPA) and the Association Psychanalytique de France (APF), whose analysts were readmitted to the IPA. Pontalis, after having been closely identified with Lacan and having minuted his seminars,[67] leaves him in 1963 and joins the APF, where he becomes editor of the *Nouvelle revue de psychanalyse*. He thus moves into a 'moderate' position and his editorial policy in *TM* reflects this. The review publishes work emanating from the Ecole Freudienne, from the APF, as well as from the long-established Société Psychanalytique de Paris (SPP, i.e. the Institut de Psychanalyse).

In the course of the period, Pontalis brings to *TM* a selection of Freud's letters to Oscar Pfister (February 1965), an article by Melanie Klein (February 1968) and studies of the pyschoanalytic philosopher Georg Groddeck by Lewinter (March 1969) and Fédida (December 1969). In addition, there are two contributions of sociological interest: a further essay by Georges Devereux, the ethno-psychiatrist, on 'La délinquence sexuelle des jeunes filles dans une société "puritaine" ' (October 1964); and a report by Françoise Morin on attitudes towards mental illness, part of a multi-disciplinary survey of public reactions to the television version of Sartre's *La Chambre* (August 1967). The interface of pyschoanalysis and literature is covered by Jean Starobinski (June 1967) and by André Green (April 1964).

Turkle notes that after the 1963 split the SFP is 'freed from its role as "official" center of resistance to Lacanism' and that 'now, further away than all the rest from its break with Lacan, it is more open to constructive dialogue with his ideas'.[68] Green is in this position. So, too, is Daniel Widlocher, later to become the first French secretary of the IPA and whose 'Lecture psychanalytique du dessin d'enfant' appears in February 1965. A more substantial embodiment of the non-sectarian spirit that prevails within *TM* is Octave Mannoni. Although publicly identified with Lacan's Ecole Freudienne, his frequent articles avoid all doctrinaire positions and deftly approach the Freudian corpus in a manner that even Sartre appreciates. In his consideration of 'L'homme aux rats' (May 1965) he discusses Freud's acceptance of the existence in the unconscious of words *qua* words – something which is taken up by Sartre in his description of language as practico-inert.[69] His investigation of *Verleugnung* (disavowal) in 'Je sais bien ... mais quand même' (January 1964) offers an analysis of belief which is adopted by *TM* in an editorial on the French nuclear deterrent (January 1965) and by Sartre in *L'Idiot de la famille*.[70]

It is worth dwelling briefly on what it is that makes Mannoni's *lacanisme* acceptable to Sartre. In the two articles cited above, as well as in an essay on J. D. Salinger (November 1964) and in an account of the Freud–Fliess relationship (June 1967), he consistently denies any positive status to psychoanalytic knowledge. He is a phenomenologist to the extent that he shows knowledge to be generated only in transference, and he is a dialectician inasmuch as he shows it to be derived from a confrontation of ignorances. Most important of all, he is hostile to both politico-economic and psychoanalytic forms of colonisation.

Mannoni never becomes a member of the Editorial Board of *TM* but nonetheless exerts real influence. Ethnographer, psychoanalyst and literary critic, his status and function approach those of Leiris. He occupies the intermediate position between Sartre and Lacan better than Pontalis does; never having declared intellectual allegiances, he never has to change them. Thanks to his inter-disciplinary position he is able to synthesise in a way which proves useful to Sartre. His study of 'Itard et son sauvage' (October 1965), for example, provides, in terms reminiscent of Lévi-Strauss's essay on Father Christmas, a bi-disciplinary link between *Les Mots* and *L'Idiot de la famille*:

L'ethnologie commence à nous dévoiler le rôle des enfants dans une organisation sociale qui tourne en grande partie autour de leur existence, et où ils sont par leur crédulité cultivée le support indispensable des vérités mythiques. En même temps la psychanalyse des enfants découvre le rôle qu'ils jouent dans les fantasmes parentaux.[71]

Mannoni's critique of Itard's pedagogic principles also plays a part in the questioning of the education system that precedes 1968.

As for Pontalis, he becomes a leading member of the APF. This association, according to Turkle, 'shares its "establishment" image with the Paris Psychoanalytical Society and its "academic" image with the Freudian school, and each of these competing groups overshadows it, one on its medical "Right", the other on its university "Left" '.[72] She suggests that Pontalis, together with Anzieu and Laplanche, suffers a loss of confidence during this period: 'When they cut themselves off from Lacan, the brilliant young Lacanians who formed the Association left themselves indelibly marked by Lacan's ideas but almost unable to have any contact with him. Many of them had been among Lacan's most cherished disciples. The breach was angry and embittered.'[73] Pontalis's writing must be seen in this context. It is tempting to identify acts of deferred obedience following the symbolic murder of the patriarch, but this is more the province of Elisabeth Roudinesco's transferential history of the French psychoanalytical movement.

A great deal of energy is invested by Pontalis and Laplanche in the *Vocabulaire de la psychanalyse* (published by the Presses Universitaires de France in 1967). It offers diachronic accounts of Freudian concepts and a synchronic view of the whole conceptual apparatus. Its ambition is to make a non-sectarian return to Freud and to strengthen the centrist position of the APF by making it the basis of a new consensus. In collaboration with Laplanche again, Pontalis presents *TM* with an article which clearly derives from their work on the lexicon and which is by far the most important theoretical contribution of the period. 'Fantasme originaire, fantasmes des origines, origine du fantasme' (April 1964) sets out to show how Freud's early work was inhibited by the primacy of certain simple binary oppositions, such as subjective–objective, internal–external, imaginary–real. It demonstrates that he was able to theorise the Oedipus complex only when the insertion of a median term, 'psychic reality', permitted him to understand fully the nature of fantasy. One of the implications of the article – the only one that I shall mention here – is that in this particular respect Freud's success must be measured beside Sartre's failure. Pontalis has long regarded Sartre as being guilty of a sterile dualism.

At the beginning of the period, Pontalis contributes a piece which is interesting for other reasons. Entitled 'Le petit groupe comme objet' (December 1963), it belongs with Pingaud's experience of group therapy and Anzieu's 'Etude psychanalytique des groupes réels' (July 1966) and joins them in a movement towards social psychology. Perhaps it indicates a need, following the 1963 split, to investigate the behaviour of psychoanalysts in groups. It can certainly be interpreted as a move to integrate into Freudian theory aspects of the group dynamics explored in Sartre's *Critique*. It testifies, moreover, to the growth of a 'group culture' heralding the events of 1968.

May 1968 itself requires little comment in this section. Certain psychoanalysts swell the subsequent tide of reaction, but *TM*'s angry criticism of them – for example, Alain Didier's review of *L'Univers contestationnaire* by 'André Stéphane' (apparently written, at least in part, by Janine Chasseguet-Smirgel of the SPP) – does not imply a repudiation of psychoanalysis itself. Seventy analysts, after all, signed a statement in *Le Monde* (on 23 May 1968) supporting the student movement. In a small measure, *TM* and psychoanalysis worked together to create the conditions of the May events. The remarks of Octave Mannoni quoted above, for instance, are recalled by Maud Mannoni in an after-the-events discussion, not just for their explanatory power, but also to be itemised as a component part of student consciousness.[74] Psychoanalytic authority nevertheless meets its May in *TM* in April 1969, with the extraordinary case of *l'homme au magnétophone*. This episode is an important moment in the history of the synthetic anthropology because, unlike the Wolf Man or the Rat Man, the Tape-recorder Man is the partial case-history of an analyst rather than that of a patient. It precipitates a confrontation between Pontalis and Pingaud on the one hand and Sartre on the other. An examination of the exchanges is therefore best prefaced by a look at Sartre's *prises de position* between 1963 and 1969.

His views, consistent with the previous professions of faith in *compréhension*, are succinctly summarised in his foreword to *Reason and Violence* by Laing and Cooper:

Je pense [...] qu'on ne peut comprendre les troubles psychiques *du dehors*, à partir du déterminisme positiviste ni les reconstruire par une combinaison de concepts qui restent extérieurs à la maladie vécue. Je crois aussi qu'on ne peut étudier ni guérir une névrose sans un respect originel de la personne du patient, sans un effort constant pour saisir la situation de base et pour la revivre, sans une démarche pour retrouver la réponse de la personne à cette situation – et je tiens […] la maladie mentale comme l'issue que le libre organisme, dans son unité totale, invente pour pouvoir vivre une situation invivable.[75]

These are the principles which will inform the empathetic study of Flaubert's breakdown in 1844. They also explain why *TM* publishes the fifth chapter of David Cooper's *Psychiatry and Anti-psychiatry* (December 1967),[76] which records the attempt to establish alternative modes of treatment within the British National Health Service. As far as psychoanalysis is concerned, Sartre presses for the recognition of the autonomy of the analysand and for a relationship of real reciprocity between analysand and analyst. In conversation with Pingaud, for example, he once more accepts psychoanalysis as a viable therapeutic practice, always provided that all parties concerned enjoy existential equality as agents rather than as patients.[77] Hence his hostility to anything that smacks of 'human engineering' and his insistence that Freudians become as theoretically reflexive as the Marxists of the PCI.[78] Hence also *TM*'s enthusiasm for self-directed therapies such as that of Louis Wolfson, whose *Le Schizo et ses langues* is described by Beauvoir as 'de tous les livres qui concernent la psychiatrie, le plus étonnant que j'aie lu'.[79]

These are exactly the issues raised by the Tape-recorder Man. In 1969, a patient known as 'A' escaped from psychiatric hospital and delivered a tape to 'L' (presumably Lanzmann) with the request that the transcript be published. As Beauvoir recalls:

Ce dialogue avait été enregistré par un patient du docteur X, qui avait surgi chez celui-ci, armé d'un magnétophone, trois ans après la fin d'une longue analyse. Inversant la situation, il s'était posé en sujet et avait exigé que le docteur répondît à ses questions: celui-ci avait manifesté devant l'appareil une véritable terreur.[80]

A full and reciprocal dialogue between equals does not ensue; instead, there is mutual symbolic violence. The analyst, accused of charlatanism and invited to analyse his own discourse, protests at the disruption of analytic confidentiality by the tape-recorder. It must be said that *TM* does not present this interaction impartially. Independently of the signed comments by Sartre, Pontalis and Pingaud, it supplies intermittent editorial commentary which reinforces the attempts of 'A' to ridicule Doctor X. In order to provide the missing intonation patterns, for example, it describes the analyst's last call for help as 'le cri lugubre final d'une baudruche qui se dégonfle comme une bête crevée'.[81] The scenario, designed to bring out the analyst's castratory propensities, ulti-mately resembles a mixture of *Huis clos* and Ionesco's *La Leçon*.

Sartre's first reaction is to assure readers that 'je ne suis pas "un faux ami" de la psychanalyse mais un compagnon de route critique et je n'ai nulle envie – et nul moyen d'ailleurs – de la ridiculiser'.[82] In this instance, he says, he wishes merely to expose a bad analyst. He is nonetheless moved by 'l'irruption du *sujet* dans le cabinet analytique ou plutôt le renversement du rapport univoque qui lie le sujet à l'objet'.[83] Objectified by a therapeutic technique that suppresses active reciprocity, 'ce sujet souhaite se comprendre en tant que sujet blessé, dévié; faute d'une collaboration intersubjec-tive, il "passe à l'acte", pour parler comme les analystes: c'est renverser la *praxis* et du même coup la situation'.[84] Sartre agrees with 'A' that the psychoanalytic relation is a feudal one which tends to passivise the patient. Analysis, in his view, is a form of violence whenever the analyst, by virtue of expertise and status and also – as in this case – by telephone call to the police, imposes a particular reality on the analysand. In these circumstances, says Sartre, the conduct of 'A' represents an acceptable counter-violence. He thus extends the views of Fanon, the most respected psychiatrist of all, in such a way as to make of the psychoanalyst a coloniser and a possessor; it is quite possible that he voices the criticisms of Lacan that many analysts would dare not utter.

Nothing is new in this episode except the force of the confront-ation. Theoretically, the situation is as it was in 'Questions de méthode': *psychoanalytic* is synonymous with *analytic* and is con-sequently opposed to, but recuperable by, the synthetic anthropo-logy. What has changed is, first, that the issues have been brought alive by a man on the run from the police less than a year after May 1968 and, secondly, that Cooper and Laing, among others, now offer a synthetic psychiatric alternative.[85]

How then do Pontalis and Pingaud respond? They protest. For Pingaud, Sartre's commentary is a case of wilful misinterpretation, for the tape in fact contains a record of the transferential moment of a therapy which might well have gone on to prove successful. As for Pontalis, he refuses to be drawn into substantive debate. Instead, he too focuses on the attitude of Sartre, noting that 'il faudra un jour écrire l'histoire du rapport ambigu, fait d'une attirance et d'une réticence *également* profondes, que Sartre entretient depuis trente ans avec la psychanalyse'.[86] Sartre's rather transparent tactic is to claim the status of 'critical fellow-traveller', hoping that this gesture will commit those inside the profession to an exchange of ideas. Pontalis bristles, wisely suspicious of the generosity of this intellectual tourist who comes to Argos with unsolicited advice:

Quant aux vertus salvatrices du dialogue, je crois ne les avoir jamais vu célébrer par Sartre – et c'est une chance! Autrement, il n'aurait pas su témoigner comme il l'a fait de l'échec de toute réciprocité ni donner à ce qu'il a nommé les 'situations limites' – la folie, entre autres – leur valeur exemplaire.[87]

However, if anyone is qualified to write the history of Sartre's ambivalence, then it is Pontalis. Here perhaps would be the place, were Pontalis not so reticent, to explore the significance of the fantasies of *Les Mots* and of the configuration of *sevrage*, resentment and the almost unmentionable stepfather. No psychoanalyst could have a better opportunity and, the reader might wonder, if Lefort, Camus, Merleau-Ponty and Lévi-Strauss have all moved onto the attack, why could not Pontalis? Perhaps the best way to defend psychoanalysis is by the silence with which it claims to speak. The worst way is undoubtedly to use its explanatory power to reify an opponent of the calibre of Sartre. Pontalis refrains from trading punches and consents to cast a professional eye on his former teacher only fifteen years later.[88] He effectively writes his way out of *TM* in April 1969, yet his resignation comes one year later on the occasion of Gorz's attack on the university system. Beauvoir, as I have mentioned, associates the two episodes – 'chez l'un et l'autre [Pingaud and Pontalis] on retrouvait cette même tendance qui leur avait fait défendre la tradition des cours magistraux'[89] – but does not emphasise the significance sufficiently. The real issue in 1969 is the same as in 1968, that is to say the institutionalisation of knowledge and the operation of processes of credentialisation in order to determine in what relation to knowledge each individual stands. This was also the crucial factor in the split of 1963. In part, therefore, Pontalis may be said to leave both Lacan and Sartre for the same reason – his unwillingness to contest the institutional legitimation of expertise.

Sartre, for his part, has no regrets: 'Pontalis n'était pas adapté à cette revue. Il était beaucoup plus bourgeois, il soutenait une théorie beaucoup plus bourgeoise en politique, il estimait que ce qu'il avait de radical passait dans la psychanalyse et dans l'étude qu'il en faisait.'[90] His view of psychoanalysis hardens accordingly. In his preface to Antonin Liehm's book on Czechoslovakia, *Trois Générations*, in 1970, he emphasises the diversionary function of psychoanalysis in the West: it makes of potential revolutionaries 'des somnambules qui se promènent sur une gouttière en rêvant à leurs couilles au lieu de regarder leurs pieds'.[91]

The ascendancy of Gorz

In this section I would like to deal with three aspects of *TM* in the period between 1963 and 1971. These are the years of its anti-Gaullism, a sustained burst of energy which lasts from the aftermath of the Algerian War to the aftermath of the May events and secures the editorial dominance of Sartre and Gorz. It was perhaps inevitable that after the Evian agreements of 1962 the attention of the militant Left – intelligentsia and student movement – should switch from North Africa to the metropolis. Sartre is terse and categorical: 'colonialisme là-bas, fascisme ici: une seule et même chose',[92] a synthetic, if overstated, view of reality (he and Beauvoir regarded the return of de Gaulle as similar to the rise of Mussolini in 1922) on which is based an efficient division of editorial labour. Sartre henceforth assumes responsibility for all that relates to imperialism and neo-colonialism – Western or Soviet – while Gorz attends to the critique of Gaullism and the neo-capitalism which develops in the framework of the Treaty of Rome. I shall consider each facet of *TM*'s programme in turn and shall end the chapter with an examination of how the relationship with academic anthropology evolves.

Looking first, then, at the now well-established Third-Worldism of the review, I shall begin by assessing the role of the ever exemplary Leiris. His only article in the period is an extract from *Fibrilles* (April 1966), the third volume of *La Règle du jeu*. Low-level involvement, however, does not diminish his significance: his experience of old age, his friendship with Césaire, his participation in the May events, his similarity with Sartre, his status as synthetic ethnographer – all these carry great weight. *Fibrilles* is particularly instructive from the point of view of ethnography. Suffused with nostalgia for both the vitality of Africa and the wisdom of the Orient, it documents the inevitability of ethnocentricity. Leiris concludes that all his travels have been motivated by non-scientific preoccupations and that they have been ambivalent enough to be counter-productive: the Dakar–Djibouti expedition of 1931, for example, which he joined in order to escape from Parisian aestheticism, launched him on his career of man of letters. In many ways, *Fibrilles* is a true contemporary of *Les Mots*. Both are committed autobiographies which seek a liberation in the comprehension of determinations. Both, however, discover that the movement between regression and progression is unending, that the understanding of constraints does not dissolve them and that the confusion of ethic and aesthetic produces only a professional code of conduct precariously founded on ambivalence. It is this discussion, rather than the conclusions bearing on ethnography, which appears in *TM*. The view that political efficacy is undermined by an overvaluation of literature is not, therefore, an isolated one. It helps to explain the lack of a formal sequel to *Les Mots* and the fact that *Fibules*, the fourth part of *La Règle du jeu*, is also abandoned.[93]

Leiris is closer to Sartre than many of those who use Sartrean terminology. His political positions are the same, most visibly in 1968 and in the support for Alain Krivine in the 1969 Presidential elections. The two men, together with Césaire and Daniel Guérin, appear as defence witnesses in the trial of Guadeloupian nationalists in March 1968. As far as the continued viability of ethnography is concerned, *Fibrilles* makes no judgements and *TM*'s readers remain uninformed of Leiris's opinion. In a speech delivered to the Havana Congress of January 1968,[94] however, he outlines a programme appropriate to the 'underdeveloped' countries. He recommends rapid technological innovation compatible with local conditions and needs, opposition to imperialist research and development projects, the incorporation into the revolutionary process of as many ancient cultural practices as possible, a 'local' ethnography designed to eliminate all sense of cultural inferiority, education and literacy campaigns, and the promotion of revolutionary art based on the absolute freedom of the artist. Far from being an attempt to radicalise European anthropology, this is a programme intended to benefit ethnographers and sociologists indigenous to the countries concerned.[95] It is difficult not to interpret this as a statement of the impending redundancy of Western anthropology. It may also be inferred that the discipline is likely to dwindle to little more than a metropolitan memory of colonisation and of empire – a memory, however, with continuing reactionary power.

TM's interest in the work of Césaire is due in part to his friendship with Leiris. (The first act of his play *Une Saison au Congo* is featured in February 1966.) Leiris publishes elsewhere,[96] however, an assessment of Césaire's literary and political importance which does not once mention Sartre – this despite the evocation in *Fibrilles* of 'l'incarnation de cet Orphée noir autour duquel un essai de Jean-Paul Sartre a fait graviter tant de lumièr-es'.[97] Instead, it gives Breton the credit for having first recognised a fellow surrealist – a more authentic one, in Leiris's eyes, for having a personal experience of oppression. He traces the genesis of *négritude* to the conjunction of Parisian surrealism and anthropo-logy in which Césaire 'découvrit [...] la beauté des civilisations négro-africaines à travers des ouvrages ethnographiques tels que ceux de Leo Frobenius et de Maurice Delafosse'.[98] This is not, however, to say that Leiris is writing against Sartre.

Twenty years after the publication of 'Orphée noir', they agree with Fanon that the political moment of *négritude* is past. Oppor-tunely, in view of the parallels between *La Règle du jeu* and *Les Mots*, *Fibrilles* presents Césaire's achievements in such a way that those of both Leiris and Sartre suffer in comparison: 'le seul de nos amis vivants en qui l'art et la politique [...] parviennent à se fondre au lieu de s'exclure l'une l'autre ou de tant bien que mal coexister'.[99]

Stimulated no doubt by Césaire, *TM*'s drama critic Renée Saurel turns to the history of the Congo conflict, and her article (March 1965) supplements Sartre's important preface to the *Présence africaine* publication *La Pensée politique de Patrice Lumumba* (1963). This preface, which unfortunately is not reproduced in *TM*, is one of his lesser known but most impressive texts. It is essential to mention it here, not simply because of its anti-imperialist thrust, but because it does what academic anthropology is reluctant to do. It studies in Lumumba an African conditioned by, and responding to, local manifestations of global forces, an African manifestly placed beyond the conceptual reach of the orthodox ethnographer.

Sartre begins by juxtaposing Fanon, the non-African theoreti-cian of violence, agrarian reform and nationalisations, and Lumumba, the Congolese preacher of non-violence who had political but no economic objectives. 'Lumumba, Fanon, ces deux grands morts représentent l'Afrique.'[100] He then traces Lumum-ba's childhood experience of peasant poverty, his acquisition of Christian egalitarianism from Protestant missionaries, and his encounter with racialism as an urban *petit bourgeois*. It is his lack of integration into class or tribe, says Sartre, which makes his pro-gramme political rather than economic. Embodying the contra-dictions of all levels of Congolese society, he could gain a real power base only by forging a nation. Sartre speaks of him as he might have spoken of Oreste: 'ce concept universel [...] permet à cet errant de profiter de ses voyages et de déchiffrer les problèmes

en fonction de l'universel'.[101] Lumumba, because he is detriba-
lised, escapes academic anthropology; he enters the synthetic, as
practitioner and as object, by virtue of his understanding of
tribalism – vestiges of pre-colonial organisation used systematically
by the colonial power for purposes of division and rule. (*TM* is well
aware that the difficulties experienced by African nations after
independence are used to justify neo-colonialism, when in fact they
are the result of colonisation. Basil Davidson argues this with
clarity in April 1971.) Sartre concludes that the failure of Lumumba
opens the door to the neo-colonialists, Belgian and North
American, and that this heralds the Latin-Americanisation of the
Congo. He predicts that 'toutes les conditions d'un castrisme seront
données'[102] and that Lumumba, the José Marti of Africa, will have
greater influence dead than alive.

Despite the interest in Lumumba, the review gives little space to
the colonial territories once or still held by the British, the Belgians
and the Portuguese. The exception is Biafra. One of the few good
words Olivier Todd has to say about *TM* is its willingness on this
occasion to go against prevailing left-wing opinion. Instead of
seeing Biafra as a second Katanga, Sartre 'publia dans *TM* un texte
de Richard Marienstrass [February 1970] qui sauva un peu le
fameux honneur de la France'.[103] He might also have mentioned
the denunciation of ethnocide by Stanley Diamond (Professor of
Anthropology at Columbia University) in the same issue. *TM*
follows with greater consistency events in South Africa. Nothing
rouses the anger of Sartre more than institutionalised racialism;
had he accepted the Nobel Prize in 1964, he would have donated
the money to the Anti-Apartheid movement.

The review also covers the first Pan-African Cultural Congress,
organised by the OAU and held in Algiers in 1969. Elias Condal's
impressions are bleak: Westernised ruling elites gather to protest
too much at past colonialism and too little at present imperialism;
they fail to offer support to African liberation movements in the
southern half of the continent and pay lip-service to a vague notion
of *africanité* in order to mask their divergences. As far as Algeria is
concerned, *TM* attempts to remain informed. Claude Collin and
the sociologist Juliette Minces give a positive account of industrial
and agricultural developments, but Mostefa Lacheraf (after five
years in a French prison) expresses alarm at the Algerian government's delay in moving towards a socialist programme. In 1964 he
explains the predominance of bourgeois nationalism in primarily
cultural terms which recall Fanon's analyses of rites of possession.

Colonisation, he asserts, weakened local Arab culture and allowed the written language to operate only as the vehicle of traditional religious thought. As a result, the only clear political perspective was that of the construction of a future based on a return to the past.

In addition to Algeria, *TM* monitors events in Guadeloupe, French Guiana and Madagascar. It also insists on considering the problems of immigrant workers in France within the context of international imperialism. The title of Sartre's 1970 article in the magazine *Tricontinental*, 'Le tiers monde commence en banlieue',[104] makes this clear. Both Gorz and Sartre follow with keen interest the affairs of the distant heirs of Richard Wright, the black Americans, many of whom perceive themselves to be a colonial working class. Between 1966 and 1971 the review features material by some of the most important Black Power leaders – Malcolm X, James Boggs, Eldridge Cleaver, James Forman, George Jackson and LeRoy Jones; James Baldwin and Stokeley Carmichael, meanwhile, participate in the Russell Tribunal. *TM* has no doubts about their importance: 'Contre l'impérialisme américain, Che Guevara réclamait que d'autres Viêt-nams se créent en divers endroits du monde. Il en existe déjà un, au cœur même de l'Amérique: le mouvement "Black Power".'[105]

Sartre's hopes for a Congolese *castrisme* and Guevara's call for a proliferation of Vietnams reflect the dual focus of *TM*'s coverage of international affairs. Its support for Castro and for Ho Chi Minh are rapidly subsumed in an all-embracing anti-Americanism which itself is rendered consistent with the review's anti-Stalinism, anti-Gaullism and anti-structuralism. These years, in fact, represent the most successful theoretical phase in the history of the synthetic anthropology; its range and power is much greater than in the early days of existentialist euphoria, and the difficulties experienced by Pontalis are evidence of the momentum which it builds up. Before turning to Gorz, I shall inspect the Cuban and Vietnamese dossiers, stressing those links which hold the different aspects of the synthetic anthropology together.

Articles by Elena de la Souchère and by the Cuban writer Nicolas Guillen had given accounts of the seizure of power by Castro in 1959. In 1960 Sartre and Beauvoir visited Havana and came away with great enthusiasm for this revolution in which received Marxist theory had played so small a part. Sartre gave his views to *France-Soir*, for greater dissemination than *TM* could offer; similarly, his comments on the Bay of Pigs episode went to *L'Express*.

The task of informing *TM*'s readers in the manner to which they were accustomed was left to a young man who subsequently gained deep first-hand knowledge of Latin America. Beauvoir reports that one of the ex-students of Althusser introduced in the autumn of 1964 as editorial assistants was Régis Debray, who 'entre autres ne revint plus'.[106] The remark is misleading, for in January 1965 appears a substantial study of 'Le castrisme: la longue marche en Amérique latine'. In it, Debray considers whether a general revolutionary strategy can be derived from the Cuban experience and how it might relate to Marxist–Leninist theory.

He begins with a critique of *golpismo*, the Latin American tradition by which different interest groups seize State power from each other without ever calling the State apparatus into question. He rejects it in favour of *focismo*, a strategy in which armed elites, based in the poorest rural areas, create, by military, educational and agricultural activity, the conditions for revolution which had not previously existed. Debray stresses the Leninist credentials of this particular option, as well as the need to attack the weakest link of the chain of oppression. It is the same consideration that leads Gorz to ascribe major political potential to students in Western Europe. Surveying events in Latin America following the Cuban Revolution, Debray recognises the widespread failure of guerrilla movements – for reasons of lack of training, lack of security, lack of adaptation of the Cuban model to local conditions and lack of co-ordination with urban political activity. He argues against the setting-up of urban guerrilla forces as well as against the patient waiting for objective revolutionary conditions to appear (the policy of the established Latin American Communist Parties). Urban political activity must be locally supportive of the work undertaken in the countryside, recognising that it will be from there that the momentum for change will come. Debray insists that political, military and economic organisation go hand in hand and specifies that 'l'accès aux communautés indiennes doit donc se conquérir sur les forces répressives qui en ont la contrôle traditionnel'.[107]

This last factor is crucial in the present context, for when Debray talks about groups of peasants stimulated by a guerrilla *foco* into acts of insurgency, he is clearly describing what Fanon had described before him; like Fanon, he is taking the objects of study of academic anthropology and making of them the subjects of history. He thus proposes a Sartrean alternative to ethnographic fieldwork which is as distinctive as the Laingian alternative to orthodox psychiatry. The impact on anthropology students made by the later image of Debray as a revolutionary worker in the field must not be underestimated. The visible distance between an academic monograph of a 'cold' society and a *castrisme*, which in a non-dogmatic and reflexive manner theorises its appropriateness to 'hot' local conditions, does much to shake the foundations of Lévi-Straussian structuralism.

Although everything in Debray's article is compatible with *TM*'s views, the closeness of the collaboration is difficult to assess. In 1966 he returned to Cuba for discussions with Castro and Guevara. In April 1967 he was arrested in Bolivia, immediately prior to the death of Guevara at the hands of the Bolivian army. Sartre, campaigning on his behalf, took the line that Debray was a journalist on trial for his opinions and likely in the near future to be assassinated: the French government should therefore apply pressure to secure the release of this working man who had been sent by *TM* to 'suivre de près les événements'.[108] Sartre's use of the enemy's rhetoric is unconvincing. Debray sent no dispatches to *TM* after his departure (there is no coverage, for example, of the 1966 Tricontinental Conference in Havana) and in any case had become known, not as a professional journalist, but as a revolutionary theorist: his *Révolution dans la révolution?* was published in Cuba in January 1967 and by Maspero in March of the same year. By the time he was sentenced to thirty years in prison in November 1967, *TM* had actually provided its readers with scant material on Bolivia and Cuba. (The only detailed account of Cuba comes from David Alexander in February and March 1967.) According to Debray, he had been sent to Latin America not by Sartre but by Maspero.[109] If *TM* fails to follow events very closely, it is perhaps because they are newsworthy enough to be handled by other publications, notably *Le Nouvel Observateur*, which features texts by Debray, Maspero and Gorz (writing as Bosquet). Two years after Debray's trial in Bolivia, Sartre (with Malraux and Mauriac) renews the campaign for his release. It meets with no immediate success, even though a new Bolivian President is in office; *TM* now proceeds to keep the matter in the public eye by publishing two reports from Debray in his prison cell – 'Un curieux réquisitoire' (May 1970) and 'Notes de prison' (June 1970).

At the same time, the review manages wide coverage of other Latin American territories. Guatemala, Mexico, Venezuela, Argentina and Uruguay all figure, but, as Robin Blackburn notes, 'the Latin American republic where [Debray's] writing has had its greatest impact is Brazil, a country where his immediate tactical prescriptions have been most in need of modification'.[110] *TM* accordingly carries many articles on Brazil, together with a special issue in October 1967. This scrutiny is justified by the fact that Brazil is felt to be the key to Latin America and to the Third World as a whole. It is a mark of this importance that the special issue should be prepared by a guest editor, a practice that becomes commonplace only after 1975, but which in 1967 testifies to the size of the Brazilian exile community in Paris. The economist Celso Furtado invites several contributions from a variety of fields, including one from the sociologist and colleague of Roger Bastide, Florestan Fernandes.

The special edition carries no discussion of Debray. It is too early, for the urban guerrilla movement in Brazil dates from 1968, and it is left to a participant, João Quartim (Marcelo de Andrade), to demonstrate the debt to *Révolution dans la révolution?* Quartim writes a number of times for *TM* (May 1969, December 1969, November 1970) and is keen to pursue the debate. He believes that the limitations of Debray's position could be discovered only in practice. By 1967, however, Guevara's disastrous errors in Bolivia had demonstrated the dangers of an ill-prepared *foco* and a naive belief in the spontaneity of the peasant masses. What the Brazilians came to call *Debrayismo* was in the end abandoned by groups which had actually tried to make it work; the priority was then shifted from the rural to the urban guerrilla. There are certain similarities with what will happen later in France. Quartim shows quite strikingly in May 1969 how the Brazilian events of 1964 anticipated those of May 1968: revolutionary conditions prevailed, only for the movement to be successfully arrested by a Stalinist Communist Party. The subsequent disappointment is translated into guerrilla warfare.

The greatest focus of the anti-imperialist struggle is of course the war in Vietnam. In the third period, there had been no mention of Indochina in *TM*. Algeria was too prominent in French minds, and perhaps it had been too easily assumed that after Dien Bien Phu colonisation had ended. The fact that the Geneva agreements were never honoured is not really noticed, and it is only with the beginnings of significant US intervention in 1963 that Vietnam returns as a subject of importance. The scene is set in November of the same year with the translation of a *Monthly Review* article by Hugh Deane. In May 1965 an editorial by Gorz analyses American policy in terms of four main aims:

1. Démontrer que le camp impérialiste peut venir à bout militairement de l'insurrection armée d'un peuple opprimé;

2. Imposer leur interprétation de la 'coexistence pacifique', interprétation qui stipule le partage du monde entre les camps impérialiste et socialiste, et qui assimile à une 'agression' de celui-ci toute révolution ou guerre de libération éclatant dans la 'sphère d'influence' de celui-là;

3. Contraindre le camp socialiste soit à empêcher, soit à renier et à laisser écraser toute révolution qui remettrait en question le *statu quo*;

4. A cette fin, menacer d'une extension de la guerre tout ou partie du camp socialiste, afin de la 'dissuader' ainsi de venir en aide aux forces révolutionnaires aux prises avec les forces impérialistes de répression.[111]

The Americans are exploiting the Sino-Soviet split, says Gorz, and the only way to stop them is to heal the rift and to give assistance to all liberation movements. This position, which is held for the duration of the war, marks a sharp shift away from *TM*'s support for the anti-Chinese Togliatti in 1963, when fear of nuclear war and the emphasis placed on peaceful coexistence were the factors that seemed of overriding importance.

Sartre's remarks of the same period (it is the time of the first American bombing raids into North Vietnam) have a slightly different tone. Declining an invitation to visit the United States, he explains rather unconvincingly that the propaganda value of such a visit would have been negative. At the same time, he evinces feelings of impotence that seem uncharacteristic. He recalls that the Algerian affair 's'est jouée entre trois partenaires: de Gaulle, l'armée et le FLN, appuyé par la population algérienne des villes [...] objectivement, notre opposition n'a servi à rien'.[112] The implication is that American imperialism will end only with the coming of the American revolution, and it is surprising that he did not feel this to be an excellent reason for going to the States. *TM* nonetheless monitors American opposition to the Vietnam War. Eric Wolf, for example, Professor of Anthropology at Ann Arbor, describes how his colleague Sahlins invented the 'teach-in' and points out that the academics involved were mainly from the arts and social sciences and less dependent on government research grants; he goes on to remark that 'par leur métier même les sociologues ont une position critique vis-à-vis de leur société; quant aux anthropologues ils ne veulent pas qu'on leur détruise leur objet d'études'.[113] Sartre's absence from teach-ins like this is regrettable.

1966, however, is the year of the first session of the Russell Tribunal, set up to investigate American contravention of international war legislation. Many of its participants are familiar to readers of *TM*: Sartre is Executive President, the Yugoslav historian Vladimir Dedijer is Chairman; among the Tribunal members are Gunther Anders, Leilo Basso, Beauvoir and Isaac Deutscher. As far as Sartre is concerned, it offers an opportunity to use the law against the legislators, thus creating possibilities of raising Western opposition to the war. In late 1966 he tends to think that the Tribunal will help undermine the illusion of Gaullist independence in matters of foreign policy, for although France has lost its empire, it engages in a substantial amount of residual colonialism and neo-colonialism on behalf of the USA, of whose empire, says Sartre, it is itself a part. Meanwhile, in August 1966, a *TM* editorial marks the latest escalation of the war – the American decision to bomb Hanoi and Haiphong. Its analysis remains the same, and it follows up with articles on draft-dodging, war atrocities and CIA activities in the universities; it features Harry Magdoff's presentation of the economic basis of American foreign policy and Chomsky's thoughts on the responsibilities of the intellectual. Some of the Tribunal investigators sent to North Vietnam report back to *TM* as well as to the Tribunal. In April 1967, Jean-Pierre Vigier confirms the American use of napalm and fragmentation bombs, and in September Gisèle Halimi describes the role of women in the war effort.

In May 1967, the first session of the Russell Tribunal is concluded in Stockholm with the announcement of its findings: the USA is declared guilty of aggression, of bombing non-military targets and of violating Cambodian neutrality; in addition, the governments of Australia, New Zealand and South Korea are found guilty of complicity. Sartre's account celebrates the first meeting of the Tribunal as that of a group in fusion. Drawing on his Hollywood culture, he recalls the members as twelve angry men who gathered as a series: unknown to each other, except by reputation, separated by language and experience, they feared the degree to which each embodied the possibility of dissent and non-co-operation. Ultimately, when their unity is forged by the objective truths placed before them, Sartre is as much excited by the dynamic as he is pleased by the fact of the moral legitimacy conferred on the Tribunal. He uses the occasion to restate the view that political consciousness is informed by ethical choices which themselves invalidate all the premises of structuralist anthropology. The argument is that of 'Détermination et liberté', advanced now in more overtly political circumstances.

In November 1967 the second convention of the Russell Tribunal in Denmark addresses the three questions which remain unanswered: Was the USA using illegal chemical weapons? Did it mistreat its prisoners-of-war? Was it guilty of genocide? Sartre is asked to draft the reply to the final question. 'Le génocide' (December 1967) is an article of major importance. It concludes the Tribunal's business and is a last word in other respects as well. The May events, the Soviet invasion of Czechoslovakia, the de-escalation of the fighting, all help move the topic of Vietnam into the background. Sartre begins by looking at the history of genocide; he finds it relatively uncommon in Europe, despite the Nazi programme, while relatively common as a European practice in the Third World. This enables him to pick up the threads of his 1956 argument and to reiterate that 'le colonialisme est en effet un système'.[114] Either it liquidates an indigenous population and replaces it with imported slave labour, or it indulges in token massacres to render the native workforce docile. Events in Vietnam, however, says Sartre, have no precedent. The purpose of the Americans is to isolate China and to show the Latin American nations that guerrilla wars cannot be won. There is no colonial economy to be protected in Vietnam: the country is merely a pawn in a global conflict. When the guerrillas move amongst the people, the solution is therefore to eliminate the people. Far from genocide being inhibited by economic considerations, as had been the case in Algeria, it is actually the only realistic policy in Vietnam. It is therefore committed intentionally and with years of premeditation.

In 'Le génocide', the synthetic anthropology is seen apprehending in fact the force and scope of rival totalisations. It is not simply that *TM* has always been revolutionary and that anti-imperialism has been a permanent plank in its platform. It is also, more crucially, that its aspirations to global efficacy make anti-imperialism the most appropriate focus of its commitment. In a sense, therefore, American policies favour the development of the synthetic anthropology; at the same time, by increasing the likelihood of a universal monoculture, they threaten the practitioners of structuralist anthropology.

On the home front, meanwhile, Gorz applies himself to co-ordinating *TM*'s activities in the fields of sociology, economics and politics. The first reveals a particular concern for three marginalised groups: immigrant workers, women and students. Little room is left for the sociology of literature, which means that Bourdieu's contribution to the special issue on structuralism – 'Champ intellectuel et projet créateur' – is given no follow-up. In the third volume of *L'Idiot de la famille*, which does indeed deal with the sociology of literature, Sartre predictably holds closer to the

Gramscian concept of hegemony than to Bourdieu's ideas on habitus and cultural legitimation. Bourdieu's main influence in the period under consideration derives from his work on the education system, and I shall mention it at the appropriate time.

TM's support for the Third World sensitises it to the fact that the term is in the process of losing its geographical specificity. Because of a labour shortage caused by economic expansion under de Gaulle, and because of the return of part of the workforce to Italy and to Algeria and the existence of higher wages in West Germany, France imports large numbers of non-French unskilled workers. Exported by the colony or neo-colony, where colonialism has undermined the agricultural systems and created unemployment, these workers arrive in France to be greeted by exploitation and racialist harassment. The situation is described in detail by Marc Nacht (July 1964) and by others. As far as Gorz is concerned, the presence of immigrant workers is primarily of political significance. In this he differs from Sartre, who tends to stress the economic aspect.[115] Gorz grants that they represent a lighter burden on the host country than indigenous workers do; because they spend their non-active lives in their native lands, moreover, they constitute part of the subsidy provided by the poor countries for the rich. Basically, however, their function is to make up a non-unionised labour force which directly weakens the bargaining position of the organised working class. They cause a number of French workers to be drawn into the *petite bourgeoisie* and to embody the racialist pretexts to which it typically has recourse. Gorz's view in 1970 is that it is wrong to regard the working class as profiting from the presence of immigrant labour: the workers suffer inasmuch as their defences are undermined, while the capitalist system benefits from the imported labour that it cannot afford to lose.

It is through sociology that feminism makes its re-entry into *TM*. It might have been supposed, given the presence of Beauvoir, that it was a permanent feature of the review's programme, but this is not the case. The gap between *Le Deuxième Sexe* and its successors is in fact one of fifteen years. It is remarkable that *TM* should fail to campaign on behalf of such a large constituency. It uses the administrative assistance of Renée Saurel and Michelle Vian, but only in 1976 is a second woman (Claire Etcherelli) appointed to the Editorial Board. Nothing is ever said in public which would suggest awareness of a repressive male ethos, but it is wise to await future biographies of Sartre before drawing conclusions in this area. Certainly, none of the male personnel go out of their way to write on the position of women. It must have been tacitly assumed that this was the province of Beauvoir; she, with her other interests, and no doubt vesting her hopes in a socialist revolution, seems content to wait for feminism to place itself on the agenda. An article in *La Nef* in 1961[116] shows that she learns from two sociologists, Andrée Michel and Geneviève Texier, that the social position of women in France is deteriorating. The development of academic sociology, meanwhile, together with the national introspection following 1962, evidently favours renewed feminist activity. *TM* picks this up and both Michel and Texier appear as contributors in 1965. The review is also anxious to investigate the position of women in the Third World. Halimi reports positively from Vietnam, but Fidéla M'Rabet tells Juliette Minces that the war effort in Algeria has left no lasting mark; in Tunisia, according to Anne Guérin, considerably more progress has been made.

The picture is mixed and made up of random observations. Nothing suggests that *TM* is prepared to undertake a comprehensive analysis of the socio-political factors relevant to feminism. Beauvoir is perhaps more directly interested in a different, but not separate, sociology, that of old age, but even *La Vieillesse* fails to find its way into the review. She does, however, with the help of Colette Audry, secure extracts from 'un excellent livre'[117] – Betty Friedan's *The Feminine Mystique*. These are published in May and June of 1964 and represent the renaissance of feminism in *TM*[118] as well as in the USA. Friedan is conscious of her debt to Beauvoir and takes up the discussion of the fallacy of the *éternel féminin* and the theme of the social construction of female identity. She brings the latter very efficiently into the context of Gorz's critique of neo-capitalism, demonstrating that American women are drawn into stereotypes created by commercial logic. Additional continuity with Beauvoir is provided by Sylvie Le Bon in February 1966.

The attention of Gorz, however, is more firmly fixed on the education system, and on higher education in particular. Clearly, many contributors and readers are located in this sector, and the hope is that participant observation will develop into revolutionary intervention. Perhaps what requires prior explanation here is the absence of discussion of the education system in previous periods. This is undoubtedly due to the influence of Sartre. Broadly speaking, his attitude is one of hostility to the institutionalisation of education, but it is a hostility which manifests itself as a lack of interest. In 1943, while demonstrating that the self and the other impinge on each other irremediably, whatever their intentions might be, he noted that both authoritarian and liberal educational practices thus condition the child equally, albeit in different ways.[119] The comment is an isolated one, but it shows that at that stage Sartre favoured an existentially authenticated autodidacticism resembling that for which Roquentin abandoned his historiography and Oreste his pedagogue. Sartre's anger is habitually directed at socialisation by the family rather than at the education system. This is one reason why he can object to the philosophy syllabus but why his critique never goes as far as that of Nizan.

Another cause of his lack of aggression is presumably his own brilliant success at university. High academic qualification, after all, is likely to inhibit a radical critique of the institutions in which it is achieved. As Bourdieu points out in 1965: 'Il n'a pas échappé à Sartre qu'une enfance passée dans un univers où les mots devenaient la réalité des choses le préparait à entrer dans un monde intellectuel fondé sur le même principe.'[120] Even so, he abandoned his teaching career very early and although his reference to 'cette putain, l'Alma mater'[121] precedes Gorz's injunction to 'Détruire l'université', he never really sees himself as a leader of students, either within or against the system. This does not mean, of course, that he has no influence over them; the anti-imperialist, anti-Gaullist, anti-Stalinist and anti-structuralist positions worked out over the years all make an impact on the student movement.

TM's coverage begins in February 1964, the year of the entry of the post-war bulge into higher education and of the greatest material strains on provision. Nacht demonstrates that the difficulties proceed from government attempts to make the system more responsive to the manpower needs of private industry. It is an article by Marc Kravetz, however, which really sets the ball rolling. Leader of the Fédération des Groupes d'Etudes de Lettres, one of the Sorbonne sections of the Union Nationale des Etudiants de France (UNEF), his line is the one which *TM* maintains an interest in. (At the end of the Algerian War, the Front Universitaire Antifasciste had split and a substantial number of militants had elected to pursue their activities within the Union des Etudiants Communistes. *TM* publishes nothing bearing on this second strand.) Kravetz's 'Naissance d'un syndicalisme étudiant' (February 1964) documents the emergence of what was known as *la ligne universitaire*. In order to sustain the student militancy of the Algerian War period and to prevent the movement being absorbed into the party political bureaucracies, it was necessary to shift union activity towards a political programme deriving from specific and widespread grievances. Hence the investigations of the tensions between the liberal university and the manpower requirements of the capitalist state. FGEL opposed both the traditional institution and the government's bid to 'industrialise' it. It analysed patterns of intake, the student's economic status and future as technician and as consumer, as well as the teaching situation, concluding that 'ce que l'étudiant apprend essentiellement à l'Université, c'est la passivité et la soumission: cela pourra lui être fort utile plus tard'.[122] It proposed, therefore, to radicalise higher education.

It will be recalled that Beauvoir declares the opposition of Pingaud and Pontalis to such theses to have remained unspoken until 1970. In this she is incorrect, for Pontalis, in February 1964, manifests considerable anxiety at the rocking of the boat and at the possible breakdown of the pedagogic consensus within the liberal university. Ostensibly written to open up the debate, his 'Un couple menacé' denounces student stirrings as objective complicity with Gaullism. Kravetz's notions of neo-capitalism, on the other hand, reveal the influence of Gorz, and it is thus possible to trace the Gorz–Pontalis disagreement to as far back as 1964.

TM's response to Kravetz is not very radical. In general, reactions are either very theoretical – J.-P. Milbergue's Althusserian analysis of the teaching situation in April 1965, for example – or very liberal. The clearest manifestation of the latter tendency is furnished by the philosopher Robert Misrahi, an occasional contributor since 1948. Misrahi rebukes Kravetz for speaking of the students' individual isolation – in his view they are a serialised group – and calls on them to make the existing system work by overcoming their fear of examinations and by asking questions in class. In the end, it is Kravetz who returns, this time with his FGEL colleague Antoine Griset. Their 'De l'Algérie à la réforme Fouchet: critique du syndicalisme étudiant' (April and May 1965) represents a considerable effort of self-criticism and marks the abandonment of *la ligne universitaire* and the surrender of control of UNEF by the FGEL. Faced with the question of why their correct analyses of the student condition have nonetheless led to demobilisation, they explain their own counter-productivity by reducing student politics to mimicry of adult union activity. They conclude that the student movement will have real purchase on the world only when it has comprehended its present status as the product of an alienated collective imagination. Their references are specifically Sartrean and they make more use of the *Critique* than does Misrahi with his allusion to the serialised group. No programme, they say, can be elaborated prior to an examination of how the movement's other-direction deforms its practice. This task is henceforth inscribed within the synthetic anthropology: 'comprendre ce qu'il fait dans ce qu'il a à faire en élucidant ce qui l'a fait'.[123]

TM continues to observe the student movement at home and abroad (in Italy, Berlin, Yugoslavia and the Congo), but its greater concern is with the position of lecturers and teachers and with the political and sociological implications of the education system as a whole. The commentators are professionals like Jeannette Colombel and René Lourau rather than student militants. Dominant among them are Bourdieu and Passeron, the authors of the two most important works on the sociology of education in the period (*Les Héritiers* (1964) and *La Reproduction* (1970), both published by the Editions de Minuit). In 1965, they highlight the central feature of the hidden curriculum of higher education – the untaught academic discourse of the lecturer. In particular, they describe the function of selection performed by what is commonly represented as pedagogic incompetence and analyse the phenomenology of the need, shared by staff and students, to imagine that communication takes place between them. Both parties, exerting a certain terror on each other, collude in a *mauvaise foi* which neither fully understands: 'En fait, le professeur est aussi résigné à ses étudiants et à leurs incapacités "naturelles" que le "bon colon" à des "indigènes" dont il n'attend pas qu'ils soient autre chose que ce qu'ils sont.'[124] This comment is a reminder not only that Bourdieu once worked in Algeria but also that all that precedes May 1968 has global ramifications. After the events, Sartre makes of Vietnam the most powerful unifying factor.[125] This is no doubt true, socio-politically speaking, but within *TM* itself, the most effective synthesising force is the cogency of Gorz's political analyses.

From the end of the Algerian War, it was evident that *TM* needed a political line that would confirm its *double refus* of capitalism and Stalinism on the theoretical basis provided by Sartre's *Critique*. Gorz's *Stratégie ouvrière et néocapitalisme*,[126] of which the second part, 'Stratégies dans le marché commun', appears in *TM* in December 1963, fulfils precisely this task and constitutes a turning-point in French socialist theory. For this reason I shall summarise its main theses. By neo-capitalism Gorz designates the economic systems of the Western industrialised nations. These are societies in which the poor are a weak and divided minority and in which material poverty, as understood by classical Marxism, is no longer a major factor impelling the advent of socialism. Instead, the majority of the proletariat are required to be skilled workers and skilled consumers. In this new context, says Gorz, the traditional strategy of the organised working class – awaiting the objective revolutionary conditions created by the increasingly catastrophic crises of capitalism – is no longer viable. (I have shown above how well this critique of European Communist Parties marries with that of Debray *vis-à-vis* the Latin American parties.)

The problem, as Gorz sees it, is to identify the needs unsatisfied by neo-capitalism and disguised by its satisfaction of other, implanted or artificially reinforced, needs. In these disjunctions lie the contradictions of the system, which must be exacerbated by political interventions. Accordingly, a political programme aiming to achieve socialism must learn to reject reformist reforms (those which reinforce neo-capitalism) in favour of non-reformist reforms (those which are expressions of authentic needs and which imply radical change). In assigning the latter to the category of *devoir-être*, Gorz shows that he regards his task to be the concrete political specification of Sartre's anti-structuralist view of ethics. *Stratégie ouvrière et néocapitalisme* thus marks out the place of praxis in the freedom no longer to conform to the norms of the existing system. It also assists Sartre in his shift of emphasis from scarcity to sovereignty, or at least permits an implied redefinition of scarcity as scarcity of sovereignty, or of material goods, or of both.

This last development underlines the significance of the work of Sahlins. I asked earlier whether his 'original affluent society' cast doubt on the validity of the Sartrean concept of scarcity. The answer is that, like the analyses of Gorz, it helps it attain a clearer formulation. Sahlins's society of hunters and gatherers is a sovereign affluent society and can be contrasted with modern France, where sovereignty is surrendered to affluence. This view is refined by Gorz, who shows how the development of monopoly capitalism in Europe causes regional imbalances which introduce economic structures of the colonial type. It also demonstrates why he attributes such political importance to the students: less affluent, they have less reason to behave defensively. The Sartrean and Gorzian points of view meet in the conviction that what the French are led to regard as affluence is a form of non-material scarcity which depends for its existence on creating material scarcity elsewhere.

It is important to stress that Gorz is not just a contributor to *TM*:

as an editor, he relays to French readers the arguments of activists of various persuasions; as a writer of editorials, he puts forward views consistent with those that Sartre expounds elsewhere, mainly in *Le Nouvel Observateur*. Above all, he brings in from Italy significant contributions to the study of neo-capitalism. Like Sartre, he considers the PCI to be politically more progressive and intellectually more alive than the PCF. It is useful to scrutinise *TM*'s debt to Italy in this period, precisely because it highlights the extent to which the editorial influences of Sartre and Gorz have changed. Sartre now derives much of his political continuity from Gorz and from *TM*, having previously seen them informed by his own. It is therefore not appropriate to reduce the review's preoccupation with Italy to the influence of Sartre's friendship with the PCI leader Togliatti. In his obituary notice for Togliatti in October 1964, Sartre merely draws in broad terms the outline of his sympathy with the PCI – a synthetic party, the only one capable of using Marxism to understand itself.

It is left to Gorz to take the review closer to the debates going on within the PCI – so close, in fact, that Sartre's high opinion is rapidly qualified. In January 1966 *TM* carries, unfortunately without contextualising them,[127] two texts dealing with the viability of the Popular Front strategy. From the dominant right wing of the Party, Giorgio Amendola justifies it in the name of working-class unity. From the left wing comes a lengthy critique of this position by Lucio Magri. It is an attempt to prevent the PCI from gravitating towards the reformist programme of the Italian Centre–Left and is much more compatible with the perspectives of Gorz and Debray than is the attitude of the PCI leadership. In the course of time, Magri becomes a commentator on whom *TM* places great reliance. Far from being a spokesman of the Togliatti so respected by Sartre, he draws his inspiration from Gramsci and considers Togliatti guilty of diminishing the intellectual vitality of the Party by making Gramsci the object of a cult. In 1966, as his importance to *TM* begins to become apparent, Magri is expelled from the cultural and press sections of the PCI.

The debates on Popular Front strategy are of relevance to the problem of the unity of the Left in France. Sartre, however, makes it quite clear in interviews given in 1965[128] that there is no party in France capable of carrying out Gorz's programme of revolutionary reforms. In deepening its critique of neo-capitalism, *TM* necessarily moves further and further away from the terms of reference of French parliamentary democracy. The more it comes to understand the system's capacity to absorb pressure for even minimal reforms, the more it turns from party political solutions towards conceptions of radical union activity and models of workers' control. It is not for nothing that Gorz's next stock-taking is entitled *Le Socialisme difficile*.[129] This collection of essays and papers written in 1965 and 1966 should be read in conjunction with all the Italian material that reaches *TM* from left-wing socialists like Leilo Basso and Vittorio Foa and communists like Magri and Bruno Trentin. In February 1967 Gorz supplies a lead-off article entitled 'Réforme et révolution'; in it, the familiar repudiations of *attentisme* and gradualism are accompanied by the acknowledgement that both sudden economic collapse and revolutionary action are out of the question. What seems to Gorz to be indicated is a socialist strategy that will progressively modify the balance of class power, creating conditions of crisis in which armed insurrection might well become appropriate.

In 1967, *TM* anticipates strategic interventions over a period of about ten years. May 1968 thus arrives nine years prematurely. Before discussing the events and their massive reverberations, I shall digress to the equally important Soviet invasion of Czechoslovakia. Before the invasion and before May 1968, Gorz celebrates the temporary victory of the Czechs in a Stalinist society where 'les libertés fondamentales et les garanties constitutionnelles n'ont cessé d'être violées au nom *d'une révolution qui n'a jamais eu lieu*'.[130] The risk, he says, is that reforms will bring token workers' control on the Yugoslav model, with government by technocracy. In order to prevent this sort of development occurring everywhere, he issues a very Gramscian call – one which will change the character of *TM* – for 'une intelligentsia marxiste liée à la classe ouvrière et capable de lui assurer l'hégémonie idéologique et culturelle'.[131]

At the time of the invasion itself, *TM* publishes one of its most angry editorials. Apparently composed by Gorz, it denounces Soviet attitudes: 'une conception purement militariste du rapport des forces mondiales; une complète indifférence pour la cause du socialisme et de la révolution dans le monde; une totale dégénérescence des dirigeants et du fonctionnement des institutions'.[132] This analysis is backed up by Sartre's preface to Liehm's collection of interviews with Czech intellectuals, *Trois Générations*. Sartre's text, which might well have been incorporated into the second volume of the *Critique* as a sequel to the study of the Stalin–Trotsky relationship, encapsulates *TM*'s basic article of faith: 'peu importent les raisons que se donne un peuple pour venir au socialisme:

l'essentiel, c'est qu'il le construise de ses propres mains'.[133] In Czechoslovakia in 1948, says Sartre, an inappropriate socio-economic model was imposed from without, one which was invalid even in its country of origin. Alienation in and by bureaucracy made of the Czechs 'les possédés du pouvoir'.[134] Atomised, they lived in mutual suspicion rather than in the reciprocity which attends shared struggle. Yet even bankrupt Stalinism contains the possibility of socialism. In 1968, the Czechs discovered that exist-ential values lead not to capitalism but to direct democracy; it was their success that brought about the invasion.

This text is of interest because of its very existence. True, the preface is a form of which Sartre is fond; true also, that Liehm is a friend and occasional contributor to *TM*. On the other hand, Sartre is at this time heavily committed to *L'Idiot de la famille*. I mention this because – and it is a fact that usually escapes notice – Sartre writes nothing at all on the May events. Interviews with *Le Nouvel Observateur* and *Der Spiegel* cannot count as substantive analyses, and in any case Sartre uses them to insist that he is a partisan but not a leader. He explicitly follows Gorz's line of '*réformisme révo-lutionnaire*',[135] and his comment that the movement reveals 'une revendication neuve, celle de la souveraineté'[136] is made by a theoretician who is happy to defer to the synthetic anthropologists in the field.

It is therefore Gorz who takes charge of *TM*'s *prises de position* during and after May. A hastily inserted editorial in the May/June number declares with a new confidence that 'nous savons désormais que la révolution socialiste n'est pas impossible dans un pays d'Europe occidentale'.[137] Gorz sticks to his analyses but is pre-pared to revise his strategy in view of the fact that 'C'est le caractère immédiatement révolutionnaire et exemplairement subversif des actions étudiantes qui a provoqué la mobilisation de la classe ouvrière.'[138] Unfortunately, due to the lack of a mature revolution-ary organisation capable of taking over the means of production, the detonation led only to small unco-ordinated explosions. Responsibility for the failure, therefore, lies with the 'principales forces d'ordre anti-révolutionnaires de la société française'[139] – the PCF and the CGT. They imposed minimalist programmes in a Stalinist manner, in order opportunistically to preserve the credibility of French communism as a reliable partner in a social-democratic government. *TM*'s extreme disillusion with the parlia-mentary Left leads it to conclude that if the strategy of revolution-ary reformism is to be revised, then it should be brought much nearer to the Guevarist schema. All the more relevant now that the element of surprise is lost, this option would permit vanguard military activity to elicit a violent response from the State and would be followed up by the mobilisation of a politically prepared working class. In fact, Gorz soon discards this scenario,[140] but nevertheless emphatically places at the top of *TM*'s agenda the problem of how to build an effective revolutionary organisation.

The most thorough analysis of the May events is supplied by Magri. In three instalments (August/September, October, November 1969) he contends that the French have failed to understand their failure. The main target of his wrath is the PCF, but the party does not bear all the blame. The French culture of preceding years, he asserts, had been technocratic or structuralist and had diminished the possibility of effective action. His accusation of theoretical bankruptcy is worth repeating:

Ce n'est donc pas par hasard que les intellectuels qui, dans les dernières années, avaient dicté les lignes de recherche et les modes actuelles, l'école de Lévi-Strauss ou celle d'Althusser, Foucault ou Lacan, n'ont joué aucun rôle important pendant les événements. De même, ce n'est pas par hasard que les intellectuels de grand renom qui ont, au contraire, appuyé pleinement le mouvement (par exemple Sartre, Kastler, le groupe du *Nouvel Observateur* et celui des *Temps modernes*, l'école de Touraine ou le groupe 'Socialisme ou barbarie', et aussi de nombreux intellectuels du PCF) aient pu ou su le faire, plus en manifestant leur solidarité qu'en apportant une contribution, qu'ils aient ressenti la crise plus comme une crise de leurs idées et de leur génération que comme une occasion de soumettre ces idées à l'épreuve des faits, de les développer dans le feu de la lutte.[141]

It is no doubt inappropriate to place Sartre and Gorz in the same generation. More importantly, Magri's suggestion that they saw May as that which confounded their previous thinking is not acceptable. I have shown in some detail the extent to which their radicalism permeated different sectors: if this process was inhibited by the PCF and by the structuralists, they themselves can hardly be held responsible. Certainly, even though both subsequently radicalise their positions further, neither gives the impression that the failure of May was in part due to his own shortcomings. Magri nevertheless remains an ally of *TM*, particularly when the PCI leadership lays down the line of 'struggle against the bourgeoisie and against the students' in 1969. Magri and Rossana Rossanda, shortly to be expelled from the Party, found the journal *Il Manifesto* and in August hold a long debate with Sartre, which is published in Italian in September and by *TM* in January 1970.

Entitled 'Masses, spontanéité, parti', it is, with the exception of the January 1973 editorial 'Elections, piège à cons', the last major text given to *TM* by Sartre during his lifetime. It contains what is perhaps his last reference to the history–structure debate of previous years. Sartre now acknowledges the value of 'le concept de "structure" introduit par Lévi-Strauss [et] que certains marxistes ont essayé, avec plus ou moins de bonheur, d'utiliser'.[142] The interview, despite Magri's contentions, reveals a Sartre confident of the importance of his own contribution to Marxism. Althusser and Lévi-Strauss, on the other hand, are now men of the past: history and the synthetic anthropology have left them behind.

More pressing are the problems of praxis. How, for example, can the need for sovereignty acquire the same mobilising power as the need for food, when food itself is not lacking? What type of political organisation does this situation require? In this perspective Sartre and *Il Manifesto* discuss the received binary opposition of spontaneism and Bolshevism. Sartre's views still derive from the *Critique* but are also marked by the experience of 1968. He insists that spontaneity is not to be thought of as the absence of organisation. The mass of oppressed and non-combative workers constitute a series; they exhibit organised behaviour, but it is behaviour organised by others from without. Consciousness of oppression and combativity, meanwhile, are manifested in conduct that is not *organised* but *organising*: the degree of organisation remains the same, while the poles of activity and passivity are reversed. The new formation is the group in fusion, in which 'les individus établissent des rapports de réciprocité, jouissent, par rapport à l'ensemble, de ce que j'ai appelé une "liberté sauvage" '.[143]

The political problem is that while one group in fusion may call others into existence, the eventual multiplicity will be a collection of groups separated by powerful geographical, economic and social variables. How are such groups to be co-ordinated? By a party, says Sartre, that will prevent each group from regressing into serialisation and minimise the extent to which inter-group relations are themselves serial. The difficulty is that a highly structured party, even with the best intentions, tends to disintegrate groups in fusion by absorbing them; a party with the worst intentions, of course, successfully suppresses them. The revolution thus requires an organisation 'perpétuellement en mesure de lutter contre sa propre institutionalité [...] J'avoue ne pas voir comment pourraient se résoudre les problèmes qui se posent à toute structure stabilisée.'[144] It is as if, in the end, Sartre's resolutely disabused conclusion to *Les Mots* is reproduced at another level, that of the group rather than that of the individual. 'On se défait d'une névrose, on ne se guérit pas de soi',[145] he had said. The struggle against counter-productivity must continue to be waged, sometimes counter-productively. Those who contest the counter-productivity of capitalism do so only because they are contaminated by it; if the alternative is total alienation, then limited infection and the desire for cure must be reckoned indices of health.

The problem of organisation thus remains unsolved, and it is up to Gorz to address it practically. In France, where the hold of the communist bureaucracies has been weakened and where capitalism is still in a state of shock following the events of May, Gorz discerns a pre-revolutionary situation. Edgar Faure's *loi d'orientation* and the promotion of *participation* in the administration of institutions of higher education become a prime target. In April 1970, *TM* rebukes Paul Ricœur for taking control at Nanterre and publishes its exhortation to 'détruire l'université'. Although Gorz's article may be described as terroristic, in that it implicitly challenges the positions of other editors, it is in no way nihilistic. Tautly argued, it asserts the double dysfunctionality of higher education. On the one hand, says Gorz, free access means that academic success is no longer a guarantee of upward social mobility; the university is no longer able to perform the function of selection necessary to the hierarchical division of labour and it is therefore an embarrassment to capitalism. On the other hand, it is incapable of providing an alternative general education which would destroy the existing division of labour. In the context of the class struggle, it is of no real use to either side. 'Elle dispense une *culture universitaire*, c'est-à-dire un savoir *séparé* de toute pratique productive ou militante.'[146] Better, then, says Gorz, to destroy it, because future violent action will further expose the crisis of bourgeois institutions and will eliminate the ghettos to which the traditional workers' organisations strive to consign the students. A major distraction will thus be removed in exemplary fashion, freeing numerous militants for more critical conflicts in the factories and in the business corporations.

This episode brings me to the third and final part of this section, the consideration of professional anthropology in the light of all that precedes. The fate of Pontalis and Pingaud leaves little doubt that Gorz's anti-academicism is formulated from a position of editorial dominance. Given the intellectual climate inside and outside *TM*, there is no reason to think that anthropology might be spared from the onslaught which has already led to the disappearance of psychoanalysis; it is, after all, an allegedly positivist academic practice suspected of collusion with colonialism. This does not bode well for Pouillon, who is also secretary of the Lévi-Straussian journal *L'Homme*, and it is not long before the question asked in turn by Oreste, Leiris, Fanon and Debray in different ways is now asked of him – 'l'ethnologie, pourquoi faire?'

On the face of it, Pouillon's predicament is serious. Lévi-Strauss is now considered a spent force and his object of study itself is vanishing. Indeed, the country which had welcomed him over thirty years previously to establish the discipline of sociology in its new higher education system – Brazil – has an extremely poor record, to say the least, regarding the human rights of the indigenous peoples; moreover, it has recently taken to sending its armed forces into the universities to root out proponents of revolutionary programmes, who owe more to Debray than to the French anthropological tradition. The *tristes tropiques*, in fact, have been caught up in the rival totalisations of imperialism and liberation struggles; they now offer better fieldwork prospects for rural and urban guerrillas than for the students of Lévi-Strauss. The significant events of the recent past – the career of Lumumba is perhaps the best example – have proved too complex for orthodox anthropological study; the fact that Lumumba's name is taken in vain by a Stalinist university in Moscow only confirms the view of Sartre and Gorz that the synthetic anthropology is at last seeing the real possibility that structures might be changed in the desired manner.

Within the profession there is a crisis of confidence. Now that the Third World starts in the suburbs, as Sartre has said, it is difficult to maintain the disciplinary boundaries between sociology and anthropology. Similarly, it is not easy to sustain the methodological stereotypes of the visiting Western observer and the visited and observed natives. Leiris in any case has gone so far as to affirm the inevitability of ethnocentricity and the primacy of personal over professional motivation. Balandier, Condominas, Jaulin and Lévi-Strauss admit as much in their more confidential texts. Métraux and Sebag, meanwhile, have committed suicide. Métraux's case is particularly revealing, for it must have been during this period of crisis (certainly between 1963, the date of his death, and 1978, when his notebooks were published) that, according to his editor, colleagues did their best to suppress the details of his professional disenchantment. The picture painted by André-Marcel d'Ans[147] is that of a discipline aspiring to academic prestige and desperately anxious to disguise the fact that the fieldwork, on which its accreditation is based, is nearly always lacking in rigour and avoided as much as possible by its practitioners.

Despite the resurgence of Marxist economic anthropology, welcomed by *TM*, it is easy to see that Pouillon's positions are bound to be exposed and tested. I shall therefore survey his editorial activity in the latter half of this period. When Beauvoir notes that she has 'un goût particulier pour les monographies',[148] she cites studies that are sociological rather than anthropological: works by Jean Duvignaud, Oscar Lewis (some of whose Mexican research appears in *TM* in April 1966), Mouloud Makal, Edgar Morin, Lawrence Wylie. When she adds that 'parmi les livres d'ethnologie, je préfère ceux qui m'indiquent sur un cas particulier comment un "primitif" intériorise sa situation',[149] she is obviously thinking of Talayesva the Sun Chief, but also mentions Theodora Kroeber's *Ishi in Two Worlds*, the account of the fate of the last Californian Yaki Indian; Paul Zumthor's review of the book (August 1965) gives a résumé of the genocide. In similar vein, Vilma Chiara (December 1968) documents the extermination of Brazilian Indians. Claude Glayman (May 1966) anticipates later debates when he assesses Colin Turnbull's *The Lonely African* and its ethical critique of colonialism. On the other hand, some familiar themes return. Julian Pitt-Rivers (June 1967) provides an essay on hospitality systems, and in the same month the shaman makes a final appearance in *TM*, in a chapter taken from A. P. Elkin's classic study of *The Australian Aborigines*. These articles, however, are best regarded as vestigial, confirming rather than quelling the disciplinary turmoil.

Michel Panoff is the first professional to acknowledge and to examine the *malaise*. In point of fact, his fieldwork in Melanesia is explicitly concerned with the effects of colonialism. His discussions of aspects of cargo-cults appear in *TM* in May 1969 and in July 1970, and in February 1965 he contributes a political history and sociology of Tahiti. He has an appropriately flexible view of the object of study and a real sense of the difficulties of working in the colonies. These emerge from a chapter of his *L'Ethnologue et son ombre*, published by *TM* in April 1968. In general, his first concern is that data should be gathered and analysed as neutrally as possible; he regards radical political interventions as counterproductive for both the fieldworker and the informants. Although it is odd for *TM* to provide a platform for these liberal academic views, Panoff is not a wholly ineffectual witness for the defence of his discipline. He challenges that familiar item of Sartrean rhetoric, the caricatural assimilation of ethnography to entomology.[150] Equally unacceptable to him, and here he appears to have Leiris in mind, is the rejection by the fieldworker of Western culture and the attempt, in British colonial idiom, to 'go native'. The main merit of his discussion of *compréhension*, which he claims is the necessary precondition of good academic fieldwork, is that he takes pains to distinguish it from identification. This is extremely useful, given that it is in precisely this respect that the methodology of *L'Idiot de la famille* may be considered suspect. At the same time, it is correct to say, as Jean Copans does,[151] that Panoff fails to persuade his readers of the scientific status of his work and that his motivations are Rousseauian. His moral and epistemological considerations are certainly politically naive, but it is no doubt instructive for *TM* readers to see, for once, a relatively open professional self-assessment.

It is revealing of the state of professional training that Panoff's book should be so full of practical advice. Indeed, both he and Copans[152] are highly critical of the absence, at undergraduate and postgraduate level, of research and teaching facilities, of funding, of curricula and of a professional *esprit de corps*. Panoff's pressure in April 1968 is reformist and aims at securing for anthropology the credibility enjoyed by other social sciences. It dramatically reveals the demoralisation in a discipline which is ripe for radicalisation and in no position to be sheltered from student criticism. The crisis which *TM* documents in 1971 is thus heavily influenced by the institutional upheavals which follow the May events. An open letter to the Dean of the Nanterre Faculty in March 1969, for example, points out that the anthropology department, which had been operating smoothly for two months, had been brought to a standstill following assaults on students by the internal security force. The signatories, including Jeanne Favret (later a contributor to *TM*) and Dan Sperber, announce their intention of going on hunger strike. Sahlins is reported as having refused to teach.

I have said that Pouillon makes no immediate response to Gorz's call for the destruction of the university, except to rebuke Courchay for the disrespect shown to Lévi-Strauss. The debate in 1971, however, is substantial: two hundred pages of argument, the bulk in the January issue, the remainder coming in June. The discussions have a dual focus which merges over the months into one. On the one hand, Copans introduces a dossier taken from the American review *Current Anthropology* in 1968 and documenting the connection between anthropology and imperialism; into this debate Pouillon is drawn. At the same time, Jean Monod presents a radical and angry view of his own professional activities; this leads to a clash with Pouillon, who then allows himself a last word.

Readers of *TM* are aware that Monod is not an orthodox ethnographer. Two previous contributions – on Parisian youth subcultures (July 1966) and on race riots in the USA (December 1967) – have indicated that his activities exclude neither the study of Western societies nor partisan political analysis. In 1971, after studies at the CNRS and fieldwork in Venezuela, he gives vent to what Balandier calls 'an accusatory anthropology',[153] comparable in spirit to the work of James Agee. He belongs to the generation of students to whom Panoff gave his fieldwork guidelines in the mid-sixties and his criticisms of prevailing pedagogic assumptions bear out much of what Panoff had to say. His critique of anthropology is nevertheless much more substantial and reaches into its intellectual core and its political function. It is striking that some of *TM*'s most anti-structuralist remarks should come from a student who spent May 1968 in the Venezuelan jungle reading Lévi-Strauss's *Mythologiques*. From Agee to Monod, *TM* retains its consistency.

Monod's research endeavours to disconfirm structuralist principles and to show that a kinship system is not so much a set of rules as a retrospective terminology, and that the problem is not how a group breaks down into family units but how the family units come to constitute a group. He concludes that structuralism imposes on foreign cultures certain predetermined schemata. By way of compensation, he accords greater attention to his own object of study's perception of him as *un riche cannibale*, the designation taken as the title of what he calls his *ethno-récit*. Unlike Leiris, he is not willing to grant the inevitability of ethnocentricity and prefers to regard the ethnocentricity of Lévi-Straussian anthropology as an expression of political interest. Lévi-Strauss had pronounced his discipline 'fille d'une ère de violence';[154] Monod, by implication, places it in the Sartrean category of *putain*, although without using the sexist language of either.

Anthropology, for Monod, operates as the tool of imperialist expansion by absorbing as objects of knowledge, and thereby devouring, foreign cultures. It eliminates them by the practice of study and may be said, in consequence, to study them by process of elimination. This view closely resembles Jaulin's concept of *ethno-cide*, formulated in his book *La Paix blanche*,[155] which is reviewed by Pouillon in the same January 1971 issue. Monod's position ultimately leaves no room for ethnography, outside the metropolis, unless it be for that of the guerrilla. As far as Pouillon can see, the difference between Monod and Jaulin is that the latter has no trace of guilt, whereas the former 'en relatant ici-même son expérience, n'a cessé de se mettre en cause et a consciemment écrit une "monod-graphie" '.[156] Pouillon's objection to Jaulin is that the hypothesis of *la paix blanche* requires anthropologists to take upon themselves all the responsibility for colonialism; it overstates its case so much as to suggest that there are no relevant political or economic considerations at all. Pouillon accepts neither that there is a mechanical relationship tying anthropology to imperialism, nor that the knowledge produced is inherently oppressive. Genuine anthropological knowledge, he believes, is available for political abuse and for political use, and it is regrettable that the former has prevailed hitherto.

In the same issue, Copans presents the dossier of American material,[157] with Kathleen Gough's 'Anthropology and imperialism' as the lead article. Gough, who went into self-imposed exile in Canada in 1967, is both example and analyst of the liberal academics compromised by the Vietnam War and led to realise the impossibility of professional decontextualisation from imperialism. American anthropology, she says, uses a conceptual apparatus derived from consensus models, has a psychologistic outlook on underdevelopment, and is paralysed by respect for its paymasters. In her view, if the discipline wishes to fulfil its humanitarian objectives, it must take Marxist analyses seriously and recognise neo-colonialism as a viable object of study. The discussion that follows acknowledges the social responsibility of the anthropologist and the need for a new theoretical basis for the study of macro-social change. On the whole, however, Gough is regarded by her American colleagues as a shade too radical. Copans, in the interests of balance, draws the attention of *TM*'s readers to the much more categorical judgements of André Gunder Frank, the economist of 'underdevelopment', who advises anthropologists to stay at home and to contribute to the elaboration of coherent anti-imperialist political programmes. Copans endorses the general view that the relationship of anthropology and imperialism is not at all clear-cut. He insists nevertheless that the profession has failed to live up to the standard of reflexivity set by Leiris in 1950: 'Vingt ans après, ce texte ['L'ethnographe devant le colonialisme'] n'a rien perdu de sa vigueur et de son exactitude.'[158]

Copans's 'Quelques réflexions', drawing together the threads of the discussion, allow him to take up a position close to that of Pouillon: anthropology is not the only discipline to be incriminated and it cannot, on its own, assume the heavy burden of the study of imperialism. Even so, French practitioners must reach a clearer understanding of their own motivations: 'Au pays des Tristes Tropiques, des Afriques ambiguës et des Exotiques quotidiens, la recherche, sinon du paradis perdu, du moins du Temps perdu (les "primitifs" vont disparaître) a toujours été un motif subjectif suffisamment puissant pour justifier le fonctionnement de cette discipline "scientifique".'[159] Like Pouillon, Copans feels that anthropology lends itself both to abuse and to use, and that use has been conspicuous by its absence. He notes that while thinkers like Sartre, Jeanson and Chomsky have used their influence in support of the national liberation struggles, anthropologists working in Chad, for example (and presumably he means Pouillon rather than Jaulin), have maintained a low profile. He sees no reason to regard this as inevitable and concludes that 'l'élaboration d'une anthropologie de la libération passe donc par la libération de l'anthropologie'.[160]

At this point, the debate is temporarily closed. The reverberations become public six months later, when a number of professionals not hitherto involved – Roberto Buijtenhuijs (a Dutch Africanist), Sidney Mintz (an American specialist of the Caribbean area), Rodolfo Stavenhagen (a Mexican sociologist based in Geneva), and Octave Mannoni – comment on the Copans dossier as well as on Pouillon's review of Jaulin; finally, there is an irate exchange between Monod and Pouillon.

Mannoni's contribution should be mentioned here, if not for any other reason than that, in the tensions between phenomenology, structuralism and Freudianism, he has retained the respect of all parties and offered comments that attempt to reconcile from a radical perspective. Mannoni believes in the validity of academic knowledge: the abandonment of methodical fieldwork by such ethnographers as Monod in favour of total identification with an oppressed population represents, he says, the acting-out of a fantasy which it is better to be conscious of. The ethnographer's activity, however, is not neutral but ambivalent. On the one hand, it appropriates a foreign culture as an object of knowledge: 'j'ai montré [...] peut-être le premier, que l'étude objective d'une population créait de son seul fait une situation coloniale'.[161] On the other, in studying what is foreign, it attains a greater understanding of the metropolis, and this is precisely what confers on ethnography a revolutionary potential. Perhaps it is this article that best defines synthetic ethnography:

Nous avons besoin des ethnographes pour comprendre (et quelquefois nous le comprenons à leur dépens) et pour modifier notre attitude occidentale, après avoir mesuré tout ce qui la sépare d'autres attitudes possibles. [...] Ils sont chargés de nous raconter des histoires vraies qui prouvent qu'on pourrait changer la vie [...] L'essentiel, c'est que d'aller chez les indigènes, ou dans les bidonvilles, ou dans les prisons, dans les usines, dans les hôpitaux psychiatriques, c'est la même chose. On y apprend ce qu'il faut combattre ailleurs.[162]

Knowledge of oppression, in other words, which, even as it is acquired increases oppression in the locality of its acquisition (the colony), must then be deployed in such a way as to promote change in the locality of its application (the metropolis). This is a brief sketch of the anthropology which *TM* has been seeking, a distant echo of Leiris's formulations resounding with new energy in the context of crisis; wholly consistent with 'Questions de méthode', it points to the recuperation of academic practico-inert in revolutionary praxis.

The problem is that this apparent reconciliation of the synthetic anthropology and academia comes shortly after Gorz has indicated all reform of the university to be a distraction. The profession thus reaches, after 1970, a position which was acceptable to *TM* only before 1970. This disjunction does not make Pouillon's task any easier. In a sense, he is lucky to be the victim of a vitriolic attack by Monod, one that invites indignation or defensive irony rather than a detailed evaluation of the issues. For Monod, there is no possibility of dialogue with one who has become the lackey of the most reactionary of the mandarins and whose polemical technique is ethnocidally to invalidate the experience of his opponent. Even for Monod, it transpires, anthropology has now become a lady: 'Emouvante vieille dame: moribonde, elle se croit irrésistible comme aux beaux jours de sa Triste Tropification.'[163] Monod pledges total support for Jaulin, implying that the latter has been ostracised as a dangerous radical by the integrated academics whose names appear regularly in *L'Homme*. Their progressive rhetoric disguises a conservatism motivated by nostalgia for a descriptive anthropology which, says Monod, does not exist. It cannot exist, for to study is to colonise and thus to annihilate: '*le politique est là, au cœur même de la question épistémologique*'.[164]

Pouillon's reply uses Monod rather disparagingly as a means of addressing Jaulin – hence the title, 'Réponse à un ventriloque'. He still resists the idea that the Western ethnographer has a necessarily evil eye, for ethnocide is a reality that will not cease simply because anthropologists abandon their profession. There are, he adds, Procrustean monographs, but not all academic work is equally reductive or equally in collusion with neo-colonialism: 'On voit mal en effet comment les *Structures élémentaires de la parenté* ou les *Mythologiques* pourraient "servir" l'impérialisme.'[165]

Monod's attack does not invite a long theoretical reply. Nevertheless, Pouillon ends with remarks which are considered and qualified and which invoke the humanism implied by his professional practice – the conviction that the species is unified while being multi-centred, a system of differences within a fundamental similarity. He concludes in the following way:

Cela suppose [...] une logique transhistorique (ce qui ne fait pas de l'histoire une illusion) et universelle. Mais cette universalité n'est pas l'extension injustifiée et violente d'une logique qui ne serait en fait que la nôtre; au contraire, la nôtre, comme les autres, n'en est qu'une spécification locale dont il faut se déprendre pour découvrir ce en quoi celles-ci et celle-là se ressemblent et s'opposent. Bref, loin d'être le pur et simple reflet du colonialisme, le produit mécanique de l'expansion européenne, l'ethnologie est plutôt ce qui mine l'assurance du monde blanc face aux autres cultures. Cela n'empêche évidemment pas qu'elle puisse être asservie et dénaturée; mais seul Gribouille peut vouloir la détruire pour la maintenir en vie.[166]

This, then, is Pouillon's *profession de foi*: it is resolutely structuralist, both in its view of history and in its desire for a continuing cultural pluralism. At the same time, it is dialectical enough to refuse any mechanistic appreciation of the political function of academic knowledge. In this way, it affirms the viability of higher education and thus implies that there are no grounds for resignation from the Editorial Board in the face of the hard line taken by Gorz. Pouillon leaves his anti-imperialist views somewhat understated; he probably feels, quite rightly, that his record on Indochina and Algeria speaks for itself; he may also feel that his record on Chad is more open to criticism. Precisely how this 1971 stance affects his subsequent editorial contribution is something that I shall take up in the Conclusion.

CONCLUSION

From 1971 to *TM*'s fortieth anniversary in October 1985 – these years represent the longest of the five periods that I have identified. There are a number of reasons for assigning the greatest amount of material to the smallest space and I shall amplify these in the course of this conclusion. The reasons are the following: first, the influence of Sartre and Gorz diminishes quite rapidly from the mid-seventies and the theoretical, if not the political, parameters of the synthetic anthropology become much less easy to discern; secondly, the editorial presence of Pouillon yields very little academic anthropology; thirdly, only one contributor, Jeanne Favret-Saada, advances significantly along the royal road of reflexivity explored by Sartre and Leiris.

In the last nine years of his life, Sartre's profile in *TM* is low. In July/August 1979 he discusses with Daniel Cohn-Bendit and Alice Schwartzer the importance of guilt in the outlook of the West Germans, and in September 1979 he chairs an Israeli–Palestinian colloquium organised, with difficulty, by Pierre Victor.[1] A terse note, the last, in March 1980, warns readers to avoid articles by Serge Thion, suspected of endorsing denials of Nazi genocide. His only sustained statement of views is the bluntly monitory 'Elections, piège à cons' (January 1973), which appropriately reiterates, through the prism of the *Critique*, the denunciation of the analytic character of liberal democracy first rehearsed in the 'Présentation' of 1945.

Sartre's active participation is reduced both voluntarily and by force of circumstance. Strikingly, he does not allow *TM* to operate at the deeper theoretical levels of his most recent work: Evelyne Pinto's essay on the third volume of *L'Idiot de la famille* (October 1974) is anomalous in this respect. This, however, is an attitude that dates from before 1968. The study of Flaubert (unfinished though it may be, and as many as three further volumes are spoken of) is an important yardstick by which *TM*'s synthetic anthropology should

203

be judged, given Flaubert's permanent status as a negative exemplar of responsibility and reflexivity. The relative absence from the review of a totalisation which it was partly designed to promote is thus unfortunate, particularly as *L'Idiot de la famille* maintains all the Sartrean lines on colonialism, racialism and possession and restates the complex view of academic anthropology that I have traced in this study.[2]

At the same time, and bearing in mind Pontalis's oblique request for greater self-understanding in 1954, it is possible to detect a real lack of reflexivity in *L'Idiot de la famille*. Sartre quotes Flaubert's evocation of a *roquentin*[3] but seems oblivious of the fact that many readers of *La Nausée* and *Les Mots* will at this point doubt the viability of a *comprehénsion* which fails to follow up the evident links between observer and observed. Nowhere is there any direct attempt to investigate the possibility of authorial identification with Flaubert. It is this totalisation, after all, which would raise the work to the highest level of synthetic anthropology and yield a *Flaubert fantôme* capable of standing beside Leiris's 'auto-ethnography'.

What does Sartre himself say of this? 'Si le Flaubert ressemble aux *Mots* par endroits, c'est parce qu'après cinquante ans d'écriture, on finit par être imbu de son propre style et que certaines formules viennent spontanément sans aucun travail.'[4] It is ingenuous or evasive of him to reduce to a technical practico-inert the elements shared by two existential psychoanalyses. He gives the strong impression that he is eager to set up a methodological barrier between *Les Mots* and *L'Idiot de la famille* in order to disguise their substantial continuity. In the interview with Contat from which the remark is taken, he implies that he himself is no longer interesting as an object of study. The inference is that the neutralisation of the observer legitimises his comprehension-based case-study, but this is difficult to accept in view of the obvious intensity of the fascination exerted by Flaubert. It is as if *Les Mots* is written in advance of *L'Idiot de la famille* and as an unannounced sequel to 'Questions de méthode' in order specifically to de-problematise the subjectivity of the synthetic anthropologist and to ensure the impartiality on which the credibility of the study of Flaubert will depend. To be able to write *L'Idiot de la famille*, Sartre thus cuts its links with *Les Mots*. This is unfortunate for *TM*, for it shares the same fate. When Sartre asserts that 'mon antipathie première s'est changée en empathie',[5] he forgets that it was on the antipathy that *TM* was built. Either this *parti pris* has been abandoned, which is unlikely – given the political consistency of the review – or it has been repudiated in the knowledge that it masks an identification. If the latter, then the synthetic anthropologist has clearly fallen at the last fence, failing to explicate his implication in his object of study.

All is not so simple, however, for there are conjunctural reasons for *TM*'s lack of interest in *L'Idiot de la famille*. They derive from the same source – a limit set to reflexivity. From this point of view, however, the motivation is more positive. In the years following 1968, Sartre is led to reconsider the status of the intellectual. His disenchantment with the mandarinate is Gorzian. It derives from the view that, while knowledge may be recuperated by the revolutionary movement, it may also be appropriated by the dominant class for its own purposes. At the time of the publication of *L'Idiot de la famille*, when the political situation is still volatile but when the forces of reaction seem to be gaining the upper hand, it is the latter possibility that seems the more likely. A highly theorised and relatively inaccessible work like the study of Flaubert thus proves an embarrassment and is kept away from the review in which all hopes of effective intervention are vested. It may therefore be that the constitutive possession of Sartre by Flaubert is indeed acknowledged, but privately, as it were, in the gigantic aside which *TM* does not publicise and which seemingly few people have read. But even if this is the case, the lack of a public working-through of authorial motivations casts doubt on its synthetic status.

Be that as it may, Sartre now resolves to 'nier le *moment intellectuel* pour tenter de trouver un nouveau statut *populaire*'.[6] The priority of *TM* becomes much more to document the needs of the immediate situation (support for the immigrant workforce, for left-wing conscripts, for Soviet Jewry, for miners working in pits with inadequate safety standards, etc.), rather than to exhaust its energies in methodological virtuosities which might be construed as self-indulgent. When Sartre agrees to take on the legal editorship of periodicals subjected to government harassment (*Interluttes*, *La Cause du peuple*, *Tout!*, *La Cause du peuple – J'accuse!*, *Révolution*), it is not to uphold the freedom of the press, but to seek, in the defence of the *gauchistes*, a new efficacy.

From 1970 onwards, meanwhile, a new factor becomes relevant: sickness and, from 1974, blindness. Sartre is increasingly severely handicapped and restricted more and more to largely symbolic activities, such as the visit to the Baader–Meinhof leaders in Germany in 1974. As a result, most of his subsequent publications take the form of dialogues with persons congenial to him. In these, the significance of Maoism for him is readily visible: it reinforces the long-standing distinction between legality and legitimacy. He continues to hold that the non-coincidence of the two justifies illegal actions by the oppressed, who wish to institute a reciprocity that has been denied them. He is struck by the moral force of the desire for direct democracy, a desire which he expresses primarily as an investment in hope, but it is a mistake to think that hope is a value extorted from a dying Sartre by a newly religious Victor in 1980. On the contrary, it makes its appearance as a 'grande force révolutionnaire'[7] seven years earlier.

At the same time, other evidence shows that Sartre was committed to a rethinking of his positions, one that would produce a third attempt at an ethic. 'La recherche morale', he tells Michel Sicard, 'oblige à considérer l'ontologie que j'ai développée jusqu'ici comme incomplète et fausse.' He speaks of 'un vrai traité philosophique [...] qui sera obligé de ne plus rien laisser debout de *L'Etre et le néant* et de la *Critique de la raison dialectique*'. It would be based on 'l'idée qu'ontologiquement les consciences ne sont pas isolées, il y a des plans où elles entrent les unes dans les autres'.[8] This may imply a return to the Husserlian empathy cast aside in 1943. It also suggests a renewed and explicit reference to the line of thinking embarked on in *La Transcendance de l'Ego*; this would entail a continuation of *Les Mots* in terms of an examination of the compulsion to become *ens causa sui*, as well as of its implications for the methodology of *L'Idiot de la famille*. In his discussions with Beauvoir in 1974,[9] Sartre is encouraged to inspect the connection between breast-feeding and reciprocity and between weaning and resentment. Jeannette Colombel reveals not only that he wished to go more deeply into the related concept of generosity (apparently by an analysis of the *pensée sauvage* of hunters and gatherers – and did he not think of the *TM* team as *des chasseurs de sens*?), but also that he planned a study of the 'premier regard de l'enfant à sa mère'.[10] There seems little doubt that loss of sight stimulated the desire for a 'morale du NOUS',[11] but whether Sartre was sufficiently Oedipal to end in blindness and in truth is a question for other commentators. A study of *TM* does little to answer these intriguing questions.[12]

In 1975, Sartre mentions that 'le travail pratique – ce que nous appelons "faire un numéro" – est assuré actuellement surtout par Pouillon et Gorz, à tour de rôle'.[13] In fact, Gorz's participation begins to wane at precisely this time. Having enthusiastically followed the affairs of the Italian *groupuscule Lotta continua* (which thereby received greater depth of coverage in *TM* than the

French Maoists who were in contact with Sartre), he changes direction and proceeds to examine the implications that information technology and ecology hold for socialist theory and organisation. His *Adieux au prolétariat*[14] is a scintillating application of Sartrean themes – passivity, resentment, scarcity, autonomy, reciprocity, patriarchy and *mentalité pré-logique* – to the specific socio-political conjuncture of the late seventies and the early eighties, but his effective withdrawal from *TM* means that his ideas, although given an airing, do not constitute a theoretical capital to be exploited editorially.

Pouillon, however, remains. Following the great debates of January and June 1971,[15] he writes only three more pieces for *TM*: a brief note in June 1979 which leads to the resignation of Christian Zimmer, the film correspondent; a sceptical comment in June 1981 on the election of François Mitterand to the Presidency; and one of the four editorial texts published in November 1982 and dealing with events in Lebanon. He writes nothing, in other words, that is specifically anthropological, nor does he take over the intellectual leadership abdicated by Gorz. As the editor best placed to promote academic anthropology, his record must be regarded as rather disappointing. I have mentioned already that the texts submitted by Pierre Clastres are particularly lightweight; the same is true of his colleague Jacques Lizot, whose 'Histoires indiennes d'amour' appear in October 1974. It is significant that the more interesting aspects of Clastres's work are featured in *L'Homme* and in Pontalis's *Nouvelle Revue de Psychanalyse* and that Pouillon is also an editor of both these publications. It is to these reviews that he transfers his own interests in history and structure, in structuralism itself, in possession and shamanism, and in psychoanalysis. His dual allegiance remains well established, but the component parts are now more readily separable – an intellectual loyalty to Lévi-Strauss and a personal and political loyalty to Sartre and to *TM*. His recent defence and illustration of Lévi-Strauss's work makes this plain.[16]

The articles which do reach *TM* from the field of academic anthropology, although few in number, maintain, at least initially, the note of disciplinary crisis sounded in 1971. Godelier reviews Colin Turnbull's account of the degradation of the Ik (March 1975); Bernard Lelong and Stefano Varese criticise the Peruvian government's handling of the Amazonian Indians (November 1972 and April 1973); Emmanuel Terray comments on the political perspectives of nationalist movements within France (August/September

1973); Jacques Dournes presents details of ethnic minorities inside Vietnam (May 1975); Georges Dupré describes the symbiosis of capitalism and traditional beliefs in the industrial Congo (August/ September 1977); Laënnec Hurbon examines the movement of Haitians from Haiti (September 1982) into Guadeloupe (April/ May 1983) and the influence of Jehovah's Witnesses in Guadeloupe (October 1983); Jacqueline Duvernay scrutinises Chaco myths in January 1984; and Claudia Fonseca offers a study of a Brazilian *favela* in June 1984.

I list these texts in chronological order to show that, where anthropology is concerned, there is a real falling-away in the early and mid-seventies and a reawakening of interest in the eighties. This broadly reflects the degree of general editorial consensus, which in the years immediately surrounding Sartre's death was distinctly weak. Younger editors came and went – Elisabeth de Fontenay, François George, Pierre Goldman, Dominique Pignon, Pierre Rigoulot, Pierre Victor – while the old guard was diminished by the loss of Bost and Gorz. Seen in this light, the role of Pouillon (together with Beauvoir and Lanzmann) has primarily been that of ensuring the survival of *TM* at a time when its existence was threatened by more fashionable publications. One aspect of this labour is visible in Appendix 5: the dramatic increase in special issues, mostly prepared by guest editors. More viable commercially, they also reflect the Gramscian ethos bequeathed by Sartre and Gorz, that is to say the conception of the review as a militant organ run not by mandarins but by intellectual labourers operating in a variety of strategically crucial locations – local government, industry, education, and so on. If Leiris were to recommend a particular input to this ethos, he would undoubtedly advise the recruitment of anthropologists from the colonised cultures. This is exactly what Pouillon secures in the eighties. Whether a corner has been turned in the post-Sartrean fortunes of *TM*, it is too soon to say, but the indications are that with the West Indian Michel Giraud and the Algerian Sami Nair (together with Henriette Asseo) a new editorial stability has been achieved. Certainly, as Appendix 5 suggests, the anti-colonialist momentum has been recaptured, and Pouillon must take much of the credit for this.

One of the factors which helped *TM* through the difficult interregnum of the seventies was the energy of its feminist contingent, which supplied analyses, *sottisiers* and film reviews on a regular basis. It was through this channel that the work of Jeanne Favret-Saada reached *TM*. There could be no more appropriate review, for she embodies and synthesises many of the strands of the history that I have endeavoured to trace. Brought up in Tunisia, she studied with Sebag at a school in which Memmi was a teacher. She subsequently undertook research on Arab political systems, working in independent Algeria after having acquired a grounding in political anthropology at the London School of Economics. After 1968, as I have mentioned, she was involved in the campaign for *autogestion* at the Laboratoire d'Ethnologie et de Sociologie Comparées in Nanterre. She is now a practising psychoanalyst as well as an ethnographer. Indeed, her first publication in *TM*, in June 1977, is her letter of resignation from Lacan's Ecole Freudienne. The terrorism and lack of reciprocity prevailing inside this supposedly anti-institutional institution raise not only intellectual objections – pedagogic, therapeutic, political – but also a revulsion at the cost of human life – Sebag's hazardous exploration of the interface of anthropology and psychoanalysis and of the relations of both with Marxism had ended in suicide. Her own success owes as much to her independence from Lacan as to her Lacanian insights.

Since she is aware of the probability of mis-recognition, she breaks with the established duality of ethnographic testimony – the academic monograph on the one hand and the confidential journal on the other. The transgression of the protocol which Balandier, Condominas, Lévi-Strauss, Métraux and even Leiris respect finally renders all the debates about scientific objectivity procedurally inseparable from a methodology and a practice of reflexivity. If ethnography is a labour of getting-to-know, says Favret-Saada, then it is this process which should be documented and communicated to the public. Hence the disclosure of her investigations into sorcery in the Bocage district of Normandy in 'Les mots, la mort, les sorts' (August/September 1977) and in 'Corps pour corps' (March 1981). The former theorises the knowledge deriving from the interactions recorded in the latter; subjectivity is banished from neither, on the grounds that if it were, both would be invalidated. The result is that *TM*, so enthusiastic in its early days for the *document brut*, witnesses the elaboration of ethnographic knowledge as never before.

Favret-Saada's opinion of fieldwork is stated in a forthright manner in her review of the Panoffs' *L'Ethnologue et son ombre*. Scientific method, as far as she is concerned, has never had any basis in morality; their attempt to give it one merely reflects changes in professional conduct since the end of direct colonisation. Her observations go to the heart of the matter.

Comment les Panoff ne voient-ils pas qu'être ethnographe, c'est aller justement là où on n'est pas désiré, aucune société sauvage n'ayant jamais inscrit dans son projet l'avènement d'un regard étranger? La relation ethnographique est *d'abord* une relation illégitime parce qu'une offre est faite en regard de laquelle n'existe aucune demande indigène.[17]

There is no inherent reciprocity, then, in the academic ties which bind students of reciprocity to their object of study – only an invasion of privacy. Readers of *TM* will recall that Jaulin had rudely demonstrated this. It follows that ethnographers abstract themselves methodologically from their field of observation at their scientific peril, for they approach their *terrain* of research in a manner that cannot but induce ambivalent attitudes on the part of its inhabitants. Since they wish to claim a positive status for their acquired knowledge, research workers tend to deny the most important aspect of their situation; they accordingly assign a primitivism to the object of study in order to guarantee their cognitive separation from it. But it is apparent that the scientific posture is typically based on a *Verleugnung*: a nostalgia for magic is projected onto the 'primitive' as a form of *mentalité pré-logique*. Favret-Saada thus has recourse to Mannoni in order to formulate a critique of Lévy-Bruhl and of all who have succeeded him. All this, thanks to Mannoni, has become recognisably Sartrean territory, but her use of the concept of *dénégation* is more synthetic than that of Sartre (at least as far as *L'Idiot de la famille* is concerned), because it acknowledges the tendency to disavowal in the observer as well as in the observed.

Her own fieldwork begins at least in part from the Freudian insight, distilled through Lévi-Strauss and Lacan, that where symbolisation is impossible, somatisation ensues. This allows her to extend Evans-Pritchard's sociology of misfortune into a study of the discourse sought and found by victims of extreme anxiety. The discourse in question is that of witchcraft. She discovers that peasant farmers of the Bocage who suffer repeated misfortune are invited by a compassionate *annonciateur* to consider themselves accursed or spellbound, whereupon they call upon a *désorceleur* either to redirect the spell whence it came or to take its ill-effects upon himself or herself. This sets in train a set of struggles for survival which neither Church nor psychiatric hospital are prepared to acknowledge. Here the methodological problem for the ethnographer is one of pragmatics. Sorcery in the Bocage is not a dominant ideology and is therefore defended by silence. There is thus no possibility of acquiring useful information, unless the ethnographer is assigned, by those within the discourse, an appropriate place from which to hear it. Favret-Saada therefore finds herself *ensorcelée* and *apprentie-désorceleuse*; violated, rather than, like Jaulin, violating, she is thus included rather than excluded.

Favret-Saada satisfies better than anyone the epistemological and existential criteria of the synthetic anthropology. Her contribution to it, made from beyond its own theoretical positions, is a sociology of resentment, a comprehension of precariously situated peasants who, reeling from the blows of an unkind fate, have recourse to discourses and to persons offering at least a mediated response to this aggression. She concludes that the sexual impotence of one of her principal contacts 'est pour lui la seule méthode qu'il ait trouvée pour s'affirmer comme un sujet autonome, face à la coalition familiale qui a décidé de son destin en ses lieu et place'.[18] So much does this recall, in different ways, not only Laing but also the Stekel, the Genet and the Flaubert of Sartre, to mention only a few, that it is regrettable that she could not meet Sartre and Flaubert in the Normandy countryside. *Les Mots, la mort, les sorts* is in a sense an excellent sequel to *Les Mots*, for, at least in respect of the informant mentioned above, it is the explication of her own implication in an *idiot de la famille* and is a more effective totalisation than the massive Sartrean labour which is kept at such a distance from *TM*.

I mentioned in the Preface that my intention was to undertake something resembling a Sartrean evaluation of the review. This is, I think, the best compliment that can be paid to a publication which, because of the premium set on reflexivity, has succeeded in sustaining a high level of intellectual tension long enough to hold the curiosity and to shape the attitudes of three generations – those whose maturation was marked by the Liberation, by the Algerian War and by May 1968. I have noted in passing that each of these three 'events' has been the occasion for reproaches to be addressed to Sartre: the criticisms of Jankélévitch in respect of the Occupation, the implied accusation of Hamon and Rotman that Sartre failed to hurry back from Brazil to defend Jeanson in 1960, and the critique by Magri of the intellectuals' record in May. Shaman or *bouc émissaire*? The time has come to pose the question.

I propose to answer it, however, within the context which I have established, that is to say with reference to *TM* and its agonistic relationship with academic anthropology. The review published Jankélévitch without comment and without making clear what sort of satisfaction was being given to him; in this it was remiss. On the other hand, it did not have to defend itself against Jeanson, who did not attack it, or against Magri, whose judgement was much too harsh. However, its own terms of reference make it much more vulnerable to accusations of lack of reflexivity in respect of its synthetic anthropology and, in particular, of its constitutive antipathy – for did not Sartre make of Flaubert both a shaman and a *bouc émissaire*? If the student movement, or at least *TM*'s favoured part of it, gathered real momentum in the sixties thanks to Kravetz's critique of its disabling identification with trade unions in general, why could Sartre not have done likewise with Flaubert in particular?

It may well have been that the circumstances – the post-1968 change in Sartre's and *TM*'s priorities, his rapidly declining health, the magnitude of the task – were unfavourable; it may have been that so much autobiographical material was destined for posthumous publication in order to render such a question redundant. I would like to suggest that, while it is obvious that *L'Idiot de la famille* was not written by a man intent on emulating Leiris, the contacts between the Sartrean and the ethnographic discourses are substantial enough to circumscribe a problematic, one which depends for its coherence on a certain mode of reflexivity.

Sartre is not usually thought of as being the philosopher of possession, resentment, generosity, empathy and reciprocity; in the anthropological context, however, these come to the fore. Observing him ethnographically – in a dual sense, that is to say within the *TM* collective and endeavouring to come to terms with Lévi-Strauss – one realises that Sartre's moral and political recuperation of himself, his redemption, takes place in the move from the micro-social to the macro-social. The Sartre who, in my view, was totally vindicated by his Third-Worldism was the Sartre who had an intimate experience – passive and active – of colonisation, *by* his family and *of* his intellectual *congénères*. Similarly, his intuitive understanding of his own generosity led him to theorise better than any of its objects its potential for humiliation. He was a *sorcier* among *sorciers*, more powerful than many others, but determined to denounce the *grands sorciers* and all their works.

As for Flaubert, Sartre colonised and possessed him because he knew how much he was colonised and possessed by him. He deployed a counter-violence similar in intensity, though not in scale, to that of the Algerians. His was more successful than theirs, in the sense that it yielded an empathy which transcended antipathy; on the other hand, it was a Pyrrhic victory over a dead man, achieved in circumstances which suggested that such a great investment might more usefully have been made in the second volume of the *Critique*. Even so, implied in *L'Idiot de la famille* is the explicit imperative of *TM*: 'coloniser, decolonise thyself!' Failure in this task means that the shaman becomes *bouc émissaire*, which is why the Sartrean answer to the question of identity implicates the present editors of *TM*, for his status is partly in their hands.

Before I consider the review's current situation, I would like to stress that my intention is not to offer a romantic perception of Sartre as an idol with feet of clay. He was not Hegel, after all, but an anti-Hegelian Hegelian, a potter with hands of clay who knew his own degree of existential compromise, even if he expressed it with inconsistent explicitness. To listen to the anthropological intertext is perforce to credit him, not with a constitutive *méconnaissance*, but with a decreasing *inconscience* and a decreasing vulnerability to the temptations of the *esprit de survol*. This is because the *loa* and the *zar* attend him constantly and benevolently. They bring a facility of symbolisation which overrides the lack of explicit linkage between *Les Mots* and *L'Idiot de la famille*; they allow psychoanalytic discourse, which would not tolerate the same lack in the same way, to be relegated to the background and thus ensure both that Pontalis's view of the Flaubert–Sartre relationship is not directly endorsed, and that Sartre does not appear to fall under the sway of the *grand sorcier* Lacan. They inform, therefore, the anti-colonialism which operates at every level of his work.

This is not to suggest that Sartre solved all the problems thrown up by his long and critical fellow-travelling with the Maussian tradition. Possession, resentment, generosity, reciprocity: however much he set his practico-inert to work, he totalised the problems by incarnating them, not by finding theoretical solutions. How far the 'morale du NOUS' is a revision and how far it is implied by the *Critique*, how far empathy and reciprocity can be conflated, how far ontology and ethics can be articulated – these questions, and more, require philosophical answers. Unfortunately, there would appear to be few philosophers in France prepared to call themselves Sartreans; the majority of those who would accept the designation work in Belgium, Holland, Italy and the USA and have only marginal contact with *TM*. The review itself, although staunchly militant, seems reluctant to acknowledge its accumulated Sartrean wisdom and to apply it critically, either in political analyses or in critiques of the dominant ideological discourses of the moment.

What, then, of *TM*? The major question that it has allowed to fade into the background is the one which was raised at its inception – the question of the indivisibility of truth: 'si la vérité est une . . .'. Perhaps it has vanished because contemporary French philosophy tends to regard it as nonsensical. This is not adequate cause for *TM* to forget it – it was, after all, Sartre's fundamental wager. It may be that it will be put back on the agenda by the appearance of the second volume of the *Critique*, and that those who feel the danger of totalisation by Armageddon will be best placed to rediscover the power and the relevance that Sartrean philosophy so obviously had in the sixties. It seems unlikely, however, that this particular deployment of the synthetic anthropology will be undertaken by the French.

An Editorial Board seemingly unsure of its continuity with its founder would be well placed, nonetheless, to work through the implications of the supra-disciplinarity which was the anti-academic expression of Sartre's grand wager. Was it a strategy designed to secure intellectual hegemony in a highly competitive field?[19] Was it something akin to the inter-disciplinarity which Robert Castel refers to as a 'grand rêve fœtal',[20] betokening Oedipal avoidances and a refusal to encounter the Other as other? Was it a grandiose narrative, of which *L'Idiot de la famille* – 'un roman *vrai*'[21] – was merely a fragment, recounted in order to confirm the intuition that all things must be intelligible if a desirable future is ever to be realised?

It was certainly not a provisional and consensual division of theoretical labour predicated on disciplinary reciprocity. For all the dream of hunters and gatherers, Sartre did not relish teamwork where his own projects were concerned.[22] *TM*, a very effective forum, fared better when other editorial personnel were strong enough to complement him creatively or when his own predisposition to colonise was deployed in the great anti-colonialist campaigns. When these two factors worked together, as in the sixties, *TM* enjoyed its most dynamic moments. The time may now be ripe for *TM*'s Editorial Board to engage in a labour of reflexivity in respect of its own history and to totalise its implication in the possessions, generosities and reciprocities of Sartre. It may then be able to determine what sort of collective liberation is indicated, if any, and what sort of instituted group and division of intellectual labour is most effective. A corporate *Les Mots*: I venture this suggestion because in the struggle against racialism and the extreme Right, *TM* will need the *loa* and the *zar*.

COMPOSITION OF THE EDITORIAL BOARD

October 1945	Aron, Beauvoir, Leiris, Merleau-Ponty (*politique*), Ollivier, Paulhan, Sartre (*directeur*).
June 1946	Resignations of Aron and Ollivier; no Editorial Board named.
January 1953	Resignation of Merleau-Ponty.
January 1954	Editorial Board named as Cau, Lanzmann, Péju (*secrétaire général*), Sartre (*directeur*).
January 1959	Two names only appear – those of Sartre and Péju.
February 1961	Sartre (*directeur*), Beauvoir, Bost, Gorz, Lanzmann, Péju (*secrétaire général*), Pingaud, Pontalis, Pouillon.
December 1961	The announcement of a *direction collective* specifies the following division of labour: *politique* – Lanzmann, Péju, Sartre; *littérature* – Beauvoir, Pingaud; *économie* – Gorz; *arts et spectacles* – Bost; *sciences humaines* – Pontalis, Pouillon.
June 1962	Péju is dismissed and Jeanson co-opted.
November 1967	Resignation of Jeanson.
May 1970	Resignations of Pingaud and Pontalis.
November 1976	Appointment of Etcherelli.
March 1977	Addition of Goldman, Rigoulot, Victor (Benny Levy).
April 1977	Replacement of Etcherelli by George.
August 1977	Return of Etcherelli.
September 1979	Murder of Goldman, whose name is nonetheless retained.
November 1979	Departure of Victor.
January 1980	Appointment of Pignon.
April 1980	Death of Sartre.
June 1980	Beauvoir named as *directrice*.
April 1981	Departure of George.
January 1982	Resignation of Rigoulot; appointment of Fontenay.
October 1982	Departure of Bost.

January 1983	Resignations of Fontenay and Pignon.
February 1983	Removal of Goldman's name.
October 1983	Retirement of Gorz.
November 1983	Recruitment of Asseo, Giraud, Nair.

The membership of the Editorial Board in October 1985, the date of *TM*'s 40th anniversary, was thus as follows: Beauvoir (*directrice*), Asseo, Etcherelli, Giraud, Lanzmann, Nair, Pouillon.

CIRCULATION FIGURES

No official figures are available; indeed, the present secretary, Etcherelli, bemoans the absence of any sort of record or archive. Philip Thody reported in 1960 that 'the number of copies of *TM* printed each month has increased from 3,500 in 1945 to 10,000 in 1959'.[1] At about the same time, Sartre commented as follows: 'Voici tantôt dix-sept ans que nous avons fait paraître le premier numéro des *TM*: nous avons gagné régulièrement des abonnés et c'est le bout du monde si quelques douzaines nous ont quittés.'[2]

Everything indicates that 10,000 represents the peak figure. It was attained in the late 1940s (Sartre refers to the review as 'lue par 10,000 personnes'[3] under the editorship of Merleau-Ponty) and may have fallen away quite rapidly after the end of the Algerian War. By January 1967 *TM* was clearly losing its ability to recognise its readership and issued an *Enquête aux lecteurs* which was an orthodox exercise in market research. Despite an undertaking to the contrary, no results were ever published. In 1975, Sartre noted that 'la revue a en gros le même tirage qu'à ses débuts, 11,000 exemplaires',[4] but this was probably an overstatement and certainly glossed over the undoubted fluctuations.

By 1981, according to Etcherelli, the print-run had fallen to 8,500 and the majority of subscribers were located abroad rather than in France. Hamon and Rotman offer *L'Arc* (8,000) and *Esprit* (10,000) as examples of continuing domestic success: they consider that *TM* 'tombe en ruines nostalgiques',[5] a view which is harsh but nevertheless indicative of current Parisian opinion.

The latest available figures confirm that a real decline has taken place. 'Les chiffres des ventes ont subi une forte baisse mais ne sont pas déshonorants: 1,500 abonnements à l'étranger, 1,000 en France et, au mieux, 1,500 exemplaires vendus en plus (sauf pour les numéros spéciaux qui ont de plus gros tirages).'[6] The article quoted here also cites the following remark by Beauvoir: 'La revue a été celle de ses fondateurs au lieu de devenir une institution apte à continuer seule.' The 40th anniversary issue in October 1985 turns its face resolutely towards the future, but whether *TM* will survive only time, the Editorial Board and the readership will tell.

217

CATEGORIES OF MATERIAL TO BE FOUND IN *LES TEMPS MODERNES*

The pie-charts below show, for each of the five periods studied, the amount of space, expressed as a percentage of the whole, which is given to different categories of feature article. A number of points should be borne in mind. The first is that the periods are not of equal length, having been delimited not to facilitate statistical analysis but to highlight the role of academic anthropology within the synthetic. It follows that the curves to be extrapolated from the charts have only limited usefulness. Secondly, the unit of account is not the page but the article. This may vary greatly in length, but an average is between fifteen and twenty pages. Serialised texts have been counted according to the number of parts. Thirdly, the categorisation is broad and corresponds to the assumed intuitions of a typical reader, as well as to the divisions of labour from time to time announced by the Editorial Board. It is also naive, in the sense that it breaks the synthetic whole into discrete and banal sections and negates the disciplinary subversion promoted by Sartre. 'Saint Genet', for example, which appeared in 1950 in six parts and straddles every category, is designated as literature. The categories are as follows:

(a) politics (pol.): political and economic theory, analysis and commentary, feminism;

(b) literature (lit.): theory of literature, literary criticism, poetry and literary prose;

(c) *sciences humaines* (*sc. hum.*): academic anthropology, sociology, psychoanalysis, linguistics, history and philosophy;

(d) other arts (arts): cinema, theatre, music, painting, sculpture, architecture;

(e) miscellaneous (misc.).

Period 1 (October 1945 to February 1951); 64 issues, 680 articles

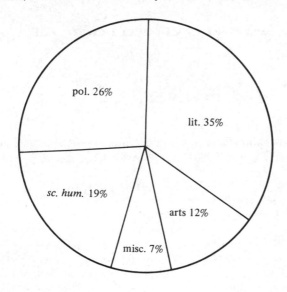

Period 2 (March 1951 to July 1956); 62 issues, 520 articles

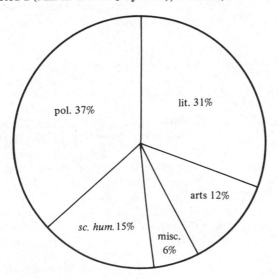

Period 3 (September 1956 to September 1963); 82 issues, 700 articles

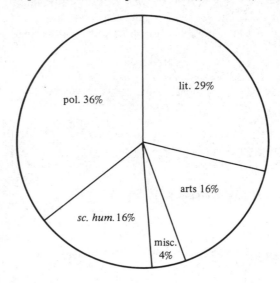

Period 4 (October 1963 to July 1971); 92 issues, 740 articles

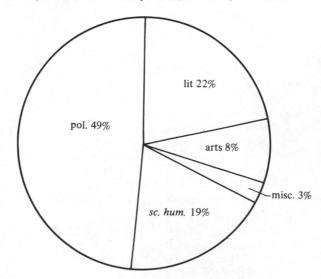

Period 5 (August 1971 to October 1985); 175 issues, 1430 articles

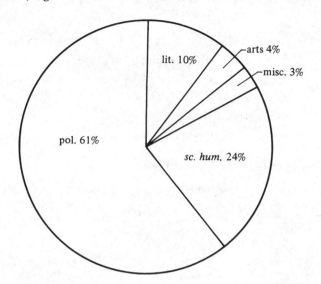

ARTICLES PERTAINING TO ACADEMIC ANTHROPOLOGY

Period 1

Aug/Sept 1946	G. Devereux	'Quelques aspects de la psychanalyse aux Etats-Unis'
Aug/Sept 1946	D. Hare	'Le vieux cacique d'Acoma'
March 1947	J. Cuisinier	'Détails'
Aug/Sept 1947	J. Cuisinier	'La France vue de Saigon'
October 1947	D. Hare	'Huit jours et une danse'
December 1947	J. Agee and W. Evans	'Louons maintenant nos grands hommes'
February 1949	M. Leiris	Review of A. Breton and A. Masson, *Martinique charmeuse de serpents*
March 1949	C. Lévi-Strauss	'Le sorcier et sa magie'
November 1949	S. de Beauvoir	Review of C. Lévi-Strauss, *Les Structures élémentaires de la parenté*
December 1949	M.-A. Galmache and J. Robichez	'Introduction à des poèmes berbères'
December 1949	L. Ménard	Review of M. Eliade, *Traité d'histoire des religions*
February 1950	M. Leiris	'Martinique, Guadeloupe, Haïti'
February 1950	A. Métraux	'Chants vaudou'
July 1950	E. Dermenghem	'Images du Maghreb'
July 1950	F. Jeanson	Review of O. Mannoni, *Psychologie de la colonisation*
August 1950	M. Leiris	'L'ethnographe devant le colonialisme'
November 1950	D. Traore	'Mariage entre femmes'
February 1951	C. Lefort	'L'échange et la lutte des hommes'
February 1951	L. Guillermit	Review of R. Benedict, *Patterns of Culture*

Period 2

March 1951	L. Guillermit	Review of R. Caillois, *L'Homme et le sacré*
April/May 1951	M. Mead	'Masculinité et féminité'
July 1951	M. Merleau-Ponty	Introduction to M. Crozier, 'Human engineering'
December 1951	J. Dechamps	'Mariages en pays soudanais'
March 1952	C. Lévi-Strauss	'Le Père Noël supplicié'
April 1952	P. Mus	'Insertion du communisme dans le mouvement nationaliste vietnamien'
Oct/Nov 1952	G. Balandier	'L'utopie de Benoît Ogoula Iquaqua'
Aug/Sept 1953	M. Ner	'La république démocratique du Viet-nam'
Aug/Sept 1953	M. Ner	'Le Viet-nam et la Chine de 1945 à 1953'
March 1955	C. Lévi-Strauss	'Diogène couché'
April 1955	R. Caillois and C. Lévi-Strauss	'Correspondance'
July 1955	C. Lévi-Strauss	'Tristes Tropiques'
Jan/Feb 1956	V. Elwin	'Maison des jeunes chez les Muria'
July 1956	G. Balandier	'Afrique ambigüe'
July 1956	J. Pouillon	'L'œuvre de Claude Lévi-Strauss'

Period 3

April 1957	J. Delange	'Ethnologie du 1er congrès des intellectuels noirs'
June 1957	A. Métraux	'Vaudou et christianisme'
July/Aug 1957	C. Roy	'Arts "sauvages"'
September 1957	R. Jaulin	'La mort sara'
Feb/March 1959	J. Pouillon	'Vaudou, "zar" et possession'
May/June 1959	J. Pouillon	'Les mémoires d'un Hopi rangé'
August 1959	J. Pouillon	Review of V. Elwin, *The Muria and their Ghotul*
November 1959	R. Jaulin	'Entre noir et blanc'
March 1961	C. Lévi-Strauss	'La geste d'Asdiwal'
May 1961	F. Fanon	'De la violence'
April 1962	C. Lévi-Strauss	'Le temps retrouvé'

April 1962	J. Pouillon	'Décolonisation et révolution'
May 1962	J. Pouillon	'Les Incas démystifiés'
July 1962	L. Sebag	'Histoire et structure – idéologie et réalité'
July 1962	G. Condominas	'Fête à Sar Luk'
July/Sept 1963	P. Verstraeten	'Lévi-Strauss ou la tentation du néant'

Period 4

December 1963	L. de Heusch	'Réflexions sur la technique'
June 1964	L. Sebag	'Analyse des rêves d'une Indienne Guayaki'
February 1965	M. Panoff	'Tahiti et le mythe de l'indépendance'
March 1965	J.-P. and M.-C. Boons	'Lucien Sebag'
March 1965	L. Sebag	'Le mythe: code et message'
May 1965	M. Godelier	'Le "mode de production asiatique"'
August 1965	P. Zumthor	Review of T. Kroeber, *Ishi in Two Worlds*
April 1966	O. Lewis	'Un paysan mexicain et sa famille'
May 1966	C. Glayman	Review of C. Turnbull, *The Lonely African*
July 1966	J. Monod	'Des jeunes, leur langage et leurs mythes'
September 1966	A. Métraux	'L'anthropophagie rituelle des Tupinamba'
November 1966	J. Pouillon	'Un essai de définition'
November 1966	M. Godelier	'La structure chez Marx'
June 1967	J. Pitt-Rivers	'La loi de l'hospitalité'
June 1967	P. Clastres	'De quoi rient les Indiens?'
June 1967	A. P. Elkin	'Medicine men et magie en Australie'
September 1967	C. Lévi-Strauss	'Vingt ans après'
December 1967	J. Monod	'Watts, L. A.'
April 1968	M. Panoff	'L'ethnologue et l'action'
October 1968	M. Sahlins	'La première société d'abondance'
December 1968	V. Chiara	'Le processus d'extermination des Indiens au Brésil'
May 1969	M. Panoff	'Aspects d'un cargo cult mélanésien'
February 1970	S. Diamond	'Un ethnocide'

February 1970	P. Clastres	Reviews of J. Meunier and A.-M. Savarin, *Le Chant de Silbaco* and of L. Bodard, *Le Massacre des Indiens*
April 1970	C. Courchay	'Gros rouges et bororos'
May 1970	J. Pouillon	'Note'
July 1970	M. Panoff	'Du suicide'
January 1971	J. Monod	'Un riche cannibale'
January 1971	K. Gough	'L'anthropologie et l'impérialisme'
January 1971	J. Pouillon	'L'ethnologie, pourquoi faire?'
May 1971	P. Clastres	'Le dernier cercle'
July 1971	P. Clastres	'Le don de la croisière'
July 1971	S. Mintz	'Le rouge et le noir'
July 1971	R. Stavenhagen	'Décoloniser les sciences sociales'
July 1971	R. Buijtenhuijs	'Anthropologie révolutionnaire'
July 1971	J. Monod	'Oraison funèbre pour une vieille dame'
July 1971	J. Pouillon	'Réponse à un ventriloque'

Period 5

November 1972	S. Varese	'Considérations d'anthropologie utopique'
November 1972	B. Lelong	'Situation historique des Indiens de la forêt péruvienne'
April 1973	S. Varese	'Au sujet du colonialisme écologique'
Aug/Sept 1973	E. Terray	'L'idée de nation et les transformations du capitalisme'
October 1974	J. Lizot	'Histoires indiennes d'amour'
March 1975	M. Godelier	Review of C. Turnbull, *The Mountain People*
May 1975	J. Dournes	'Les marches sauvages'
Aug/Sept 1977	J. Favret-Saada	'Les mots, la mort, les sorts'
Aug/Sept 1977	G. Dupré	'Sorcellerie et salariat'
March 1981	J. Favret-Saada and J. Contreras	'Corps pour corps'
September 1981	B. Wongar	'Nabaru – la famille'
September 1982	L. Hurbon	'La fuite du peuple haïtien'
December 1982	J.-L. Siran	'Pour Mauss'

April/May 1983	L. Hurbon	'Immigrés haïtiens et dominicains en Guadeloupe'
July 1983	M. Izard	Review of M. Leiris, *L'Afrique fantôme* (3rd edn)
October 1983	L. Hurbon	'Les témoins de Jéhovah en Guadeloupe'
November 1983	S. Nair	Review of P. Bruckner, *Le Sanglot de l'homme blanc*
December 1983	D. Ducosson	'Adolescents des "ghettos" de Pointe-à-Pitre'
January 1984	J. Duvernay	'Tous sauf un'
March/April/May 1984	B. Etienne	'L'Islam à Marseille'
June 1984	C. Fonseca	'La violence et la rumeur: le code d'honneur dans un bidonville brésilien'
October 1984	M. Giraud	Review of C. Lévi-Strauss, *Le Regard éloigné*
February 1985	M. Abelès, P. Alliès and W. Dressler-Holohan	'Dossier: l'anthropologie politique de la France'
October 1985	M. Giraud	'Nationalisme et question coloniale'

SPECIAL ISSUES

Period 1

11/12	Aug/Sept 1946	USA
23/24	Aug/Sept 1947	Italy
46/47	Aug/Sept 1949	Germany

Period 2

93/94	Aug/Sept 1953	Indochina
112/113	May 1955	'La gauche'

Period 3

127/128	Sept/Oct 1956	China
129/130/131	January 1957	Hungary
132/133	Feb/March 1957	Poland
184/185	Sept/Oct 1961	Merleau-Ponty
207/208	Aug/Sept 1963	'Littératures'

Period 4

246	November 1966	Structuralism
253 bis	July 1967	'Le conflit israélo-arabe'
257	October 1967	Brazil
272	February 1969	Japan
276 bis	August 1969	Greece
279	October 1969	Italy

Period 5

hors série	April 1972	*'La Cause du peuple'*
311	July 1972	Northern Ireland
323	June 1973	Chile
324/325/326	Aug/Sept 1973	'Minorités nationales en France'

333/334	April/May 1974	'Les femmes s'entêtent'
335	June 1974	'*Lotta continua*: la leçon italienne'
340	November 1974	'Normalisation de l'école – scolarisation de la société'
343	February 1975	Gramsci
354	January 1976	'Justice, discipline, production'
hors série	April 1976	'Espagne 1976'
358	May 1976	'Petites filles en éducation'
361/362	Aug/Sept 1976	'Les Etats-Unis en questions'
376/377	Nov/Dec 1977	'Vivre à l'Est'
hors série	December 1977	'Le Maghreb'
380	March 1978	'Dossier Chine'
hors série	June 1979	'La question sépharade en Israël'
396/397	July/Aug 1979	West Germany
398	September 1979	'La paix maintenant?' (Israeli–Palestinian colloquium)
402	January 1980	Indochina
406	May 1980	'L'URSS et la science'
408/409	July/Aug 1980	Afghanistan
410	September 1980	'L'histoire anachronique'
420/421	July/Aug 1981	Argentina
432/433	July/Aug 1982	'Algérie: espoirs et réalités'
441/442	April/May 1983	'Antilles'
hors série	June 1983	'La politique économique de la gauche en question'
445/446	Aug/Sept 1983	Poland
452/453/454	Mar/Apr/May 1984	'L'immigration maghrébine en France'
456/457	July/Aug 1984	Turkey
464	March 1985	'La Nouvelle Calédonie'
468/469	July/Aug 1985	'Le système soviétique: consensus dans la dictature'
471	October 1985	'Spécial quarantième anniversaire'

NOTES

Unless otherwise stated, the place of publication for works mentioned below is Paris for books in French and London for books in English.

Preface

1 For convenience I propose to adopt this abbreviation.
2 For circulation figures, together with other tabulated data, statistical and non-statistical, see the appendices.
3 See F. Mulhern, *The Moment of 'Scrutiny'* (Verso, 1981), p. x.
4 See M.-A. Burnier, *Les Existentialistes et la politique* (Gallimard, Idées edn, 1966) (a survey of the first two decades); and A. D. Ranwez, *Jean-Paul Sartre's 'Les Temps Modernes', a Literary History, 1945–1952* (Whitston, New York, 1981).
5 Such a sociological study, covering the period 1945–60, has recently been published by Anna Boschetti, but too late to be considered here: see her *Sartre et 'Les Temps Modernes'* (Minuit, 1985).
6 See J.-P. Sartre, *Les Carnets de la drôle de guerre, Cahiers pour une morale, Lettres au Castor et à quelques autres* (2 vols.), all published by Gallimard (1983); and *Le Scénario Freud* (Gallimard, 1984).

Introduction

1 See S. de Beauvoir, *La Force de l'âge* (Gallimard, 1960), p. 577.
2 This discovery accompanies that of the Heideggerian concept of historicity, a coincidence which Sartre himself describes as providential. See *Les Carnets de la drôle de guerre*, pp. 224 *et seq.*
3 The 'Présentation' had already appeared, in abridged translation, in *Horizon* in Britain and in *Partisan Review* in the USA. It was subsequently featured in Elio Vittorini's Italian periodical *Il Politecnico*.
4 J.-P. Sartre, 'Présentation des *Temps Modernes*', *Situations II* (Gallimard, 1948), p. 12.
5 *Ibid.*, p. 12.
6 In the epigraph to this study I have quoted the allusion to Gide's *Les Nourritures terrestres* made by Sartre in his subsequent recollection of

the origins of *TM*. The same reference is, however, subjected to a political critique in *Les Carnets de la drôle de guerre*, pp. 177 *et seq*. As for Flaubert, the size, the date and the non-completion of *L'Idiot de la famille* all testify eloquently to the extent to which, in Sartre's mind, he survives the dismissal effected in the 'Présentation'.

7 See *Libération*, 8/9, 10 June 1985.

8 Alluding to *Socialisme et liberté*, they recall that 'en faisaient partie Yvonne Picard, morte en déportation, et François Cuzin, fusillé par les Allemands' (*Le Monde*, 26 July 1985). Cuzin was the philosopher with whom Jankélévitch unfavourably compared Sartre and Merleau-Ponty.

9 'De temps en temps un explorateur revenu de la capitale [Jankélévitch was in hiding in Toulouse during the war years] nous apportait dans nos cavernes une liasse de journaux parisiens, et nous apprenions avec stupéfaction que Paris avait ses événements littéraires, son théâtre, ses garçons de café hégéliens et tout ce qu'il faut à un grand pays pour tenir son rang. Elle était belle, décidément, la république des lettres de 1944' ('Dans l'honneur et la dignité', *TM*, vol. 3, no. 33 (June 1948), p. 2250).

10 Sartre, 'Présentation des *Temps Modernes*', *Situations II*, p. 26.

11 *Ibid.*, p. 23.

12 J.-P. Sartre, *Esquisse d'une théorie des émotions* (Hermann, 1938), p. 8.

13 Lévi-Strauss was in any case the first Frenchman to use the term *anthropologie* in anything resembling the British and American uses; the established term had been *ethnologie*. French and British segmentations of knowledge differ somewhat and the guidelines of John and Doreen Weightman (see G. Charbonnier, *Conversations with Claude Lévi-Strauss* (Cape, 1969), p. 9) have been followed here.

14 See J.-P. Sartre, 'La liberté cartésienne', *Situations I* (Gallimard, 1947).

15 Although Hegel did not constitute part of Sartre's formal philosophical training, his work gained currency in France in the 1930s. Accounts of this process may be found in V. Descombes, *Le Même et l'autre* (Minuit, 1979); and in M. Poster, *Existential Marxism in Postwar France* (Princeton University Press, New Jersey, 1975).

16 See J.-P. Sartre, *L'Etre et le néant* (Gallimard, 1943), p. 138.

17 *Ibid.*, p. 299.

18 *Ibid.*, p. 38.

19 See J.-P. Sartre, *L'Imagination* (PUF, 1936), chapter 4; and 'Une idée fondamentale de la phénoménologie de Husserl: l'intentionnalité', *Situations I*

20 E. Husserl, *Cartesian Meditations* (trans. D. Cairns) (Martinus Nijhoff, The Hague, 1973), p. 41.

21 See Sartre, *L'Imagination*, pp. 153–62.

22 Husserl, *Cartesian Meditations*, pp. 134–5.

23 See J. Colombel, *Sartre ou le parti de vivre* (Grasset, 1981), p. 16.

24 Sartre, 'Présentation des *Temps Modernes*', *Situations II*, p. 13.

25 See S. de Beauvoir, *Le Sang des autres* (Gallimard, 1945), p. 177.
26 See J.-P. Sartre, *Situations VIII* (Gallimard, 1972), p. 95.
27 For Sartre and Surrealism, see G. Idt, *'Le Mur' de Jean-Paul Sartre* (Larousse, 1972), pp. 180–5.
28 D. Hollier (ed.), *Le Collège de sociologie (1937–1939)* (Gallimard, 1979).
29 See A. Métraux, 'Rencontre avec les ethnologues', *Critique*, no. 195/6 (August/September 1963), pp. 677–84.
30 See J.-P. Sartre, 'Un nouveau mystique', *Situations I*, pp. 201–2.
31 M. Leiris, *L'Afrique fantôme* (Gallimard, 1934). For evidence of Sartre's admiration of *L'Age d'homme*, part of Leiris's autobiographical undertaking which *TM* will in due course encourage, see *Les Carnets de la drôle de guerre*, p. 175.
32 See, in particular, L. Lévy-Bruhl, *Les Fonctions mentales dans les sociétés inférieures* (Alcan, 1910); and *La Mentalité primitive* (Alcan, 1921).
33 De Beauvoir, *La Force de l'âge*, p. 151.
34 Sartre, *Esquisse d'une théorie des émotions*, p. 58.
35 See H. Davies, '*Les Mots* as *essai sur le don*: contribution to an origin myth', *Yale French Studies*, no. 68 (New Haven, 1985).
36 See M. Leiris, 'Oreste et la cité', *Les Lettres françaises*, no. 12 (1943).
37 Beauvoir, Bost and Pouillon write to defend Sartre 'au moment [. . .] où Sartre – mais il y était habitué – est encore une fois pris comme bouc émissaire' (*Le Monde*, 26 July 1985).
38 The contents of *TM* are conditioned by a variety of factors other than editorial policy – the pressure of copy dates, the other commitments of individual members of the Editorial Board, the unpredictability of personal contact and acquaintance, the availability of translation and serialisation rights, the commercial interests of the publishing houses, political censorship, and so on. Where such factors are known, they can be mentioned, but it has to be assumed that some of them operate continuously. My investigations, although empirical rather than theoretical, concentrate less on this level of contingent detail and more on the underlying rationale that makes up the project of *TM*.
39 S. de Beauvoir, *Pour une morale de l'ambiguïté* (Gallimard, 1947), Idées edn, p. 249.
40 J.-P. Sartre, *Qu'est-ce que la littérature?* (Gallimard, 1948), Idées edn, p. 96.
41 Hollier (in *Politique de la prose* (Gallimard, 1982), pp. 147–8) labours hard to preserve the bananas as a monument to Sartre's *mauvaise foi*, on the grounds that Sartre actually preferred tinned fruit. It is true that there is ambivalence here, as elsewhere in Sartre; for a more balanced view, see George H. Bauer, 'Just desserts', *Yale French Studies*, no. 68 (1985).

1 The first six years: the participation of Leiris and Lévi-Strauss

1 See, for example, J. Poirier, *Histoire de l'ethnologie* (PUF, 1974), p. 118. This journey helped to establish Leiris's credentials both professionally and politically: according to Claude Wauthier (in his *L'Afrique des Africains* (Seuil, 1977), p. 230), Griaule was one of the few French ethnographers whose work commands a measure of respect in Africa today.

2 Anthropologists, he says, 'need to be familiar with the principles, methods and results of other branches of the study of man: philosophy, psychology, history, etc.' ('French sociology', in *Twentieth Century Sociology*, ed. G. Gurvitch and W. E. Moore (Philosophical Library, New York, 1945), p. 536).

3 See Sartre, 'L'homme et les choses', *Situations I*.

4 'Nos goûts s'accordaient rarement', she notes in *La Force des choses* (Gallimard, 1963), p. 60.

5 *Ibid.*, p. 97.

6 Sartre, *Qu'est-ce que la littérature?*, p. 17.

7 To be found in M. Leiris, *Mots sans mémoire* (Gallimard, 1969).

8 See Sartre, *Qu'est-ce que la littérature?*, p. 18.

9 See *Obliques*, no. 18/19 (Nyons, 1979).

10 See S. de Beauvoir, *L'Amérique au jour le jour* (Paul Morihien, 1948), p. 206.

11 J. Agee and W. Evans, *Let Us Now Praise Famous Men* (Houghton Mifflin, Boston, 1941), p. xv. The complete French edition appeared only in 1972 (published by Plon). The extract carried by *TM* in December 1947 was translated for Beauvoir by Michelle Vian. A flippant introduction by Boris Vian was refused by Merleau-Ponty and may be found in *Chroniques du menteur* (Christian Bourgois, 1974).

12 For example, 'La croyance aux génies *zar* en Ethiopie du Nord', *Journal de psychologie normale et pathologique*, vol. 35 (January–March 1938); and *La Langue secrète des Dogons de Sanga*, Travaux et mémoires de l'Institut d'Ethnologie, no. 50 (1948).

13 Elisabeth Roudinesco (in *La Bataille de cent ans: histoire de la psychanalyse en France*, vol. 1 (Ramsay, 1982), p. 331) notes that Mauss had a very low opinion of *L'Afrique fantôme*, which he regarded as likely to damage the nature of the relationship between ethnographer and natives. She goes on to say that Marie Bonaparte disapproved of its critique of colonialism. It is not too fanciful to speculate that this endorsement of the civilising mission of Western imperialism, of which Sartre must have been aware, helped consolidate his own opposition to Freudian psychoanalysis.

14 Burnier, *Les Existentialistes et la politique*, p. 39.

15 Lefort, speaking from a Trotskyist position, is bitterly critical of the Viet Minh policy of unity with the bourgeoisie. He deems Ho Chi Minh's strategy to be counter-revolutionary and based on a dogmatic

hypostatisation of history as a sequence of stages that must be passed through in the correct order. Tran Duc Thao, on the other hand, regards the bourgeoisie as a progressive element and considers Ho Chi Minh's reading of the balance of forces to be accurate.

16 J.-P. Sartre, 'Merleau-Ponty', *Situations IV* (Gallimard, 1964), p. 243.

17 Tran Duc Thao, 'Sur l'Indochine', *TM*, vol. 1, no. 5 (February 1946), p. 897.

18 Tran Duc Thao, 'Les relations franco-vietnamiennes', *TM*, vol. 2, no. 18 (March 1947), p. 1055. Tran Duc Thao's contributions are few in number: relations with Sartre broke down when, in a difference of opinion concerning the publication of interviews conducted between them, Tran Duc Thao had recourse to the law. He subsequently returned to Vietnam only to be purged from Hanoi University in 1958. In 1967, at the time of the Russell Tribunal, Sartre attempted to trace him but met with no success. (See O. Todd, *Un fils rebelle* (Grasset, 1981), pp. 219–22.)

19 M. Leiris, review of A. Breton and A. Masson, *Martinique charmeuse de serpents*, in *TM*, vol. 4, no. 40 (February 1949), p. 364.

20 Wright was a frequent contact in this period – in Paris, where he participated in some of the meetings of the Rassemblement Démocratique Révolutionnaire, and in the USA, where he escorted Beauvoir through Harlem in 1947. He also wrote the introduction to the American edition of *La Putain respectueuse* in 1948.

21 J.-P. Sartre, *Réflexions sur la question juive* (Gallimard, 1946), Idées edn, p. 183.

22 De Beauvoir, *L'Amérique au jour le jour*, p. 62.

23 F. Jeanson, 'Sartre et le monde noir', *Présence africaine*, no. 7 (1949), p. 194.

24 Quoted in M. Contat and M. Rybalka, *Les Ecrits de Sartre* (Gallimard, 1970), p. 216.

25 J.-P. Sartre, 'Orphée noir', in L. S. Senghor, *Anthologie de la nouvelle poésie nègre et malgache de langue française* (PUF, 1948), p. xliii.

26 *Ibid.*, p. xliv.

27 *Ibid.*, p. xxvii.

28 *Ibid.*, p. xl.

29 Other theoreticians also help to pave the way. In March 1946, for example, Paulhan (who also contributes occasional pieces under the name of Maast) takes up the discussion of what Sartre in his pre-war criticism had referred to as the *crise linguistique*. Maurice Blanchot (June 1946) and Nathalie Sarraute (February 1950), for their part, follow up Sartre's criticisms of Mauriac in *Situations I* and debate the degree of artifice which may be allowed to inform the construction of characters who appear to be free agents.

30 M. Merleau-Ponty, review of *Les Cahiers de la Pléiade* (April 1947), *TM*, vol. 3, no. 27 (December 1947), p. 1152.

31 It appeared in *TM*, vols. 2–3, nos. 17–22 (February–July 1947).

32 I have attempted to explore this aspect of the novel in '*La Nausée* as a narrative of compensations', *Australian Journal of French Studies*, vol. 15, parts 5, 6 (1978). Much more sustained discussions exist, however, notably the following: S. Doubrovsky, 'Le neuf de cœur', *Obliques*, no. 18/19, and 'Feuillet sans date', in M. Issacharoff and J.-C. Vilquin, *Sartre et la mise en signe* (Klincksieck, 1982, and French Forum, Lexington, Kentucky, 1982); Hollier, *Politique de la prose*; J. Pacaly, *Sartre au miroir* (Klincksieck, 1980).

33 J.-P. Sartre, 'Ecrire pour son époque', in Contat and Rybalka, *Les Ecrits de Sartre*, p. 671.

34 M. Merleau-Ponty, 'Commentaire', *TM*, vol. 5, no. 50 (December 1949), p. 1119.

35 See his discussions of his own class background and of Kaiser Wilhelm in *Les Carnets de la drôle de guerre*, pp. 355 *et seq.*

36 M. Leiris, *Biffures* (Gallimard, 1948), p. 20.

37 See C. Lévi-Strauss, *Les Structures élémentaires de la parenté* (Mouton, 1967), 2nd edn, part 2, chapter 29.

38 Leiris, *Biffures*, p. 231.

39 Leiris, preface to J.-P. Sartre, *Baudelaire* (Gallimard, 1947), Idées edn, p. 9.

40 In *Le Problème moral et la pensée de Sartre* (Seuil, 1947), Jeanson explores in considerable detail the ethical potential of *L'Etre et le néant*.

41 De Beauvoir, *La Force des choses*, p. 69.

42 J.-P. Sartre, *Saint Genet* (Gallimard, 1952), p. 177.

43 C. Lévi-Strauss, 'Introduction à l'œuvre de Marcel Mauss', in M. Mauss, *Sociologie et anthropologie* (PUF, 1950), p. xx; quoted in Sartre, *Saint Genet*, p. 59.

44 J.-P. Sartre, 'L'engagement de Mallarmé', *Obliques*, no. 18–19 (Nyons, 1979), p. 178.

45 Sartre, *Saint Genet*, p. 508.

46 Sartre, 'Présentation des *Temps Modernes*', *Situations II*, p. 30.

47 *TM*, vol. 3, no. 32 (May 1948), p. 1996. I have tried to show elsewhere (in *Yale French Studies*, no. 68) how *Moses and Monotheism*, *Totem and Taboo* and Lévi-Strauss's critique of the latter in *Les Structures élémentaires de la parenté* all make their presence felt in *Les Mots* and how *homage*, in the context of Mauss's *Essai sur le don*, is not as innocent a term as it may seem. It is, incidentally, Lévi-Strauss's identification of Mauss with Moses that elicits the attack by Lefort with which this chapter ends.

48 C. Lévi-Strauss, 'Le sorcier et sa magie', *TM*, vol. 4, no. 41 (March 1949), p. 387.

49 Sartre, *Saint Genet*, p. 140.

50 C. Lévi-Strauss, *Anthropologie structurale* (Plon, 1958), p. 200.

51 See Sartre, *Esquisse d'une théorie des émotions*.

52 C. Lévi-Strauss, 'L'efficacité symbolique', in *Anthropologie structurale*, chapter 10.

53 F. Pasche, 'Le psychanalyste sans magie', *TM*, vol. 5, no. 50 (December 1949).

54 Lévi-Strauss, *Anthropologie structurale*, p. 33.

55 R.-L. Wagner, 'Le langage et l'homme', *TM*, vol. 3, no. 30 (March 1948). Wagner was a friend of Sartre and Paul Nizan at the Ecole Normale (see A. Cohen-Solal and H. Nizan, *Paul Nizan, communiste impossible* (Grasset, 1980), p. 38).

56 Sartre, *Situations I*, p. 241.

57 M. Merleau-Ponty, *Sens et non-sens* (Nagel, 1948), p. 164.

58 It does not, however, attack the Party's policies, some of which, on Indochina, for example, are close to those of *TM*.

59 See F. Jeanson, *Sartre dans sa vie* (Seuil, 1974), p. 180.

60 J.-P. Sartre, *Situations VI* (Gallimard, 1964), p. 52.

61 She reports that 'les numéros [...] s'enlevèrent comme des petits pains' (quoted in C. Francis and F. Gontier, *Les Ecrits de Simone de Beauvoir* (Gallimard, 1979), p. 157).

62 See de Beauvoir, *La Force des choses*, p. 235.

63 See Lévi-Strauss, *Les Structures élémentaires de la parenté*, p. 563.

64 *TM*, vol. 5, no. 49 (November 1949), p. 949.

65 G. Gurvitch, preface to Mauss, *Sociologie et anthropologie*, p. viii.

66 Lévi-Strauss, 'Introduction à l'œuvre de Marcel Mauss', *op. cit.*, p. xxvii.

67 *Ibid.*, p. xxx.

68 *Ibid.*, p. xxxix.

69 *Ibid.*, p. xxxv.

70 See chapter 4 (pp. 151 *et seq.*).

71 C. Lefort, 'L'échange et la lutte des hommes', *TM*, vol. 6, no. 64 (February 1951), p. 1409.

72 See Poster, *Existential Marxism in Postwar France*, pp. 201–5.

73 Lefort, 'L'échange et la lutte des hommes', *op. cit.*, p. 1415.

2 From 1951 to 1956: the rise of structuralism

1 Sartre, 'Merleau-Ponty', *Situations IV*, p. 246.

2 *Ibid.*, p. 244.

3 *Ibid.*, p. 252.

4 De Beauvoir, *La Force des choses*, p. 271.

5 G. Balandier, 'Le bilan de la sociologie au XXe siècle', *Critique*, vol. 5, no. 34 (March 1949), p. 270.

6 M. Crozier, 'La civilisation technique', *TM*, vol. 7, no. 76 (February 1952), p. 1497.

7 M. Crozier, 'Human engineering', *TM*, vol. 7, no. 69 (July 1951), p. 75.

8 *TM*, vol. 7, no. 69 (July 1951), p. 44.

9 See *TM*, vol. 6, no. 64 (February 1951). Louis Guillermit takes exception to a cultural relativism based on scepticism.

10 See A. Robinet, *Merleau-Ponty* (PUF, 1963, revised edn 1970), p. 74.

11 See, for example, M. Merleau-Ponty, 'De Mauss à Claude Lévi-Strauss', in *Signes* (Gallimard, 1960).

12 J. Pouillon, review of G. Freyre, *Maîtres et esclaves*, *TM*, vol. 8, no. 90 (May 1953), p. 1837.

13 *Ibid.*, p. 1838.

14 Sartre, 'Présentation des *Temps Modernes*', *Situations II*, p. 29.

15 J.-P. Sartre, *Situations VII* (Gallimard, 1965), p. 112.

16 See C. Lefort, 'De la réponse à la question', *TM*, vol. 10, no. 104 (July 1954).

17 See M. Merleau-Ponty, *Les Aventures de la dialectique* (Gallimard, 1955), chapter 5.

18 J.-P. Sartre, 'Réponse à Claude Lefort', *TM*, vol. 8, no. 89 (April 1953).

19 Sartre, *Situations VII*, p. 48.

20 Sartre, *Situations VI*, p. 203.

21 G. Balandier, 'L'expérience de l'ethnologue et le problème de l'explication', *Cahiers internationaux de sociologie*, vol. 12 (1956), p. 124.

22 See his reference to nomadic Brazilian Indians in *Situations VII*, p. 56. The footnote dealing with Roger Bastide's account of slavery in Brazil (p. 55) dates from 1965 and does not appear in the *TM* article in 1953.

23 *Ibid.*, p. 50.

24 Merleau-Ponty, *Les Aventures de la dialectique*, pp. 256–7.

25 See S. de Beauvoir, 'Merleau-Ponty et le pseudo-sartrisme', *TM*, vol. 10, no. 114/15 (July 1955).

26 *TM* vol. 7–8, nos. 80, 81 (June and July 1952).

27 Of all the dramatic episodes in the history of *TM*, the quarrel of Sartre and Camus made the greatest public impact. It is also true to say that it had very little effect on the direction of the review; the link with Camus had always been tenuous. One of the more curious aspects of the affair – which began with Jeanson's hostile account of *L'Homme révolté* in May 1952 – is the fact that *TM* had already carried an extract from the book (a discussion of Nietzsche) in August 1951. There was no contact at all after 1952. Camus refused to contribute to the collection of articles on the Henri Martin affair in 1953; J.-J. Brochier (*Albert Camus, philosophe pour classes terminales* (Balland, 1970), p. 45) quotes him as saying that 'c'est compromettre désormais les valeurs de la liberté entre autres valeurs, que de les défendre auprès des *TM* et de ceux qui les approuvent'. *TM* thereafter studiously ignored Camus, with the exception of some subsequent theatre reviews by Renée Saurel. His attitudes to the Algerian question received no attention whatever. (Merleau-Ponty's unwitting involvement in the quarrel is described in S. de Beauvoir, *La Cérémonie des adieux* (Gallimard, 1981), p. 344, where Sartre also impugns Jeanson's motives.)

28 M. Merleau-Ponty, *Signes* (Gallimard, 1960), p. 91.

29 *Ibid.*

30 C. Audry, review of K. Horney, *L'Autoanalyse, TM*, vol. 9, no. 92 (July 1953), p. 185.

31 J.-B. Pontalis, *Après Freud* (Gallimard, 1966, Idées edn, 1968).

32 *Ibid.* (Idées edn), p. 21.

33 J.-B. Pontalis, 'La psychanalyse en question', *TM* vol. 9, no. 98 (January 1954), p. 1271.

34 J.-B. Pontalis, 'Nos débuts dans la vie selon Melanie Klein', *TM*, vol. 10, no. 105 (August 1954), p. 370.

35 Pontalis, 'La psychanalyse en question', *op. cit.*, p. 1275.

36 J.-B. Pontalis, 'Les mauvais chemins de la psychanalyse ou Karen Horney critique de Freud', *TM*, vol. 9, no. 99 (February 1954), p. 1502.

37 J.-B. Pontalis, 'Freud aujourd'hui', *TM*, vol. 11, no. 125 (June 1956), p. 1890.

38 *Ibid.*, p. 1894.

39 *Ibid.*, *TM*, vol. 12, no. 126 (July 1956), p. 177.

40 *Ibid.*, p. 178.

41 *Ibid.*

42 *Ibid.*

43 *Ibid.*, p. 179.

44 See M. Leiris, 'Henri Martin et le colonialisme', in J.-P. Sartre, *L'Affaire Henri Martin* (Gallimard, 1953), pp. 71–9.

45 In *Après Freud* the article is reproduced as 'Michel Leiris ou la psychanalyse sans fin', perhaps to dissociate it from Freud's *Analysis Terminable and Interminable*, to which it makes no reference.

46 See Sartre, 'L'engagement de Mallarmé', *op. cit.*, p. 191.

47 See Francis and Gontier, *Les Ecrits de Simone de Beauvoir*, p. 170.

48 S. de Beauvoir, *Faut-il brûler Sade?* (Gallimard, 1955, Idées edn), p. 63.

49 I am conscious that my commentary shows how far Sartre's best play can be impoverished by reductive readings. In 'L'idéologie théâtrale du *Diable et le Bon Dieu*' (*Etudes sartriennes 1, Cahiers de sémiotique textuelle 2*, Université de Paris X, 1984) I have tried to show how the anthropological problematic is also a theatrical one.

50 Quoted in de Beauvoir, *La Force des choses*, p. 218.

51 *Ibid.*, p. 369.

52 J.-B. Pontalis, 'La maladie de Flaubert', *TM*, vol. 9, nos. 100, 101 (March, April 1954), p. 293.

53 I use this preposition advisedly, in view of Josette Pacaly's thesis that Sartre's most anxious defences were set up to ward off all that might threaten from the rear (see her *Sartre au miroir, passim*).

54 Pontalis, 'La maladie de Flaubert', *op. cit.*, p. 311.

55 A. Memmi, *La Statue de sel* (Gallimard, 1966), Folio edn. p. 109.

56 *Ibid.*, p. 346.

57 In due course, it will be Jeanson who leads the way into underground activism in support of the Algerian insurgents. His co-authored work

(F. and C. Jeanson, *L'Algérie hors la loi* (Seuil, 1955)) appears when his editorial work in *TM* has already ceased.

58 J.-P. Sartre, 'Le colonialisme est un système', in *Guerre d'Algérie et colonialisme*, pamphlet published by the Comité d'Action des Intellectuels contre la Poursuite de la Guerre en Afrique du Nord (1956), p. 70.

59 *Ibid.*, p. 68.

60 *Ibid.*, p. 73.

61 *TM*, vol. 11, no. 121 (January 1956), p. 1081.

62 C. Lévi-Strauss, 'Diogène couché', *TM* vol. 10, no. 110 (March 1955), p. 1210.

63 I have tried to carry this suggestion a little further in 'Sartre et Margaret Kennedy: l'intertexte maternel', in the proceedings of the 1985 Colloque de Lyon to be published by the Presses Universitaires de Lyon.

64 G. Balandier, 'La situation coloniale: approche théorique', *Cahiers internationaux de sociologie*, vol. 11 (1951), p. 74.

65 Lévi-Strauss, *Anthropologie structurale*, p. 397.

66 *Ibid.*, p. 399.

67 Lévi-Strauss, 'Diogène couché', *op. cit.*, p. 1216.

68 C. Lévi-Strauss, *Tristes Tropiques* (Plon, 1955), p. 62.

69 Lévi-Strauss, 'Histoire et ethnologie', in *Anthropologie structurale*, chapter 1.

70 C. Lefort, 'Sociétés "sans histoire" et historicité', *Cahiers internationaux de sociologie*, vol. 12 (1952).

71 Lévi-Strauss, 'Diogène couché', *op. cit.*, p. 1193.

72 *Ibid.*, p. 1200.

73 Lévi-Strauss, *Anthropologie structurale*, p. 417.

74 Lévi-Strauss, 'Diogène couché', *op. cit.*, p. 1214.

75 *Ibid.*, p. 1217.

76 Lévi-Strauss, *Tristes Tropiques*, p. 454.

77 J. Pouillon, 'L'œuvre de Claude Lévi-Strauss', in *Fétiches sans fétichisme* (Maspero, 1975), p. 311.

78 *Ibid.*, p. 317.

79 *Ibid.*, p. 316.

80 *Ibid.*, pp. 320–1.

81 Marcel Detienne notes (in 'Le Grec à deux têtes', *Critique*, no. 394 (March 1980), p. 210) that 'vers les années 60 [. . .] toute une part de la phénoménologie, avec la philosophie existentielle, réhabilitait l'être-au-monde du primitif et découvrait dans la mythologie une première métaphysique'. He cites the work of Dufrenne and Gusdorf, of which there is not a trace in *TM*.

3 Algeria: intellectual rivalries in time of war

1 J.-P. Sartre, 'Correspondance', *TM*, vol. 18, no. 194 (July 1962), p. 182.

2 *Ibid.*, p. 183.

3 Todd, *Un fils rebelle*, pp. 114–15.
4 M. Leiris, 'Hommage à Alfred Métraux', *L'Homme*, vol. 4, no. 2 (1964), p. 12.
5 A. Métraux, 'Entretiens', *ibid.*, p. 23.
6 C. Lévi-Strauss, 'Hommage à Alfred Métraux', *ibid.*, p. 8.
7 *Ibid.*
8 M. Leiris, *La Possession et ses aspects théâtraux chez les Ethiopiens de Gondar* (Plon, 1958).
9 Here Pouillon adds in a footnote: 'C'est parce qu'il en est ainsi que l'analyse sans préjugés est possible et qu'en même temps la psychologie relève en fin de compte de l'éthique.'
10 J. Pouillon, 'Vaudou, "zar" et possession', *TM*, vol. 14, nos. 156/7 (February/March 1959), reprinted in *Fétiches sans fétichisme* (Maspero, 1975), pp. 332–3.
11 *Ibid.*
12 *Ibid.*
13 J. Pouillon, 'Les mémoires d'un Hopi rangé', *TM*, vol. 14, no. 159/60 (May/June 1959), reprinted in *Fétiches sans fétichisme*, p. 337.
14 G. Condominas, *De l'exotique au quotidien* (Plon, 1962).
15 The formal record of Condominas's fieldwork among the Mnong Gar peoples of southern Vietnam is to be found in *Nous avons mangé la forêt de la pierre-génie Gôo* (Mercure de France, 1957).
16 Lévi-Strauss, *Tristes Tropiques*, p. 277.
17 Pouillon deals with the problem of ethnocide in 1971 (see chapter 4, pp. 199 *et seq.*).
18 H. Hamon and P. Rotman, *Les Porteurs de valises* (revised edn, série Points, 1981), p. 158. Sartre was in Brazil during the trial of the *réseau Jeanson*; Hamon and Rotman give details of how his written testimony was forged, with his consent, by Lanzmann and Péju (pp. 304–6).
19 J. Delange, 'Ethnologie du 1ᵉʳ congrès des intellectuels noirs', *TM*, vol. 12, no. 134 (April 1957), p. 1612.
20 *Ibid.*, p. 1613.
21 A. Memmi, *Portrait du colonisé* (Pauvert, 1966), p. 80.
22 *Ibid.*, p. 34.
23 A. Memmi, 'Sociologie des rapports entre colonisateurs et colonisés', in *Cahiers internationaux de sociologie*, vol. 23 (1957), p. 92.
24 F. Fanon, *Peau noire, masques blancs* (Seuil, reprinted 1975), p. 109. Fanon had an equally disillusioning effect on Octave Mannoni; see Mannoni's *Clefs pour l'imaginaire* (Seuil, 1969), pp. 290–300.
25 F. Fanon, 'De la violence', *TM*, vol. 16, no. 181 (May 1961), reprinted in *Les Damnés de la terre* (Maspero, reprinted 1968), pp. 22–3.
26 See, for example, *ibid.*, p. 143.
27 J.-P. Sartre, preface to F. Fanon, *Les Damnés de la terre*, in *Situations V* (Gallimard, 1964), pp. 180–1.
28 Like the *enfant qui meurt de faim*, the *grand sorcier* is a figure which haunts the Sartrean discourse. *TM* has already entertained one mani-

festation – the Mussolini of Silone's *Une Poignée de mûres*; Flaubert will later be called upon to assume the mantle.

29 Sartre, preface to Fanon, *Les Damnés de la terre*, pp. 190–1.
30 *Ibid.*, p. 192.
31 References in the first chapter of *Les Damnés de la terre* show that Fanon was familiar with the *Critique*.
32 A. Gorz, *Fondements pour une morale* (Galilée, 1977).
33 A. Gorz, *Le Traître* (Seuil, 1958), p. 51.
34 *Ibid.*, p. 75.
35 Although Beauvoir notes that 'Gorz qui dans *Le Traître* dénonce ses marmonnements continue à marmonner' (*Tout compte fait* (Gallimard, 1972), p. 46).
36 Sartre, *Situations IV*, p. 41.
37 *Ibid.*, pp. 54–5.
38 *Ibid.*, p. 57.
39 Sartre, *Situations V*, p. 192.
40 See, for example, Act V, scene 1, *passim*.
41 See M. Contat, *Explication des 'Séquestrés d'Altona' de Jean-Paul Sartre*, Archives des lettres modernes, no. 89 (Minard, 1968), p. 67.
42 J.-P. Sartre, *Un théâtre de situations* (Gallimard, Idées, 1973), p. 101.
43 J.-P. Sartre, 'Le fantôme de Staline', *Situations VII*, p. 276.
44 *Ibid.*, p. 281.
45 *Ibid.*, pp. 253, 293.
46 M. Crozier, 'La civilisation technique', *TM*, vol. 7, no. 76 (February 1952), p. 1511.
47 *Ibid.*, p. 1512.
48 *TM*, vol. 17, no. 192 (May 1962), p. 1780.
49 P. Bourdieu, 'Les sous-prolétaires algériens', *TM*, vol. 18, no. 199 (December 1962), p. 1050.
50 De Beauvoir, *La Force des choses*, p. 479.
51 A. Gorz, 'Avant-propos', *TM*, vol. 18, no. 196–7 (September/October 1962), p. 389.
52 A. Gorz, 'Le vieillissement', *TM*, vol. 17, no. 187–8 (December 1961, January 1962), p. 647.
53 *Ibid.*, p. 830.
54 *Ibid.*, p. 837.
55 J.-P. Sartre, *Critique de la raison dialectique* (Gallimard, 1960), p. 9.
56 *Ibid.*, p. 24.
57 *Ibid.*, p. 28.
58 *Ibid.*, p. 30.
59 *Ibid.*, p. 38.
60 *Ibid.*, pp. 52–3.
61 *Ibid.*, p. 94.
62 *TM*, vol. 13, no. 141 (November 1957), p. 761.
63 See Sartre, *Critique*, p. 75; and Pouillon, review of Desanti, *TM*, vol. 13, no. 137/8 (July/August 1957), p. 294.

64 J. Pouillon, review of Goldmann, *TM*, vol. 13, no. 141 (November 1957), p. 907.

65 *Ibid.*, p. 898.

66 Contat and Rybalka, *Les Ecrits de Sartre*, p. 368.

67 C. Lévi-Strauss, *La Pensée sauvage* (Plon, 1962), pp. i–ii.

68 M. Merleau-Ponty, *Signes* (Gallimard, 1960), p. 35. This passage is quoted by Sartre in the recently published and fascinating English translation of his first attempt to compose a memorial article for Merleau-Ponty. See J.-P. Sartre, 'Merleau-Ponty [1]', *Journal of British Society for Phenomenology*, vol. 15, no. 2 (May 1984).

69 Merleau-Ponty, *Signes*, p. 37.

70 *Ibid.*, p. 46.

71 J.-P. Sartre, 'Merleau-Ponty', *Situations IV*, p. 207.

72 J.-P. Sartre, *Situations IX* (Gallimard, 1972), p. 32.

73 Sartre, *Situations IV*, p. 283.

74 M. Merleau-Ponty, 'L'œil et l'esprit', *TM*, vol. 17, no. 184/5 (September/October 1961), p. 198.

75 Sartre, *Situations IV*, p. 270.

76 *Ibid.*, pp. 283–5.

77 J. Lacan, 'Maurice Merleau-Ponty', *TM*, vol. 17, no. 184/5 (September/October 1961), p. 250.

78 *Ibid.*

79 *Ibid.*, p. 252.

80 J.-B. Pontalis, 'Note sur le problème de l'inconscient chez Merleau-Ponty', *TM*, vol. 17, no. 184/5 (September/October 1961), p. 288.

81 *Ibid.*, p. 289.

82 *Ibid.*, p. 294.

83 He does, however, pursue his unfavourable contrast of Sartre with Merleau-Ponty; see 'Présence, entre les signes, absence', in *Entre le rêve et la douleur* (Gallimard, 1977).

84 *TM*, vol. 17. no. 188 (January 1962), p. 855.

85 J.-B. Pontalis, 'Homo psychanalyticus', *TM*, vol. 17, no. 188 (January 1962), p. 990.

86 J. Laplanche and S. Leclaire, 'L'inconscient, une étude psychanalytique', *TM*, vol. 17, no. 183 (August 1961), p. 91.

87 By the time Lacan gives his own opinion (in a preface to a study by Anika Lemaire), the second schism (that of 1963) has taken place and he is no longer a colleague of Laplanche and Leclaire. Lemaire, who seems to be unaware that 'L'inconscient' was published in *TM*, covers the whole debate in her chapters 8, 9, 11. See A. Lemaire, *Jacques Lacan* (Denart, Brussels, 1970).

88 See his disparaging comment to this effect in his memorial article on Togliatti (*Situations IX*, p. 138). The chronology suggests that this is a direct reply to Pontalis.

89 C. Lévi-Strauss, *Anthropologie structurale deux* (Plon, 1973), p. 11.

90 *Ibid.*, p. 17.

91 Sartre, *Situations IX*, p. 9.
92 Sartre, *Critique de la raison dialectique*, p. 107.
93 The second volume of the *Critique de la raison dialectique* has now appeared (Gallimard, 1985), but too recently to be considered here.
94 *New Left Review*, no. 100 (November 1976–January 1977).
95 Sartre, *Critique de la raison dialectique*, p. 156.
96 *Ibid.*, p. 687.
97 De Beauvoir, *La Force des choses*, p. 610.
98 Sartre, *Critique de la raison dialectique*, p. 487.
99 *Ibid.*, p. 753.
100 De Beauvoir, *La Force des choses*, p. 522.
101 G. Gurvitch, 'Dialectique et sociologie selon J.-P. Sartre', *Cahiers internationaux de sociologie*, vol. 31 (1961), p. 124.
102 Lévi-Strauss, *La Pensée sauvage*, p. ii.
103 *Ibid.*, p. 331.
104 *Ibid.*, p. 326.
105 Sartre's familiarity with Lévy-Bruhl is difficult to measure. His use of the concept of *mentalité pré-logique* was clearly subversive, something that Lévi-Strauss fails to appreciate. Sartre later observes that in 1963–4 he studied the sociological view of moral constraint: 'il y avait toute une critique de Lévy-Bruhl d'abord, puis de Lévi-Strauss' (see the interview with Michel Sicard, *Obliques*, no. 18/19 (1979), p. 14). My attempts to trace these notes have met with no success.
106 Lévi-Strauss, *La Pensée sauvage*, p. 329.
107 *Ibid.*, p. 341.
108 *Ibid.*, p. 330.
109 *Ibid.*, p. 329.
110 Sartre, *Critique de la raison dialectique*, p. 203.
111 See *ibid.*, p. 627.
112 J.-P. Sartre, *Situations X* (Gallimard, 1976), p. 190.
113 L. Sebag, *Marxisme et structuralisme* (Payot, 1964).
114 *Ibid.*, p. 96.
115 L. Sebag, 'Histoire et structure', *TM*, vol. 18, no. 195 (July 1962), p. 288.
116 Sebag, *Marxisme et structuralisme*, p. 152.
117 L. Sebag, *L'Invention du monde chez les Indiens Pueblos* (Maspero, 1962).
118 L. Sebag, 'Le mythe: code et message', *TM*, vol. 20, no. 226 (March 1965), p. 1608.
119 *Ibid.*, p. 1610.
120 See P. Ricœur, *La Symbolique du mal* (Aubier, 1960).
121 Sebag, 'Le mythe: code et message', *TM*, *op. cit.*, p. 1618.
122 *Ibid.*, p. 1622.
123 L. Sebag, 'Analyse des rêves d'une Indienne Guayaki', *TM*, vol. 19, no. 217 (June 1964), p. 2226.
124 *Ibid.*, p. 2229.

125 M. Godelier, *Horizons, trajets marxistes en anthropologie* (Maspero, 1973), p. 253.
126 Contat and Rybalka, *Les Ecrits de Sartre*, p. 420.
127 P. Verstraeten, 'Lévi-Strauss ou la tentation du néant', *TM*, vol. 19, no. 206 (July 1963), p. 72.
128 *Ibid.*, p. 78.
129 *Ibid.*, p. 83.
130 *Ibid.*, p. 91.
131 *Ibid.*, p. 92.
132 *Ibid.*, p. 95.
133 Verstraeten, *TM*, vol. 19, no. 207/8 (August/September 1963). p. 509.
134 *Ibid.*, p. 518.
135 *Ibid.*, p. 552.

4 The critique of academic knowledge

1 De Beauvoir, *Tout compte fait*, p. 152.
2 A further sign of instability is the market research exercise undertaken in January 1967. Readers were asked, by questionnaire, to identify themselves in terms of conventional sociological categories and to say if they considered *TM* to have fulfilled the promises of 1945. The results were never published and my own inquiries into the nature of the responses have not proved fruitful.
3 It is at this time that Gorz (whose real name is Gérard Horst) gains a large readership in *Le Nouvel Observateur*, where he writes under the name of Michel Bosquet.
4 In 1965: interview with P. Verstraeten, 'L'écrivain et sa langue', *Revue d'esthétique* (July–December), reprinted in *Situations IX*, pp. 75–7; lectures given in Tokyo and published as *Plaidoyer pour les intellectuels* (Gallimard, Idées, 1972). In 1966: interview in *Cahiers de philosophie* entitled 'L'anthropologie', in *Situations IX*, pp. 83–9; interview with B. Pingaud, *L'Arc*, no. 30, pp. 88–90.
5 In Contat and Rybalka, *Les Ecrits de Sartre*.
6 Ibid., p. 741.
7 The advice of Lévi-Strauss was accepted in the writing of *La Vieillesse* (Gallimard, 1970), just as it had been in *Le Deuxième Sexe*.
8 C. Courchay, 'Gros rouges et bororos', *TM*, vol. 25, no. 285 (April 1970), p. 1704.
9 J. Pouillon, 'Note', *TM*, vol. 25, no. 286 (May 1970), p. 1936.
10 I should add that the 'post-structuralist' consideration of this matter in Derrida's *De la grammatologie* (Minuit, 1967) arouses no comment whatever in *TM*.
11 L. de Heusch, 'Vers une mytho-logique?', *Critique*, no. 219–20 (August/September 1965), p. 695.
12 The same point is made by Dan Sperber in *Le Structuralisme en anthropologie* (Seuil, 1968), pp. 71 *et seq.*

13 De Heusch, 'Vers une mytho-logique?', *op. cit.*, p. 716.
14 J. Pouillon, 'La structure du pouvoir chez les Hadjeraï (Tchad)', *L'Homme*, vol. 4, no. 3 (September–December 1964), reprinted in *Fétiches sans fétichisme*.
15 *Ibid.*, in *Fétiches sans fétichisme*, p. 197.
16 See *Situations IX*, p. 85; and *L'Arc* no. 30, p. 90.
17 J. Pouillon, 'Structure: un essai de définition', *TM*, vol. 22, no. 246 (November 1966), reprinted in *Fétiches sans fétichisme*, p. 14.
18 *Ibid.*, in *Fétiches sans fétichisme*, pp. 16–17.
19 *Ibid.*, p. 20.
20 *Ibid.*, p. 23.
21 *Ibid.*, p. 27.
22 See *Fétiches sans fétichisme*, p. 159.
23 J.-F. Steiner, *Treblinka* (Fayard, 1966).
24 A.-J. Greimas, 'Structure et histoire', *TM*, vol. 22, no. 246 (November 1966), p. 821.
25 *Ibid.*, p. 823.
26 *Ibid.*, p. 826.
27 Sartre, *Situations IX*, p. 52.
28 See his interview with Pingaud in *L'Arc*, no. 30.
29 M. Amiot, 'Le relativisme culturaliste de Michel Foucault', *TM*, vol. 22, no. 248 (January 1967), p. 1296.
30 G. Balandier, *Anthropologie politique* (PUF, 1967), p. 25.
31 The first chapter of M. Sahlins, *Stone Age Economics* (Tavistock, 1974).
32 Godelier, *Horizons, trajets marxistes en anthropologie*, p. 55.
33 Sartre, *Critique de la raison dialectique*, pp. 202–3.
34 See R. Bastide, *Anthropologie appliquée* (Payot, 1971), chapter 5.
35 Godelier, *Horizons, trajets marxistes en anthropologie*, p. 188.
36 De Beauvoir, *Tout compte fait*, p. 153.
37 *TM*, vol. 21, no. 238 (March 1966), p. 1681.
38 See N. Poulantzas, 'La *Critique de la raison dialectique* et le Droit', *Archives de philosophie de droit*, vol. 10 (Sirey, 1965); and a brief comment by Gorz in his *Le Socialisme difficile* (Seuil, 1967), p. 215.
39 N. Poulantzas, 'Vers une théorie marxiste', *TM*, vol. 21, no. 240 (May 1966), p. 1968.
40 Godelier, *Horizons, trajets marxistes en anthropologie*, p. 193.
41 See *ibid.*, part 5, chapter 4.
42 *Ibid.*, p. 206.
43 See De Beauvoir, *Faut-il brûler Sade?*, p. 160.
44 See my article, '*Les Mots* as *essai sur le don*: contribution to an origin myth', in *Yale French Studies*.
45 See J.-B. Pontalis, preface to J.-P. Sartre, *Le Scénario Freud* (Gallimard, 1984).
46 De Beauvoir, quoted in Francis and Gontier, *Les Ecrits de Simone de Beauvoir*, p. 335.

47 J.-P. Sartre, *Kean* (Gallimard, 1954), p. 74.

48 J.-P. Sartre, *Les Mots* (Gallimard, 1964), p. 160.

49 Sartre, *Critique de la raison dialectique*, p. 493.

50 De Beauvoir, quoted in Francis and Gontier, *Les Ecrits de Simone de Beauvoir*, p. 335.

51 Sartre, *Les Mots*, p. 141.

52 *Ibid.*, p. 211.

53 See *L'Arc*, no. 30, p. 96.

54 See the David Levine drawing on the cover of the Folio edition of *Les Mots* illustrating Sartre's assertion that 'En face d'un enfant qui meurt, *La Nausée* ne fait pas le poids' (*Le Monde*, 18 April 1964).

55 I look into these questions in my article, 'Margaret Kennedy et l'intertexte maternel' (Presses Universitaires de Lyon, forthcoming).

56 See, for example, Sartre's contribution to *Que peut la littérature?*, ed. Y. Buin (UGE, 10/18, 1965).

57 M. Beaujour, 'Fuite hors du temps: le langage poétique ou la révolution', *TM*, vol. 23, no. 264 (May/June 1968), p. 1956.

58 De Beauvoir, quoted in Francis and Gontier, *Les Ecrits de Simone de Beauvoir*, p. 456.

59 De Beauvoir, *Tout compte fait*, p. 153.

60 B. Pingaud, *Inventaire* (Gallimard, 1965).

61 *Ibid.*, p. 12.

62 *Ibid.*, p. 27.

63 De Beauvoir, *Tout compte fait*, p. 154.

64 S. de Beauvoir, *La Cérémonie des adieux* (Gallimard, 1981), p. 356.

65 A. Wilden, *The Language of the Self* (Delta Books, New York, 1968), p. 301.

66 S. Turkle, *Psychoanalytic Politics: Freud's French Revolution* (Burnett Books, 1979), part 2.

67 See the issues of the *Bulletin de psychologie* between 1957 and 1960.

68 Turkle, *Psychoanalytic Politics: Freud's French Revolution*, p. 131.

69 See the 1965 interview with Verstraeten, in *Situations IX*, p. 53.

70 J.-P. Sartre, *L'Idiot de la famille* (Gallimard, 1971), pp. 427 *et seq.*, p. 720.

71 O. Mannoni, 'Itard et son sauvage', *TM*, vol. 21, no. 233 (October 1965), p. 662.

72 Turkle, *Psychoanalytic Politics: Freud's French Revolution*, p. 130.

73 *Ibid.*, p. 131.

74 See M. Mannoni, 'Psychoanalysis and the May Revolution', in C. Posner (ed.), *Reflections on the Revolution in France: 1968* (Penguin, 1970), p. 221.

75 J.-P. Sartre, foreword to R. D. Laing and D. Cooper, *Reason and Violence* (Tavistock, 1964), p. 7.

76 D. Cooper, *Psychiatry and Anti-psychiatry* (Tavistock, 1967).

77 See *L'Arc*, no. 30.

78 See Sartre, *Situations IX*, p. 138.

79 De Beauvoir, *Tout compte fait*, p. 164.
80 *Ibid.*, p. 154.
81 'Dialogue psychanalytique', in *Situations IX*, p. 356.
82 J.-P. Sartre, 'L'Homme au magnétophone', *ibid.*, p. 329.
83 *Ibid.*, p. 331.
84 *Ibid.*, p. 333.
85 A more explicitly socio-political view of madness is expressed in Sartre's letter to the University of Heidelberg *Sozialistischen Patientenkollektiv*, in *Obliques*, no. 18/19 (Nyons, 1979). It is curious that Franco Basaglia's work in Italy receives no coverage in *TM*.
86 J.-B. Pontalis, 'Réponse à Sartre', in *Situations IX*, p. 360.
87 *Ibid.*
88 See his preface to *Le Scénario Freud*.
89 De Beauvoir, *Tout compte fait*, p. 154.
90 De Beauvoir, *La Cérémonie des adieux*, p. 356.
91 Sartre, *Situations IX*, p. 261.
92 Sartre, *Situations V*, p. 163.
93 Another part, however, entitled *Frêle bruit*, is announced in J. Pouillon and P. Maranda, *Echanges et communications* (Mouton, 1970).
94 See M. Leiris, *Cinq études d'ethnologie* (Gonthier, 1969), chapter 5.
95 See, by way of example, the final chapter of Métraux's *Les Incas* (Seuil, 1983 edn), written by Abdòn Yaranga Valderrama, a Peruvian Indian.
96 See M. Leiris, 'Qui est Aimé Césaire?', *Critique*, no. 216, reprinted in *Brisées* (Mercure de France, 1966).
97 M. Leiris, *Fibrilles* (Gallimard, 1966), p. 53.
98 Leiris, *Brisées*, p. 270.
99 Leiris, *Fibrilles*, p. 57.
100 Sartre, *Situations V*, p. 194.
101 *Ibid.*, p. 209.
102 *Ibid.*, p. 253.
103 Todd, *Un fils rebelle*, p. 226.
104 See Sartre, *Situations VIII*.
105 *TM*, vol. 23, no. 264 (May/June 1968), p. 2038.
106 De Beauvoir, *Tout compte fait*, p. 153.
107 R. Debray, 'Le castrisme: la longue marche en Amérique latine', *TM* vol. 20, no. 224 (January 1965), p. 1207.
108 See *Le Monde*, 11 October 1967.
109 R. Debray, 'Ce que je demande à mes amis', *Le Nouvel Observateur*, 1 November 1967.
110 R. Blackburn, preface to R. Debray, *Strategy for Revolution* (Cape, 1970), p. 20.
111 A. Gorz, 'Le test vietnamien', *TM*, vol. 20, no. 228 (May 1965), p. 1922.
112 Sartre, *Situations VIII*, pp. 14–15.

113 E. Wolf, 'Intellectuels américains contre la guerre du Vietnam', *TM* vol. 21, no. 235 (December 1965), p. 1106.

114 J.-P. Sartre, 'Le génocide', *TM*, vol. 23, no. 259 (December 1967), p. 957.

115 See Sartre, *Situations VII*, pp. 302–7.

116 S. de Beauvoir, 'La condition féminine', in Francis and Gontier, *Les Ecrits de Simone de Beauvoir*, pp. 401–9.

117 De Beauvoir, *Tout compte fait*, p. 502.

118 The history of *TM*, however, shows this resurgence of feminism to be little more than a burst. All is ended by 1968. There is then another gap of five years before *TM* introduces its long-running section 'Le sexisme ordinaire' in December 1973; this leads to the special issue entitled 'Les femmes s'entêtent' in April/May 1974. In this respect, *TM* reflects the intellectual currents at large: of the three ventures that develop out of the failure of 1968 – fashionable *lacanisme*, Maoism and feminism – it at least backs the most important. It is nevertheless disappointing that Beauvoir is so silent in the 'low' years.

119 Sartre, *L'Etre et le néant*, p. 480.

120 P. Bourdieu and J.-C. Passeron, 'Langage et rapport au langage dans la situation pédagogique', *TM*, vol. 21, no. 232 (September 1965), p. 463.

121 Sartre, *Situations VIII*, p. 250.

122 M. Kravetz, 'Naissance d'un syndicalisme étudiant', *TM*, vol. 19, no. 213 (February 1964), pp. 1454–5.

123 A. Griset and M. Kravetz, 'De l'Algérie à la réforme Fouchet: critique du syndicalisme étudiant', *TM*, vol. 20, no. 228 (May 1965), p. 2066.

124 Bourdieu and Passeron, 'Langage et rapport au langage dans la situation pédagogique', *op. cit.*, p. 441.

125 See his conversation with *Il Manifesto* in *Situations VIII*, p. 273.

126 A. Gorz, *Stratégie ouvrière et néocapitalisme* (Seuil, 1964).

127 For a succinct presentation of this context, see J. Halliday, 'Structural reform in Italy – theory and practice', *New Left Review*, no. 50 (July/August 1968).

128 See Sartre, *Situations VIII*, pp. 146–74.

129 Gorz, *Le Socialisme difficile*.

130 A. Gorz, 'Un socialisme à refaire', *TM*, vol. 23, no. 263 (April 1968), p. 1780.

131 A. Gorz, 'D'un printemps à l'autre', *TM*, vol. 24, no. 274 (April 1969), p. 1847.

132 'De sang froid', *TM*, vol. 24, no. 266/7 (August/September 1968), p. 195.

133 Sartre, *Situations IX*, p. 231.

134 *Ibid.*, p. 238.

135 J.-P. Sartre, *Le Nouvel Observateur*, 26 June 1968, p. 196.

136 *Ibid.*, p. 204.

137 'Un commencement', *TM*, vol. 23, no. 264 (May/June 1968), p. i.
138 *Ibid.*, p. ii.
139 *Ibid.*, p. iv.
140 See his comments in Posner (ed.), *Reflections on the Revolution in France: 1968*, pp. 264–5.
141 L. Magri, 'Réflexions sur les événements de mai', *TM*, vol. 25, nos. 277–80 (August–November 1969), p. 457. *TM*, so used to perceiving, is for once the object of another's perceptions. I comment at greater length on its Italian connection in 'L'Immagine dell'Italia in *Les Temps Modernes*', in the proceedings of the colloquium, *Sartre e l'Italia*, Leghorn, 1985 (forthcoming).
142 Sartre, *Situations VIII*, p. 286.
143 *Ibid.*, p. 265.
144 *Ibid.*, pp. 282–3.
145 Sartre, *Les Mots*, p. 211.
146 A. Gorz, 'Détruire l'université', *TM*, vol. 26, no. 285 (April 1970), p. 1557.
147 A. Métraux, *Itinéraires I* (Payot, 1978), pp. 9–16. This volume of *carnets* covers the period 1935–53. The second volume, still awaited, will be of great interest to historians of anthropology.
148 De Beauvoir, *Tout compte fait*, p. 162.
149 *Ibid.*, p. 163.
150 See M. and F. Panoff, *L'Ethnologue et son ombre* (Payot, 1968), pp. 82, 108. Written by a husband and wife team, the chapter in *TM* is credited to Michel Panoff.
151 See J. Copans, 'Le Métier d'anthropologue (ii)', *L'Homme*, vol. 9, no. 4 (October–December 1969), pp. 79 *et seq.*
152 See other articles by Copans in *L'Homme*, vol. 6, no. 3 (July–September 1966), and vol. 7, no. 4 (October–December 1967).
153 G. Balandier, 'From one anthropology to another', *The Human Context*, vol. 7 (1975), p. 295.
154 Lévi-Strauss, *Anthropologie structurale deux*, p. 69.
155 R. Jaulin, *La Paix blanche* (Seuil, 1970).
156 J. Pouillon, 'L'ethnologie, pourquoi faire?', *TM*, vol. 26, no. 293/4 (January 1971), p. 1196.
157 Later expanded into the book *Anthropologie et impérialisme*, ed. J. Copans (Maspero, 1975).
158 J. Copans, 'Quelques réflexions', *TM*, vol. 26, no. 293/4 (January 1971), p. 1169.
159 *Ibid.*, p. 1181.
160 *Ibid.*, p. 1193.
161 O. Mannoni, '"Terrains" de mission?', *TM*, vol. 26, no. 299/300 (June/July 1971), p. 2353.
162 *Ibid.*, pp. 2352–3.
163 J. Monod, 'Oraison funèbre pour une vieille dame: lettre à quelques ethno-loques', *TM*, vol. 26, no. 299/300 (June/July 1971), p. 2393.

164 *Ibid.*, p. 2397.
165 J. Pouillon, 'Réponse à un ventriloque', *TM*, vol. 26, no. 299/300 (June/July 1971), p. 2405.
166 *Ibid.*, p. 2407.

Conclusion

1 Victor (Benny Levy), nominally an editor of *TM* from 1977 to 1979, had little influence on the review; in 1978 he withdrew in circumstances described by an unsympathetic Beauvoir. See *La Cérémonie des adieux*, pp. 139 *et seq.*

2 Sartre published only two texts on Flaubert in *TM*: 'La conscience de classe chez Flaubert' (May and June 1966) and 'Flaubert: du poète à l'artiste' (from August to October 1966). Contat and Rybalka subsequently note that 'Sartre n'a pas été entièrement satisfait des deux études [...] il a complètement refondu son manuscrit' (*Les Ecrits de Sartre*, p. 429). They are not strictly correct, for the second piece consists of 180 pages which survive more or less in their original form (*L'Idiot de la famille*, vol. 1, part 2, book 3, chapter 7).

3 Sartre, *L'Idiot de la famille*, vol. 1, p. 688.

4 Sartre, *Situations X*, p. 94.

5 Sartre, *L'Idiot de la famille*, vol. 1, p. 8.

6 Sartre, *Situations VIII*, p. 374.

7 P. Gavi, J.-P. Sartre and P. Victor, *On a raison de se révolter* (Gallimard, 1974), p. 183.

8 *Obliques*, no. 18/19, p. 15.

9 See De Beauvoir, *La Cérémonie des adieux*.

10 Colombel, *Sartre ou le parti de vivre*, p. 137.

11 See *Obliques*, no. 18/19.

12 Only after Sartre's death, and when the *inédits* emerge, does he begin to become an object of study in *TM*. His own posthumous texts are the following: 'Journal de Mathieu' (September 1982); 'Lettres à Simone Jollivet' (November 1982); 'Premières lettres de guerre à Simone de Beauvoir' (February, March and June 1983); 'La lutte, est-elle intelligible?' (October 1985).

13 Sartre, *Situations X*, p. 215.

14 A. Gorz, *Adieux au prolétariat* (Galilée, 1980). The preface to the 1981 edition appears in *TM* in March 1981.

15 The only reminder of these comes from Jean-Louis Siran ('Pour Mauss', December 1982), but his critique of positivist anthropology is much more 'post-modern' than Sartrean.

16 See *Magazine littéraire*, no. 223 (October 1985).

17 J. Favret-Saada, 'En ethnologie le crime ne paie plus', *Critique*, no. 271 (December 1969), pp. 1076–7.

18 J. Favret-Saada, *Les Mots, la mort, les sorts* (Gallimard, 1977), p. 248.

19 See Boschetti, *Sartre et 'Les Temps Modernes'*.

20 R. Castel, *Le Psychanalysme* (Maspero, 1973), p. 15.
21 Sartre, *Situations X*, p. 94.
22 See the exchange with Rybalka in *Situations X*, p. 113.

Appendices

1 P. Thody, *Jean-Paul Sartre* (Hamish Hamilton, 1960), p. 193.
2 Sartre, *Situations IV*, p. 218.
3 Gavi, Sartre and Victor, *On a raison de se révolter*, p. 28.
4 Sartre, *Situations X*, p. 215.
5 H. Hamon and P. Rotman, *Les Intellocrates* (Ramsay, 1981), p. 206.
6 J. Savigneau, 'Que deviennent "Les Temps modernes"?', *Le Monde*, 1 April 1983.

SELECT BIBLIOGRAPHY

All texts in English were published in London, unless otherwise stated; similarly, the place of publication of texts in French is Paris unless otherwise stated.

The standard bibliographies of the work of Sartre and Beauvoir are comprehensive; only texts which postdate them have been listed. The reader is therefore referred to the following:

Contat, Michel and Rybalka, Michel, *Les Ecrits de Sartre*, Gallimard, 1970
  The Writings of Jean-Paul Sartre, trans. R. C. McCleary, Northwestern University Press, Evanston, USA, 1974
  'Les écrits de Sartre 1973–1978', *Obliques*, no. 18/19, Nyons, 1979
Francis, Claude and Gontier, Fernande, *Les Ecrits de Simone de Beauvoir*, Gallimard, 1979

The list below does not include articles from *TM* cited in the text. Nor does it include books in which these articles appear unless they bear a specific relation to academic anthropology.

Agee, James and Evans, Walker, *Let Us Now Praise Famous Men*, Houghton Mifflin, Boston, 1941
Balandier, Georges, 'Le bilan de la sociologie au XXe siècle', *Critique*, vol. 5, no. 34, March 1949
  'La situation coloniale: approche théorique', *Cahiers internationaux de sociologie*, vol. 11, 1951
  Afrique ambiguë, Plon, 1956
  'L'expérience de l'ethnologue et le problème de l'explication', *Cahiers internationaux de sociologie*, vol. 21, 1956
  Anthropologie politique, PUF, 1967
  'From one anthropology to another: Evans Pritchard, Luc de Heusch and Jean Monod', *The Human Context*, vol. 7, 1975
Bastide, Roger, *Anthropologie appliquée*, Payot, 1971
Bauer, George H., 'Just desserts', *Yale French Studies*, no. 68, 1985
Beauvoir, Simone de, Bost, Jacques-Laurent and Pouillon, Jean, 'Correspondance', *Le Monde*, 26 July 1985
Boschetti, Anna, *Sartre et 'Les Temps Modernes'*, Minuit, 1985

Brochier, Jean-Jacques, *Albert Camus, philosophe pour classes terminales*, Balland, 1970
Buin, Yves (ed.), *Que peut la littérature?*, UGE 10/18, 1965
Burnier, Michel-Antoine, *Les Existentialistes et la politique*, Gallimard, Idées, 1966
Castel, Robert, *Le Psychanalysme*, Maspero, 1973
Charbonnier, Georges, *Conversations with Claude Lévi-Strauss*, trans, John and Doreen Weightman, Cape, 1969
Cohen-Solal, Annie and Nizan, Henriette, *Paul Nizan, communiste impossible*, Grasset, 1980
Colombel, Jeannette, *Sartre ou le parti de vivre*, Grasset, 1981
Condominas, Georges, *Nous avons mangé la forêt de la pierre-génie Gôo*, Mercure de France, 1957
   De l'exotique au quotidien, Plon 1962
Contat, Michel, *Explication des 'Séquestrés d'Altona' de Jean-Paul Sartre*, Minard, 1968
   'Les philosophes sous l'Occupation', *Le Monde*, 28 June 1985
Cooper, David, *Psychiatry and Anti-psychiatry*, Tavistock, 1967
Copans, Jean, 'La monographie en question', *L'Homme*, vol. 6, no. 3, 1966
   'Le métier d'anthropologue', *L'Homme*, vol. 7, no.4, 1967
   'Le métier d'anthropologue' (ii), *L'Homme*, vol. 9, no.4, 1969
   (ed.) *Anthropologie et impérialisme*, Maspero, 1975
Davies, Howard, '*La Nausée* as a narrative of compensations', *Australian Journal of French Studies*, vol. 15, part 6, September–December 1978
   'L'idéologie théâtrale du *Diable et le Bon Dieu*', *Cahiers de sémiotique textuelle 2*, 1984
   '*Les Mots* as *essai sur le don*: contribution to an origin myth', *Yale French Studies*, no. 68, 1985
   'Sartre et Margaret Kennedy: l'intertexte maternel', Proceedings of the 1985 Colloque de Lyon, *Sartre aujourd'hui, Sartre lecteur, Sartre lu*, Presses Universitaires de Lyon, forthcoming
   'L'Immagine dell'Italia in *Les Temps Modernes*', Proceedings of the 1985 colloquium, *Sartre e l'Italia*, Leghorn, forthcoming
Debray, Régis, *Révolution dans la révolution?*, Maspero, 1967
   'Ce que je demande à mes amis', *Le Nouvel Observateur*, 1 November 1967
   Strategy for Revolution, Cape, 1970
Derrida, Jacques, *De la grammatologie*, Minuit, 1967
   L'Ecriture et la différence, Seuil, 1967
Descombes, Vincent, *Le Même et l'autre*, Minuit, 1979
Detienne, Marcel, 'Le Grec à deux têtes', *Critique*, no. 394, March 1980
Doubrovsky, Serge, 'Le neuf de cœur', *Obliques*, no. 18/19, Nyons, 1979
   'Feuillet sans date', in M. Issacharoff and J.-C. Vilquin, *Sartre et la mise en signe*, Klincksieck, 1982 and French Forum, Lexington, Kentucky, 1982

Elkin, A.P., *The Australian Aborigines*, Angus and Robertson, Sydney, 1964

Elwin, Verrier, *The Muria and their Ghotul*, Oxford University Press, Bombay, 1947

Esprit, '*La Pensée sauvage* et le structuralisme', no. 322, November 1963

Fanon, Frantz, *Peau noire, masques blancs*, Seuil, 1952, 1975

    Les Damnés de la terre, Maspero, 1961, 1968

Favret-Saada, Jeanne, 'En ethnologie le crime ne paie plus', *Critique*, no. 261, December 1969

    Les Mots, la mort, les sorts, Gallimard, 1977

Favret-Saada, Jeanne and Contreras, Josée, *Corps pour corps*, Gallimard, 1981

Freyre, Gilberto, *Casa Grande e Senzala*, José Olympio, Rio de Janeiro, 1933

Gide, André, *Voyage au Congo*, Gallimard, 1927

Godelier, Maurice, *Horizons, trajets marxistes en anthropologie*, Maspero, 1973

Gorz, André, *Le Traître*, Seuil, 1958

    Stratégie ouvrière et néocapitalisme, Seuil, 1964

    Le Socialisme difficile, Seuil, 1967

    Fondements pour une morale, Galilée, 1977

    Adieux au prolétariat, Galilée, 1980

Gurvitch, Georges, preface to Marcel Mauss, *Sociologie et anthropologie*, PUF, 1950

    'Dialectique et sociologie selon J.-P. Sartre', *Cahiers internationaux de sociologie*, vol. 31, 1961

Halliday, Jon, 'Structural reform in Italy – theory and practice', *New Left Review*, no. 50, July/August 1968

Hamon, Hervé and Rotman, Patrick, *Les Porteurs de valise*, Albin Michel, 1979, revised edn, série Points, 1981

    Les Intellocrates, Ramsay, 1981

Heusch, Luc de, 'Vers une mytho-logique?', *Critique*, nos. 219–220, August/September 1965

Hollier, Denis, *Politique de la prose*, Gallimard, 1982

    (ed.), *Le Collège de sociologie (1937–1939)*, Gallimard, Idées, 1979

Husserl, Edmund, *Cartesian Meditations*, trans. D. Cairns, Martinus Nijhoff, The Hague, 1973

Idt, Geneviève, '*Le Mur*' *de Jean-Paul Sartre*, Larousse, 1972

Jankélévitch, Vladimir, Interview, *Libération*, 8/9, 10 June 1985

Jaulin, Robert, *La Paix blanche*, Seuil, 1970

    La Mort sara, Plon, 1971

Jeanson, Francis, *Le Problème moral et la pensée de Sartre*, Seuil, 1947

    'Sartre et le monde noir', *Présence africaine*, no. 7, 1949

    Sartre dans sa vie, Seuil, 1974

Jeanson, Francis and Jeanson, Colette, *L'Algérie hors la loi*, Seuil, 1955

Laing, R. D. and Cooper, David, *Reason and Violence*, Tavistock, 1964

Laplanche, Jean and Pontalis, J.-B., *Vocabulaire de la psychanalyse*, PUF, 1967

Lefort, Claude, 'Sociétés "sans histoire" et historicité', *Cahiers internationaux de sociologie*, vol. 12, 1952

Leiris, Michel, *L'Afrique fantôme*, Gallimard, 1934, 1951, 1983
  'La croyance aux génies *zar* en Ethiopie du Nord', *Journal de psychologie normale et pathologique*, vol. 35, January–March 1938
  'Oreste et la cité', *Les Lettres françaises*, no. 12, 1943
  L'Age d'homme, Gallimard, 1946
  preface to Jean-Paul Sartre, *Baudelaire*, Gallimard, 1947
  Biffures, Gallimard, 1948
  La Langue secrète des Dogons de Sanga, Travaux et mémoires de l'Institut d'Ethnologie de l'Université de Paris, no. 50, 1948
  Fourbis, Gallimard, 1955
  La Possession et ses aspects théâtraux chez les Ethiopiens de Gondar, Plon, 1958
  'Hommage à Alfred Métraux', *L'Homme*, vol. 4, no. 2, 1964
  Brisées, Mercure de France, 1966
  Fibrilles, Gallimard, 1966
  Cinq études d'ethnologie, Gonthier, 1969
  Mots sans mémoire, Gallimard, 1969

Lemaire, Anika, *Jacques Lacan*, Denart, Brussels, 1970

Lévi-Strauss, Claude, 'French sociology', in G. Gurvitch and W. E. Moore, *Twentieth Century Sociology*, Philosophical Library, New York, 1945
  Les Structures élémentaires de la parenté, PUF, 1949 and Mouton, Paris and The Hague, 1967
  'Introduction à l'œuvre de Marcel Mauss', in Marcel Mauss, *Sociologie et anthropologie*, PUF, 1950
  Tristes Tropiques, Plon, 1955
  Anthropologie structurale, Plon, 1958
  La Pensée sauvage, Plon, 1962
  'Hommage à Alfred Métraux', *L'Homme*, vol. 4, no. 2, 1964
  Anthropologie structurale deux, Plon, 1973

Lévy-Bruhl, Lucien, *Les Fonctions mentales dans les sociétés inférieures*, Alcan, 1910
  La Mentalité primitive, Alcan, 1921

Mannoni, Octave, *Psychologie de la colonisation*, Seuil, 1950
  Clefs pour l'imaginaire ou l'Autre Scène, Seuil, 1969

Mauss, Marcel, *Sociologie et anthropologie*, PUF, 1950

Mead, Margaret, *Male and Female*, Penguin, 1962

Memmi, Albert, 'Sociologie des rapports entre colonisateurs et colonisés', *Cahiers internationaux de sociologie*, vol. 23, 1957
  Portrait du colonisé, Pauvert, 1966
  La Statue de sel, Gallimard, 1966

Merleau-Ponty, Maurice, *Sens et non-sens*, Nagel, 1948

Les Aventures de la dialectique, Gallimard, 1955
Signes, Gallimard, 1960
Métraux, Alfred, *L'Ile de Pâques*, Gallimard, 1941
Le Vaudou haïtien, Gallimard, 1958
Les Incas, Seuil, 1961 and 1983
'Rencontre avec les ethnologues', *Critique*, no. 195/6, August/ September 1963
'Entretiens', *L'Homme*, vol. 4, no. 2, 1964
Religions et magies indiennes d'Amérique du Sud, Gallimard, 1967
Itinéraires I, Payot, 1978
Monod, Jean, *Un riche cannibale*, UGE, 1972
Mulhern, Francis, *The Moment of 'Scrutiny'*, Verso, 1981
Pacaly, Josette, *Sartre au miroir*, Klincksieck, 1980
Panoff, Michel and Panoff, Françoise, *L'Ethnologue et son ombre*, Payot, 1968
Pingaud, Bernard, *Inventaire*, Gallimard, 1965
Poirier, Jean, *Histoire de l'ethnologie*, PUF, 1974
Pontalis, J.-B., *Après Freud*, Gallimard, Idées, 1968
Entre le rêve et la douleur, Gallimard, 1977
Posner, Charles (ed.), *Reflections on the Revolution in France: 1968*, Penguin, 1970
Poster, Mark, *Existential Marxism in Postwar France*, Princeton University Press, New Jersey, 1975
Pouillon, Jean, *Fétiches sans fétichisme*, Maspero, 1975
Pouillon, Jean and Maranda, Pierre, *Echanges et communications*, Mouton, Paris and The Hague, 1970
Poulantzas, Nicos, 'La *Critique de la raison dialectique* et le Droit', *Archives de philosophie de droit*, vol. 10, Sirey, 1965
Ranwez, Alain D., *Jean-Paul Sartre's 'Les Temps Modernes', a Literary History, 1945–1952*, Whitston, New York, 1981
Ricœur, Paul, *La Symbolique du mal*, Aubier, 1960
Robinet, André, *Merleau-Ponty*, PUF, 1963, revised edn 1970
Roudinesco, Elisabeth, *La Bataille de cent ans: histoire de la psychanalyse en France*, vol. 1, Ramsay, 1982
Sahlins, Marshall, *Stone Age Economics*, Tavistock, 1974
Sartre, Jean-Paul, 'L'engagement de Mallarmé', *Obliques*, no.18/19, Nyons, 1979
'Lettre au *Sozialistischen Patienten-kollektiv*', *Obliques*, no.18/19, Nyons, 1979
'L'espoir maintenant', interview with Benny Lévy, *Le Nouvel Observateur*, nos. 800–2, 10–30 March 1980
Cahiers pour une morale, Gallimard, 1983
Les Carnets de la drôle de guerre, Gallimard, 1983
Lettres au Castor et à quelques autres, Gallimard, 1983
Le Scénario Freud, Gallimard, 1984

'Merleau-Ponty [1]', *Journal of the British Society for Phenomenology*, vol. 15, no. 2, May 1984

Critique de la raison dialectique, vol. 2, Gallimard, 1985

Sartre, Jean-Paul and Sicard, Michel, 'Entretien', *Obliques*, no.18/19, Nyons, 1979

Savigneau, Josyane, 'Que deviennent "Les Temps Modernes"?', *Le Monde*, 1 April 1983

Sebag, Lucien, *L'Invention du monde chez les Indiens Pueblos*, Maspero, 1962

Marxisme et structuralisme, Payot, 1964

Senghor, Léopold Sedar, *Anthologie de la nouvelle poésie nègre et malgache de langue française*, PUF, 1948

Sperber, Dan, *Le Structuralisme en anthropologie*, Seuil, 1968

Steiner, Jean-François, *Treblinka*, Fayard, 1966

Thody, Philip, *Jean-Paul Sartre*, Hamish Hamilton, 1960

Todd, Olivier, *Un fils rebelle*, Grasset, 1981

Turkle, Sherry, *Psychoanalytic Politics: Freud's French Revolution*, Burnett Books, 1979

Vian, Boris, *Chroniques du menteur*, Christian Bourgois, 1974

Wauthier, Claude, *L'Afrique des Africains*, Seuil, 1977

Wilden, Anthony, translation with notes and commentary of Jacques Lacan, *The Language of the Self*, Delta Books, New York, 1968

NAME INDEX

257

SUBJECT INDEX

19054

4 3 3 9 5 0 1 0 0 3 0 9 8 4 4 2 7 7 2 6 0 1 2

CHARTERHOUSE LIBRARY

019054